THE FORGING OF AN AMERICAN JEW

THE FORGING OF AN AMERICAN JEW

The Life and Times of Judge Julian W. Mack

by

HARRY BARNARD

HERZL PRESS NEW YORK

Also by HARRY BARNARD:

EAGLE FORGOTTEN:
The Life of John Peter Altgeld
RUTHERFORD B. HAYES AND HIS AMERICA
INDEPENDENT MAN:
The Life of Senator James Couzens
ALONG THE WAY:
The Life of Dr. Preston Bradley
THE STANDARD CLUB'S FIRST 100 YEARS:
A History of the Chicago Club
THIS GREAT TRIUMVIRATE OF PATRIOTS:
The Story Behind the George Washington–
Robert Morris– Haym Salomon Monument

This life of a good and
true man is dedicated
to the memory of Bea's
Harry Schneiderman,
my dear Chicago friend.

Contents

Acknowledgments

Julian W. Mack, a citizen of four American cities—San Francisco, Cincinnati, Chicago, and New York—along with his numerous other good causes collaborated in the founding and perpetuation of that splendid New York institution of higher learning, the New School for Social Research. It was fitting, therefore, that, through the affectionate interest of friends and kin of Judge Mack, a grant from the New School should have helped make this biography possible; this assistance, for a portion of the time involved, I am pleased to acknowledge. It made the work easier.

I acknowledge also the cooperation given to me, through interviews or correspondence, by scores of individuals whose lives were touched by Julian Mack, especially in New York; Cambridge, Massachusetts; Chicago; Cincinnati; San Francisco; Washington, D.C.; Jerusalem, Tel Aviv, and Zikhron Ya'akov in Israel. Many of the names are listed in the after-pages.

Gratefully, too, I acknowledge the cooperation given me by the directors and staffs of various libraries—assistance always invaluable in a work of this kind—including the American Jewish Archives in Cincinnati; the Zionist Archives in New York; the University of Louisville; Harvard University; the University of Chicago; Northwestern University; Yale University; the American Jewish Historical Society in Waltham, Massachusetts; the Hebrew University in Jerusalem; the Library of Congress; the Huntington Library in Pasadena; the Jewish Historical Society of London; *The New York Times; The Chicago Tribune; The Chicago Daily News*; the San Francisco Public Library; *The Los Angeles Examiner*; the Chicago Historical Society; the Chicago Public Library; the Newberry Library; the Chicago Bar Association; the Chicago Law Institute; the Mercantile Exchange Library of San Francisco; the Spertus College of Judaica in Chicago; North Shore Congregation Israel Library; Temple Emanu-El of San Francisco; the National Archives; the Hoover Institution of War, Revolution, and Peace at Palo Alto; the American Jewish Committee in New York; the Jewish

Information Bureau in New York; the University of Cincinnati; the Cincinnati Public Library; the Wilmette (Illinois) Public Library; the Oral History Project of Columbia University; Tufts University; the YIVO Institute in New York; Chicago Center for Research Library, and, of course, the New School. No work like this ever comes into being without the aid of librarians.

What has been set down in this book is my own choice, including judgments and conclusions. However, I wish to acknowledge helpful suggestions and counsel, as well as materials, from a score of Mack friends or kin, which would include Max Lowenthal, Horace M. Kallen, Robert Szold, Justice Felix Frankfurter, J.M. Kaplan, Benjamin V. Cohen, Lawrence Berenson, Alvin Johnson, Judge Justine Wise Polier, Roger N. Baldwin, Dean Roscoe Pound, the two William J. Macks (brother and nephew, respectively, of Julian Mack), Richard J. Mack, Justice John M. Harlan, Henry P. Chandler, Willard L. King, Judge Murray Gurfein, Matilda Brunswick, Rifka Aaronsohn, Charles P. Schwartz, Lewis L. Strauss, Marjorie Mack Krause, Julian W. Mack of San Francisco, Professor James Gutmann, Professor Mark Brunswick, Bernard G. Richards, and Professor Nathaniel L. Nathanson, among others listed elsewhere.

In research, I had the assistance of one who someday will pass his father in works of this kind, my history-minded son, David Barnard. I had also counsel on legal matters along with other important cooperation from his lawyer-brother, my other son, Ronald L. Barnard. As for style, perhaps some of the literary gift of my novelist daughter, Judith Barnard Papier, rubbed off on me and may be apparent; if so, I am indebted to her—for that and for her continued moral support. And, not least—on the contrary, most—as in other books of mine, I am indebted for the help of my own Henrietta Szold, another woman of valor: my patient, perceptive wife, Ruth.

To the editor of the Herzl Press, Marie Syrkin, whose own career is so much a part of the great matters in which Judge Mack was concerned, I am, it goes without saying, much indebted; also to the meticulous scholarship of Gertrude Hirschler, assistant editor, as well as to the able assistance of Gertrude H. Sneider.

HARRY BARNARD

Julian William Mack

by HORACE M. KALLEN

No one person's recollection, no, nor the rememberings of the thousands whose lives touched the life of Julian Mack can ever approach the substance of this high-minded being or recapture the zest for life or the impartiality that was yet all sympathy, which his presence communicated. From 1911 to 1941—during thirty years—a judge on the federal bench, by universal consent one of the most hard-working, competent and judicious of his time, he refused to imprison the citizen in the judge, or to let the bench contain him. He went all out for applied democracy in one or another field of community life, and there is hardly a major social cause which he did not illumine and defend.

Born in San Francisco, grown to manhood in Cincinnati, he came to be known and cherished not only in those cities and in Chicago, New York, Washington and Miami, but at Versailles and Vienna and Geneva and Jerusalem. His life and works are an outstanding testimony of how freedom releases Jewish men and women to put distinguished powers and unyielding democratic faith into the common hopper of the American way. His story provides an outstanding testimony of how championing equal liberty for the Jew as Jew inevitably calls for strengthening the civil liberties of every human being.

The outer man, especially to those who knew Judge Mack only from his public appearances, gave little hint of the inner spirit. A stocky figure, short and stout, whose voice had in later years become a little plaintive and a little strident, he gave, in his prime, an impression of great drive and vital force. Chief Justice Stone of the United States Supreme Court writes of him as he was in 1917. "He had great intellectual vigor and physical endurance. He was a practical-minded man because of his long experience in the courts. He had a good understanding of human psychology. While he was not a man who could be easily taken in he was a man of broad sympathies, high intelligence, and was tolerant enough to know that men could be conscientious in beliefs which were wholly foreign to his own." Later, and especially as deafness crept up on him, he appeared inattentive, often seeming unconscionably to sleep while others were talking. But when it came to dealing with issues, people who counted on these appearances speedily found how deceitful they could be. There are many who have reason to remember his outraged roar, and more who still must smile as they recall the mighty ring of his laughter.

It is true, however, that Judge Mack exercised upon people seeing or hearing him for the first time no particular attraction. It is in working with him that they came to admire him and to love him. In fact, his smile, his zest, his directness, his outgivingness, made him one of the most engaging persons in public life. Not by any means an orator, Julian Mack held his own at meetings, in conferences, in committees, against masters of all the rhetorical tricks, by the extraordinary lucidity of his thinking, the sincerity and force of his spirit. People discovered in a very brief time how rare were their fellow-worker's qualities of mind and heart. Justice Stone, who served with him on President Wilson's Board of Inquiry on Conscientious Objectors, writes: "His vitality and vigor, his lively interest in everything worth thinking about, and his enlightened intelligence, attracted me from the start." No one else could find the dynamic core of a problem so rapidly, or expound its nature and implications so simply, with such unusual clearness, and with such justice and sympathetic understanding for the aspects to which he himself might be even passionately opposed. Because of this generosity of spirit—which is commoner in science than in law, and is indeed the point of departure of scientific method—one felt Judge Mack's own views to be all the more compelling. "The great thing about him," writes his colleague, Judge Augustus N. Hand, "was his ability to act with judgment and detachment whenever he had to resolve contested issues in the courts, plus a kindly nature and warm heart that were guided by a high intelligence." These are the attributes of a just mind, that held it to be a part of the sportsmanship of equity, which legal justice achieves at its best, never to leave anyone in doubt what its own views were. Though he presided over many great trials—notably those of Harry M.

Daugherty, Attorney-General during the Harding Administration, and Col. Thomas W. Miller, Alien Property Custodian of World War I—often involving much prejudice and the most complicated and confusing issues, he never once lost the confidence of the Bar and the respect and affection of the Bench. In 1935, when he sat in the case of the reorganization of the notorious Associated Gas and Electric Company, counsel for this holding concern took recourse to charging Julian Mack, then the oldest Federal judge in the District, with personal bias and prejudice. Judge Mack at once asked Robert P. Patterson, the youngest judge, to pass on the charges, volunteering, although the final decision was lawfully his own, to accept Patterson's opinion without question. Patterson found the charges false. He declared in his memorandum: "There is not a trace of bias or prejudice against the debtor in any of these [Judge Mack's] remarks or rulings." And he dismissed the complaint as "frivolous."

And what else, indeed, could the finding have been? Unfairness was as foreign as obscurity to the spirit of Julian Mack. Whether in the practice of the law, the judgment of the court, or the handling of the problems that came before him from the various causes of human freedom and human welfare that he served, he invariably transformed the most confused and obfuscated matter into an issue simple and clear, with its scientific and ethical bearings unmistakable. Judge Mack was roused to anger not so much by ill-will as by deceit and hypocrisy. These traits would bring forth his roars; on these he would crack down with righteous indignation. Nevertheless, his bitterest foes and most obstinate opponents—and his life-long service to the welfare and freedom of men brought him many such—fought him without hatred and opposed him without rancor. Insisting that he was wrong, they also conceded that he was generous and just. Many who opposed him, as I can testify, loved him.

The causes to which Julian Mack gave himself are extraordinarily varied, yet extraordinarily consistent with one another. His career as a liberal jurist and a democratic humanist began with the conventional participation of a not poor young man blessed with a social conscience in the charities of Chicago, the city where he chose to make his home. He had gone from his high school in Cincinnati straight to the Harvard Law School, and thence, with his degree of Bachelor of Laws and the Parker Fellowship, to the Universities of Berlin and Leipzig, where he spent three years in graduate study. When he returned in 1890, at the age of twenty-four, he took his bar examinations and settled in Chicago to practice law. Within five years he became professor of law at Northwestern University, and seven years after was called to the University of Chicago. In the interim he had married that lovely and charming lady, Jessie Fox of Cincinnati; he had been drawn into the service of the Jewish Charities of Chicago; he had begun to concern himself with the social implications of the law and the moral implications of municipal government. In 1903 he served for five months on Chicago's Civil Service Commission. The same year he ran for election to a Circuit Court judgeship of Cook County, Illinois. He was elected, and thus began a career on the bench of city, state and nation which stopped only with his retirement in 1941.

Judge Mack served on the Circuit Court of Cook County for eight years. Three of those, from 1904 to 1907, he presided over Chicago's famous Juvenile Court. Although Denver, with her unique Ben Lindsey, disputes its priority, this Court and the law which established it signalize a new vision and a new method in the treatment of youthful "lawbreakers" which, initiated by Americans in Chicago, have been imitated and emulated everywhere in the world. They owe their creation to the persistent social conscience of the members of the Chicago Woman's Club. Lawyers and clergymen everywhere were well aware that the population of the prisons of the world averaged under twenty-five years of age. With the common law, they were content to attribute this fact to original sin, to natural perversity, to deficiency in grace; they looked upon the "juvenile delinquent" with a hostile eye; they were concerned not to save but to punish. So, in England, children of nine used to be hanged.

But the members of the Woman's Club looked at the matter differently. They felt that family, church, and State as well, might be accessories to delinquency before the event, and the State could at least supplement and, where necessary, replace, family and church where they fail. From 1883 the clubwomen labored to implement this view, drawing to their side jurists and politicians, until at last the Juvenile Court Law was framed and passed and the Court established. Judges were assigned to it annually from among the members of the Cook County Circuit Court, on the basis, in part at least, of the recommendation of the Club's Juvenile Court Committee. Among the male collaborators of these humane and wise women had been Julian Mack. He had served on the Circuit Court but a year, when they asked him to go on the Juvenile Court. "He gave up," says Mrs. Joseph T. Bowen, describing the early days of the Juvenile Court in 1927, "most complicated and interesting legal work in order that he might help with the Children's Court. How well he did it! We look back with the greatest pleasure and thrill of pride not only to his decisions but to the educational campaign which he conducted at the time in order that the Juvenile Court might be interpreted to the people." As an instrument of this campaign he organized the Juvenile Protective Association which in 1907 absorbed the Woman's Club Committee. He helped secure the collaboration with the Court, of Chicago's Psychopathic Institute. He insisted that for the community the question regarding any child is not *Are you guilty?* but *How and why have you become as you are? What can best be done to save you from ever being brought to court at all?*

Among Judge Mack's fellow-workers were Jane Addams, Julia C. Lathrop, Graham Taylor, Florence Kelley and other Chicagoans who were laboring to make the democratic way more effective in the Middle West. Mack held court on Halsted Street, across the way from Hull House. The children who came before him were never charged with crime. He handled them as wards of the state under his powers of Chancery. He brought to bear on their problems the then new working conceptions of the psychologist and psychiatrist, of public health, of probation and of education. The precedents he set endure, and, in spite of much obstruction, his tradition grows.

Concurrently, he carried his share of the load as a member of the Jewish community of Chicago. A member of Temple Sinai, thinking of Jewish life and Judaism in the manner of its brilliant and temperamental rabbi, Emil G. Hirsch, he listened to sermons and served on charitable boards. Nor was his service limited to the Jewish needy and the Jewish immigrant. It embraced the entire miscellany which was pouring into Chicago. He helped Grace Abbott found her Immigrants' Protective League and was its president while he remained in Chicago, and at its call always thereafter. To the newly-formed profession of social worker his leadership was encouragement and inspiration; in 1912 he was chosen president of their National Conference. He was a founder of the Survey Associates, a board member since their organization, and the board's chairman from 1927 to his death.

But perforce the Jewish tragedy in Europe gave the Jewish need there and at home a special urgency. Jewish social workers formed a National Conference of their own and made Judge Mack president of that. In 1906, when, following the pogroms of Kishinev and Gomel, the American Jewish Committee was organized, Judge Mack was among the original fifty, who elected him vice president, and thus a member of the Executive Committee of fifteen. During the twelve years of his membership on the Executive Committee, he participated in all the major undertakings of the Committee—its legal and educational work in favor of a liberal immigration policy, its diplomatic efforts to safeguard equal rights for all Americans regardless of race or religion; its studies of the general condition of the emancipation. He resigned from the Committee over issues of the internal organization of the American Jewish community and the philosophy of Jewish relationships. It was as a spokesman for the American Jewish Congress that he labored to coordinate the Committee's endeavors at the Peace Conference to achieve "full rights for the Jews in all lands and the abrogation of all laws discriminating against them" with Zionist purpose and Diaspora aspiration.

For his studies of the situation of Jews tended to shift the direction of his thought, and gradually to bring his sense of the meaning of democracy away from the prevailing assimilationist conception of Reform Judaism to that of the older, somewhat overlaid one of which Thomas Jefferson was the avatar. This led him to Zionism. The symbolic expression for the Judaist conception was "the melting pot"; the symbolic expression for the Jeffersonian one became "cultural pluralism." As was the case with Louis Brandeis, it was no more Julian Mack's sympathy for the Jews as pitiful victims of injustice than his revision of his idea of democracy that made a Zionist of him as well. "We ask no more" he told the peacemakers at Versailles, "for the Jew than we do for any one else." Nor, as a loyal servant of freedom and justice, would he stop with less. In his conversion to Zionism, Judge Mack's intimate friendship with that brave, romantic man of science from Palestine, Aaron Aaronsohn, was an important contributing factor. Others were the ideas and example of Louis Brandeis, and discussions with Felix Frankfurter.

When Julian Mack felt persuaded that instead of a "melting pot," democracy consists in the cooperative union of the different on equal terms, that a civilization is free and fertile in the degree that differences are neither suppressed nor penalized, but liberated, encouraged, and pooled in the common enterprise of the community, whether local or world-wide, he gave himself to Zionism with the same unflinching, lucid and realistic devotion as to his other causes. He labored to apply the rule of *e pluribus unum* to the special tasks which, with the coming of the First World War, fell to the Jews of America, as Jews. During a considerable part of that period as a member of the governing bodies of both the American Jewish Committee and the Zionist Organization of America, he labored to harmonize the two sects of opposed interests. After the Balfour Declaration, because of his efforts (seconded by those of Louis Marshall and Cyrus Adler), the American Jewish Committee called a special meeting and adopted a resolution welcoming the opportunity "to aid in the realization of the British Declaration, under such protectorate or suzerainty as the Peace Congress may determine, and, to that end, to cooperate with those who, attracted by religious or historic associations, shall seek to establish in Palestine a center for Judaism, for the stimulation of our faith, for the pursuit and development of literature, science and art in a Jewish environment, and for the rehabilitation of the land." In the first American Jewish Congress which resulted at last from the efforts at unity, Judge Mack sat as

President of the Zionist Organization. A unanimous vote designated him as one of the seven spokesmen of American Jewry at Versailles. There he was the choice for chairman of the *Comité des Délégations Juives auprès de la Conférence de la Paix,* and Louis Marshall took over when Judge Mack had to return to the United States.

At home, during World War I, his duties had been diverse and heavy. Early in 1917 he had been called by the Committee on Labor of the Council for National Defense to serve as chairman of the Section on Compensation and Insurance for Soldiers, Sailors and Their Dependents. The plans he worked out and put in force were a new departure in the method of paying the state's debt to the citizen soldier, fundamentally more democratic, more regardful of the self-respect of the citizen, than the pension system. In face of potential industrial disputes dangerous to the war effort, he was also assigned the task of umpire for the War Labor Board, as an arbitrator acceptable to workers and managements alike. But his most signal task was his assignment, with Dean (now Chief Justice) Harlan F. Stone and Major Richard C. Stoddard, to review the treatment of conscientious objectors. For this there had been no provision in the Articles of War, the Draft Act, or by other Congressional action. The treatment of the conscientious objector had, until then, often been characterized by blindness, brutality and stupidity. President Wilson's directive to the Board, of which he appointed Judge Mack chairman, was to sift the bona fide objectors from the dubious ones, and to assign them to non-combatant service if they would accept it, or to "farm-furlough." The tasks called for visits to all the Army camps, for interviewing all the objectors, and distinguishing the true from the untrue. Later, the President requested the Board to examine the court martial records of all conscientious objectors who had been tried. "For the successful prosecution of this important work," writes Justice Stone, "there could not have been a more ideal man than Judge Mack." The principles developed and the policies initiated by the Board, experimental and tentative as they were, represented a concrete step forward in the realization of the "democracy" men were then fighting to make the world safe for. Without its precedent, the decenter mode of dealing with the few conscientious objectors of World War II could hardly have been implemented.

Julian Mack's labors in the Zionist Organization, in the American Jewish Congress, and in all the other societies, philanthropic, educational and humanistic, which drew upon his generous spirit, were neither stopped nor diminished by this public service. He made time for everything and did five men's work. In 1918, when it became clear to him that the democratic unity he sought for American Jewry was unattainable, he had resigned from the Executive of the American Jewish Committee, but had retained his membership in the general body. With Louis Brandeis, Nathan Straus, Felix Frankfurter, Stephen Wise, he was the dynamic center of the American Zionist enterprise. He became the organization's president during its critical years. He was still its president when, in 1921, "the Mack-Brandeis group" resigned in a body from the executive of the Zionist Organization of America over a fundamental issue of *method* in developing the National Home in Palestine under the terms of the Balfour Declaration. Taking as its directive Louis Brandeis' statement of 1920—"the whole of politics is to proceed efficiently in the building up of Palestine"—this group, led by Judge Mack, proceeded to the formation of the Palestine Development Council, the Palestine Cooperative Company, the Palestine Endowment Funds. He gave great sympathy and understanding to the second American Jewish Congress after it was formed. He was Honorary President of the World Jewish Congress from its organization to the day of his death.

Judge Mack's service on the Chicago Juvenile Court had brought home to him the central import of the problems of education. They remained one of his deepest concerns the rest of his life. When, for his fiftieth birthday, his friends insisted on making him a special gift, and he finally agreed, he asked that it consist of a fund on which he might draw for loans or stipends to able but needy students working their way through college. It is a fund that ought to be kept up in his memory. The philosophy of education that had come out of his thinking and doing on this subject was the progressive one identified with John Dewey, and it governed his attitudes and actions whether as a Trustee of the Hebrew University in Jerusalem, as staunch supporter of the New School for Social Research from the very first, as a founder and later Chairman of the Board of the Jewish Institute of Religion, or as a thrice-chosen member of the Board of Overseers at Harvard College. To this last post, it is significant that he was twice nominated on petitions circulated by the members of the Harvard Liberal Club—first in 1927 and again in 1937. In 1927 he got a majority of the votes cast and the largest vote of any candidate. In 1937 Charles Francis Adams and George Peabody Gardner, Jr. polled not many more votes. Julian Mack's service to the University in the capacity as Overseer was varied. He was on the Visiting Committee for the Law School, the Germanic Museum, the German Department, and the Semitic Department. He helped largely in the establishment of the Kuno Francke Professorship in Germanic Art and Culture, and the Nathan Littauer Professorship in Jewish Literature and Philosophy. But to Harvard liberals his most significant service to their alma mater lay in the stand he took in 1922 against President A. Lawrence Lowell's proposal to set up a *numerus clausus* for Jewish students. Without his sharp intervention, this expression of snobbism and prejudice might have won out by default.

Perhaps the most characteristic, the most expressive fact of Julian Mack's conception of education is the one institution in Palestine to which he expressly gave his name. This is the Julian W. Mack School and Workshops in Jerusalem. It owes its birth, its growth, and its survival to Judge Mack who, in 1920, arranged that an American educator bring to the service of the children of Jerusalem what was most functionally democratic in the American theory and practice of education. The school was first known as "The School of the Parents' Education Association." It was a cooperative undertaking which brought together Jewish children of all classes, sects and origins, and sought, by adapting progressive methods of education to the vital needs of Palestine, to unify their diversity into a free, harmonious Palestinian Jewish type. It employed what Henrietta Szold describes as "an ethical method of acquiring knowledge," and the hope and wish of the school's principal, of Judge Mack, and of the people who joined him in its support was to extend its type of service to all the underprivileged and marginal children of Jewish

Palestine. It was seventeen years before this could be undertaken in Jerusalem alone, and when it was, Julian Mack gave it his name, and the Julian W. Mack School and Workshops in Palestine stand as the unique symbol of his first and most lasting interest in education.

Take the record of Julian Mack's achievement as a lawyer and a judge, take the tale of his services as a democrat, a public servant, a humanitarian, a Jew and a humanist, and you have a record large enough for half a dozen lives, not only one. Yet throughout the days of his maturity Julian Mack was not a well man. With the most discriminating taste in food and drink, with a knowledgeable zest unusual even in a gourmet, he had to follow a diabetic's regimen, and once or twice suffered illnesses that brought him close to death. Nobody would have known it from him. His life was, through its long last illness, right up to its contracted last moment, one brave, willing affirmation. He took what he had to take, and he stood up, without flinching, saying *Yes* to life. Thinking of him, one thinks of the words of another great Jew, Baruch Spinoza: "A free man thinks of nothing less than death, and his wisdom is not a meditation upon death but upon life." Julian Mack was a free man.

Note: Professor Horace M. Kallen's profile of Julian W. Mack has been included not only because it is a splendid appreciation of Judge Mack by one who was very close to him and played a very important role in his career, but also because it supplies a quick answer to the question which nowadays may occur to many people: "Who was Judge Mack?"

H.B.

---

*Reprinted from *American Jewish Year Book*, Vol. 46, 1944.

THE JUDGE

1. Pioneers in California

Julian Mack was born in San Francisco. American Jewish life, in which he was to play so meaningful a role, was then—in 1866, the year of his birth—still relatively undeveloped. Not until the 1830's had there been a substantial Jewish community in the United States. True, there already were some Jews in the United States long before the 1830's, enough in number for synagogues to have been established by the time of the American Revolution.

But until the 1830's American Jews were so few in number that they still seemed "quaint"—Mark Twain's word—wherever they appeared. Then came the extensive migration of German Jews, mainly from Bavaria. That was the beginning. Julian Mack's maternal grandfather, Abraham Tandler, was part of that beginning. He was one of the pioneers of the first real influx of Jews to America.

It was Abe Tandler's early arrival in this country that permitted Julian Mack in 1909, when he testified before the celebrated and controversial United States Immigration Commission, to look the elegant Senator Henry Cabot Lodge of Massachusetts in the eye and say to him:

"I do not know that you could claim to be any more of an American than I am. . . ."

Julian Mack was right, of course. Moreover, his manner, his diction, and his education were as properly American as those of Henry Cabot Lodge.

True, those early American Jews from Germany were mainly smalltown types, of modest families engaged in petty trade. At first, like the earlier Yankee peddlers of New England, they settled for the most part in small towns. Later on, the term "German Jew" was to evoke the image of a big-city banker. It was to suggest worldly-wise personages, "Our Crowd" figures—more German than Jewish—to be reckoned with in American finance, industry, politics, and even "Society," such names as Guggenheim, Schiff, Warburg, Ochs,

3

Loeb, Lewisohn, Straus, Baruch, and Pulitzer. But these emerged later, or arrived in later migrations.

Even so, many of the earlier German Jewish immigrants were fairly well educated, with secondary-school diplomas, in spite of their modest beginnings in Bavaria. They were equipped for rising rapidly, as a class, especially as America was then in one of its great periods of growth. A few failed. Some returned to the old country. A good many ceased to be Jews. But those who "made it," and at the same time remained "Jewish," helped lay the foundations for Reform Judaism.

It was as a Reform Jew that Julian Mack was reared in California and Ohio, which meant for him, at least, that he was not very religious. In fact, he considered himself non-religious, though distinctly a Jew.

Abraham Tandler was still in his teens when he came over from the village of Ichenhausen, Bavaria, about 1831. His ship docked at Philadelphia and there he started his life in America. Among other Bavarian Jews in Philadelphia, he found Fanny Schwabacher, who had come over with her family from Feldheim, Bavaria. Before long Abe and Fanny were married.

To make a living, Tandler began as a peddler of notions, operating mainly in the countryside, with farmers as his main customers. That was the way much merchandise was being sold at the time, non-Jewish New England itinerant merchants having blazed that commercial trail long before. Some of these peddlers, Yankees as well as Jews, would in time become store owners, bankers, and manufacturers.

Tandler's peddling took him as far west as Louisville, Kentucky, which struck him as an especially favorable location because it was not so well settled as Philadelphia. In 1837 he opened a carpet and rug business there, and it was in Louisville that three daughters were born to Abe and Fanny Tandler. One of them, Rebecca, was to be the mother of Julian Mack.

There were then few other Jews in Louisville. Gradually, however, enough of them settled there to form a congregation; that is, a "minyan" of ten men. Founded in 1845, this congregation—its members all in modest circumstances—held services above

Tandler's store. Tandler became its first president. Out of this synagogue later came Louisville's affluent Congregation Adath Israel, a center of Reform Judaism. But the founders of the original congregation emphasized that their synagogue "was for the worship of our God according to the *orthodox* principles of Judaism." They kept "kosher," they observed the traditional rituals of prayer, and separated the sexes at the services. Their liturgical language was Hebrew exclusively.

To Julian Mack all this would have been strange. Yet he himself stemmed from an Orthodox Jewish family. Later, there was to be a switch to Reform in Louisville, as elsewhere in America. It came to Congregation Adath Israel in the 1850's. But by then the Tandlers were pioneers once more—in California.

Julian's maternal grandfather had caught the California Gold Rush fever in 1851—against the wishes of his wife. He had been doing quite well with his carpet store in Louisville. At least Fanny Tandler thought so. She saw no reason for her husband to become a prospector for gold with the risk of being killed in some mountain canyon, as she had heard had been the fate of many such prospectors. Abe, however, had no intention of braving such perils. His idea was to sell merchandise to the miners. Almost any kind of merchandise was bringing unheard-of prices in San Francisco: a dozen eggs brought three dollars; flour, twenty dollars a barrel—all very profitable.

But Fanny Tandler could not forget San Francisco's reputation. Men in San Francisco outnumbered women fifty to one. "There are *some* honest women in San Francisco, but not very many," a French writer reported that year. Was this, Fanny Tandler wondered, a place in which to bring up three Jewish daughters? Still, while on a buying visit in Philadelphia in the spring of 1851, Abe felt the excitement over boats that landed daily, loaded with passengers and goods destined for the new American "Promised Land." Many Philadelphians had the California fever, including Abe Tandler's brother-in-law, Jacob Lang, husband of his sister, Julia, and Lang's brother-in-law, Jacob Sellers. When Lang and Sellers decided to go west, Tandler made up his mind to become their partner and go to California with them. He wrote to Fanny that she should carry on in Louisville "until further notice." That meant taking care of the three girls as well as the carpet store, while Abe and his partners opened one general store in San Francisco, then another in Sacramento. At about the same time, a Polish Jew named Goldwasser, whose great-grandson, Barry Goldwater, some 100 years later would be a candidate for President of the United States, embarked on a similar career.

All seemed to go well for Tandler in California. Then, in the first of a series of fires that struck the city, the San Francisco store was burned out. There was no insurance. But if Fanny had expected this disaster to cool Abe's ardor for California, she was mistaken.

He returned to Louisville in July, 1852, in advance of a telegram to Fanny that stated he was safely back "in the States"—that is, in New York. The telegram had been delayed by a congestion in communications caused by the death of Henry Clay.

Abe Tandler, however, was not chastened. He had returned not to stay but only to buy more merchandise and to take Fanny and the girls to California—by boat from Philadelphia to Panama, on horseback across the Isthmus, and then by boat again on the Pacific north to San Francisco.

At one o'clock in the morning of March 6, 1853, after a 14-day voyage from Panama, the Babcock Line steamer *Cortes* docked at San Francisco. As noted in the next day's *Daily Alta California*, its passengers included "Mr. Tandler, wife, and children." The "children" were Emma, Julia, and Rebecca, who was then nine.

William Jacob Mack, who was to marry Rebecca, was then still in Bavaria. He did not get to California until 1859.

2. Father William

In 1856, three years after the arrival of the Tandler family in San Francisco, young William Jacob Mack, of Altenkunstadt, Bavaria, first settled in Cincinnati, Ohio. He had been prompted to emigrate to the United States by a widely-shared motive—disinclination to serve in the army of the King of Bavaria.

What Jewish boy, in the 1850's, would have wanted to be in the Bavarian army? What could he have expected there? Only extra indignities because of his Jewishness. Bavaria had not yet granted its Jews even the limited civil rights accorded them in the other German states. Later, Bavaria would be known as more liberal than other parts of the German empire—more liberal than Prussia, for example. But in young William Mack's time Bavaria was decidedly backward with respect to its Jewish subjects. Some of the most outrageous anti-Semitic episodes in European history had taken place in Bavaria, including several in the city of Nuremberg.

So it made the best of sense, even to William's broken-hearted parents, Jacob and Rettel Mack, and to his three young sisters, that Will should go to America and join his older brother, Max, in Cincinnati. Besides, the economic opportunities for Jews in villages like Altenkunstadt, which had always been limited, were becoming even narrower. As elsewhere in Europe, the Industrial Revolution was depopulating villages also in Bavaria. Ambitious young Jews had two sensible choices. They could either move to a large city such as Munich, Frankfurt, or perhaps Berlin, or they could emigrate to America. Since the crushing of the 1848 Revolution many young Central Europeans, non-Jews as well as Jews, had been going to America. Some outstanding names, such as Schurz and Brandeis, were to figure in this migration. And, in due time, the name of Louis D. Brandeis would often be paired with that of Julian W. Mack.

When Will Mack arrived in Cincinnati, he found there, in addition to his brother Max, a number of other Altenkunstadters, including several Mack cousins. Max helped set up Will as a peddler, with merchandise from a dry goods enterprise in which Max was junior partner. However, the financial panic of 1857 was severely felt in Cincinnati. As a result, Will Mack decided to make a change; in 1859 he went to San Francisco, where the Tandlers had settled six years earlier.

"Not troubling myself unnecessarily," he wrote to Max while hunting for his first business connection there, and incidentally displaying the family trait of good humor, "but taking everything easy, as I find that the best course, decidedly."

Finally, Will found a position with a wholesale firm in crockery, glassware, and china, R. A. Swain & Co., whose owner, R. A. Swain, took a liking to him.

In January, 1859, as Will Mack was establishing a foothold in San Francisco, there took place a mass meeting that indicated the existence of a Jewish community in that city, and the fact that Jews were considered an integral part of the community at large. The meeting was one of protest, in response to the notorious Mortara case.* At that meeting, on Saturday, January 15, 1859, there sat on the platform a group of San Francisco's leading citizens, Jews and non-Jews, headed by Judge Solomon Heydenfeldt, San Francisco's most prominent Jew, who had been Chief Justice of the California Supreme Court and the first Jew to hold judicial office in that state. Seated on the platform near Judge Heydenfeldt was Abraham Tandler, who was to become Will Mack's father-in-law. So Abe Tandler, too, had become a "leading citizen" of the San Francisco community. Indeed, by the time Will Mack had settled into his job with Swain & Co. Tandler was an officer of several Jewish organizations in the city, including the leading synagogue, Congregation Emanu-El. By then, too, his three attractive daughters had grown up. And Will Mack, in a small way, was also beginning to prosper.

The fact that non-Jews joined in the Mortara protest was important. But of significance, too, in the life of Julian Mack, and in

---

*Edgar Mortara, the son of a Jewish family in Italy, had been surreptitiously baptized in infancy by a Catholic nursemaid. Then, in 1858, when he was not yet seven years old, he had been abducted from his parents' home with the presumed knowledge of the Vatican, and turned over to the Church. The incident caused a universal outcry.

the lives of other American Jews, was another fact: Not all Californians were then friendly toward Jews. Only a short time before, some Californians had noisily supported a proposed "Sunday Closing Law" directed mainly at Jewish merchants. During the debate on this law some nasty comments had been made openly about California's Jews. The Hon. William Stowe, Speaker of the State House of Representatives, for instance, had loudly called for the expulsion of all Jews from the state, or at least for a special tax on Jews, as in medieval Europe.

"Jews," the Hon. Mr. Stowe had declared, were "nothing but a set of hawkers . . . parasites who came to California only to amass ill-gotten riches and then return to Jerusalem."

To be sure, the execrable Stowe, whose kind were to spark murderous race riots in California against Chinese, Mexicans, and Indians, was not a wholly representative Californian of the period. In addition to the leaders at the Mortara case meeting, Californians such as young Samuel Clemens (who wrote under the pseudonym of Mark Twain) strongly deplored prejudice against Jews. Yet, though neither Abe Tandler nor Will Mack personally experienced anti-Semitism in California, the episode of Speaker Stowe and his cohorts did signify that, even at a time when there were few Jews in America, the virus of anti-Semitism could exist here.

Just ahead, in 1861, was the American Civil War, though it was to be quite remote from San Francisco. "Whilst our brethren in the East are unfortunately engaged in a most terrible and destructive Civil War, which has cost so many innocent lives . . . peace reigns in our midst, our homes and firesides are blessed with plenty, with all the comforts of life; commerce follows its usual channels. . . ." So Henry Seligman, of *the* Seligman family, and Abe Tandler's fellow trustee in San Francisco's Congregation Emanu-El, summed up the situation in his annual report, as president of the congregation, in October, 1862.

For Will Mack, at Swain's crockery place, the war even proved to be a boon of sorts. To raise needed war funds, Congress in Washington had acted to increase tariffs on imports, including crockery. This gave Will Mack the idea to persuade Mr. Swain to send him to Europe on a buying expedition to purchase a large

number of items before the new tariff went into effect. So successful
was his expedition that Swain gave Will a part interest in the
business. That meant dividends in addition to his salary of $500 a
month.

"You speak very coolly about my returning with $50,000 in gold
dust," he had written to his brother Max earlier from Europe. "I
assure you, it is not such an easy thing to make money here as one
supposes in the States."

Yet, with his new status, Will felt he was earning enough to turn
his attention seriously to Rebecca Tandler, now twenty, a slender
girl with dark eyes and a pleasingly open face.

He had not been in any hurry to get married, having kept in mind
that he first had to be well established in some trade. Then, too,
with his strong family sense, he wanted to be in a position to help
bring his parents and his sisters, Lottie, Jette, and Rosina, to
America. So he kept his emotions in check—a trait he was to pass on
to his son Julian. But the attractive Rebecca remained in his mind.
He began to take special notice of her as she sang in the choir of
Congregation Emanu-El. As for "Beckie," she found him attractive
also—a handsome, stable, promising businessman of thirty,
indubitably a good match.

If, as it seems, Will Mack's interest in Beckie Tandler was initially
sparked by her singing in a synagogue choir, there was significance
in this matter over and beyond their romance. What was a girl doing
in a synagogue choir? In Jewish ritual such innovations in the
worship service meant that San Francisco's Congregation Emanu-El had gone through the Jewish controversy between traditionalists and modernists—and that the modernists were winning. For the
introduction of a mixed choir in a synagogue, along with the use of
the organ at services, was part of a far-reaching movement, Reform
Judaism, which had begun in Germany and now had come also to
America.

Later the Reform movement was to address itself to more basic
issues: "decorum" at synagogue services, the role of the rabbi, the
use of Hebrew in daily worship, the Mosaic dietary laws, and even
beliefs concerning God. It would also raise the question of whether
or not Jews should continue to hope for the restoration of Jewish

nationhood in Palestine. Most strongly religious Jews were adamant on this last point, for this hope formed an integral part of their Judaism. In their view, the original covenant concerning the Promised Land and the ancient belief in the Messianic restoration could not be abandoned.

But the modernists, to whose ranks Congregation Emanu-El belonged, took an opposing stand. Desire for a return to Palestine, they said, would mean, among other things, casting the shadow of dual allegiance over their citizenship in their new homelands. Besides, they insisted, a restoration of the Biblical homeland and the Temple of Jerusalem was no longer a sound idea theologically or historically, let alone practically. Their "Jerusalem" was wherever Jews were free citizens. They disdained any bonds, except sentimental ones, with ancient Jerusalem, or with Palestine. This question was to be of great concern also to Julian Mack.

In time, of course, Emanu-El was to change, as would most Reform congregations. And so would Julian Mack. For another movement in the Jewish world was then also beginning to set off lightning flashes. In 1862 there appeared a book, *Rome and Jerusalem*, by a German Jew named Moses Hess. The theme of this book in substance was that of the modern movement which came to be known as Zionism.

It is interesting, of course, that Reform Judaism and Zionism, two movements which in their beginnings were so hotly antagonistic, should have had their start at the same time. It is of interest also to note that when a kind of truce between the two movements occurred, Julian Mack would be a striking symbol of that truce.

When Will Mack arrived in San Francisco, the controversy over Reform Judaism was already simmering. Hoping to avoid an open break with the traditionalists, the modernists called themselves "moderate reformers." But the way the wind was blowing may be seen from a notice that the congregation ran at the time in the Jewish periodical, *The Occident*:

WANTED

By Congregation Emanu-El, of San Francisco, an authorized Rabbi and Preacher, to lecture in English and German

languages alternatively . . . *Applicants must belong to the*
school of moderate reformers . . .

As a clincher, the notice added:

Applicants are required to have the approval of Isaac Mayer
Wise in Cincinnati.

Isaac Mayer Wise had been the founder of Reform Judaism in the
United States. The mention of his name in the notice made it clear
that Congregation Emanu-El of San Francisco had "gone Reform."
One of the signatures in the notice was that of "A. Tandler."

As a result of that notice, young Dr. Elkan Cohn, who in Berlin
had been a student of Leopold Zunz, founder of the school known
as *Die Wissenschaft des Judentums,* became the new rabbi of
Emanu-El. In the "Chronicle" of Emanu-El it was recorded that
Dr. Cohn was "not a half-hearted Reformer. Sabbath after Sabbath,
he attacked the rust of centuries." To be sure, he met with some
strongly voiced opposition, but the majority of the congregation
stood with Julian's grandfather, Abe Tandler, in supporting him.

Like Abe Tandler, Julian Mack's father fitted in well with the
modernists. In Bavaria, Will Mack had been reared as a fairly
"observant" Jew, but he had already been exposed to Reform
doctrines back in Altenkunstadt by a leading German reformer, Dr.
Leopold Stein, rabbi of Burg and Altenkunstadt, whose ideas had
influenced the Macks. Thus it was easy for Will Mack in San
Francisco to become one of the modernist Emanu-El circle,
including the Tandlers.

Before long, Will was seeing a good deal of Beckie Tandler. "He is
of a good family in Altenkunstadt with many friends in Cincinnati,
and by his great ability he has already a good business. . . . For a
long time, he wanted to marry Rebecca. Since we were completely
in accord with this idea, because we think that it will be good for
Rebecca, we gave our word for it." So Abe Tandler wrote to his
sister, Babette Bacharach, of Chicago, in April, 1864.

The marriage, duly recorded in the *Daily Alta Californian,* took
place June 7, 1864, in the Tandler suite of a hotel on Stockton Street
which Tandler then owned and operated.

Dr. Cohn conducted the ceremony, not yet wholly modernized,

under a traditional marriage canopy. He asked Will, as he stood before him, to repeat the ancient vows of the *ketuba*, the Jewish marriage contract by which Jewish bridegrooms for centuries had pledged to "honor, support and maintain" their wives. Then both Will and Beckie signed the *ketuba*, which was an interesting mixture of Old Testament and California statutes:

> In the name of God! On this date, the third day of the month of Sivan, in the year 5624 since the creation of the world, in the City and County of San Francisco, State of California . . . Mr. William J. Mack and Miss Rebecca Tandler are joined in Marriage according to the Statutes of Moses and Israel. . . .

Then, again in accord with the ancient ritual, the couple sipped wine from one glass, after which, with a vigorous stamp of his foot, Will crushed a small glass goblet to bits.

As usual, there was some discussion among the guests about the meaning of this glass-breaking ceremony. Did it recall, as one traditional version had it, the lamented destruction of the ancient Temple in Jerusalem? Or did it merely symbolize the mixing of the bitter with the sweet in married life?

As a Reform rabbi, Dr. Cohn favored the latter interpretation. On frequent occasions he emphasized that Jews should no longer lament the Temple in Jerusalem, and that, decidedly, they should not hope for a revived Jewish state. All that was a thing of the past and done for; the Jews were no longer a separate nation. In America, they were Americans, as completely as any other Americans. Dr. Cohn laid great stress on this. He also questioned the concept that Jews constituted a distinct race. He was certain that being a Jew was mainly, if not wholly, a matter of religion.

3. The Second Son

Will and Beckie Mack faithfully heeded the ancient Hebraic command to be fruitful and multiply. Over the next twenty years, Beckie presented to Will Mack thirteen children, of whom eleven survived.

Julian was their second child. He was also a second son, an order of birth which, according to Dr. Sigmund Freud (with whom Julian was to become friends some sixty years later), may have been significant in the formation of his character. For Dr. Freud surmised that second sons were likely to be especially successful.

The first son, Henry William, was born in the spring of 1865. Then, on July 19 of the following year, Julian arrived. An interesting pattern in the naming of the Mack children was started when Julian was given the name Julian William Mack. Three other sons also received the middle name of William. Still another son was named William Jacob, the same as his father. Was this Will Mack's way of assuring himself immortality? Be that as it may, it was Julian who eventually assured remembrance for the name of Will Mack.

Julian William Mack displayed definite "identification" with his father. A chubby boy, he was markedly good-humored and friendly, emulating Will Mack's philosophy of "taking everything easy." He was a boy who got along well with everyone.

"Very interesting" as a baby, his mother described him.

But Julian knew that his elder brother Henry was his mother's favorite. Probably this fact played a role in his developing personality. Perhaps this was the origin of his later great interest in food—why he was "the biggest eater" of the two boys, "the one it was always a pleasure to feed." He seemed to have sensed that when a mother offers food, she offers love, and that it would please her if he consumed his meals with gusto. He never lost that gusto; he became a gourmet, a fact that would often be commented upon.

Henry, Julian's older brother, was of a passive nature, a lad (and man) willing to be led. In later life, when Julian suffered from an illness so serious that the doctors feared for his life, Henry said: "I'd

14

rather God took me, and let Julian live; he's the important one."

By the time Julian was four, the family included two more youngsters—another brother, Lawrence William, and his first sister, Hilda, who became quite important to Julian. Indeed, Hilda was to influence his choice of the city in which he started his career. He was especially affectionate toward her in their early childhood and always seemed to favor her. She returned that feeling. It may be that, even more than his mother, Hilda was Julian's first "love object."

Julian accumulated some pleasant childhood memories. There was, for example, the celebrated link-up in May, 1869, of the transcontinental railroad. It was a big occasion for San Francisco, observed with parades, cannon salutes and fireworks. There was also a furor among members of Congregation Emanu-El because Rabbi Cohn marched in one of the parades which was held on a Saturday, but both the Tandlers and Julian's parents defended him and won the argument.

In July, 1869, Julian's father went on the first transcontinental trip of the new railroad. Traveling to New York, wonder of wonders for that time, he slept on the train in a bed, a "hotel on wheels"—a pioneer passenger on the new "Pullman Palace Sleeping Cars." He brought back gifts and many stories that delighted Julian: of the train's huffing climb over the mountains, the passage through the "Mormon country" of Utah, the swift ride across the western plains, with armed guards on the lookout for Indians. "The children are delighted with their father," wrote Beckie, "but say he must never go away from us again."

All in all, it was a family of exuberant, life-loving folk. The dinner parties, the trips they took together, the concerts, the temple services, the preparations for religious holidays, the family "sings," the socials at their "Allemania" club, the visits with grandparents and aunts—these made for a close-knit, gregarious family life, precisely the environment for producing, among other factors, a self-assured boy and man.

This Jewish way of life, based on the precept that it was necessary to be concerned for the welfare of others, became Julian's model. Much of the family's table talk was about the grandparents in

Bavaria, to whom money periodically had to be sent. Or about Uncle Max in Cincinnati, who, it was said, did not relax enough from his work, causing worry to Julian's parents. This concern extended even to people only remotely related—cousins of various degree, in-laws, in-laws' cousins, and even mere acquaintances.

Grandma Fanny Tandler was constantly visiting the sick, for she was the head of the Hebrew Ladies' Benevolent Society in the city. And Grandpa Tandler was an official of the Men's Benevolent Society of Emanu-El, as well as of the fraternal order B'nai B'rith. Julian got the point. Brothers and sisters helped brothers and sisters, uncles helped nephews, and cousins helped cousins. Somebody was always helping somebody from "the old country" to come to America. Reform Jewish doctrine especially emphasized such charity, perhaps as compensation for having dropped other phases of the ancient faith. All this was significant in the forging of Julian as an American who was a Jew. In a later period, the era of Hitler, no one would be more zealous than Julian Mack in efforts to help fellow Jews get out of Germany, not only to America but also to Palestine.

Julian also grew up with a lack of interest in money-making, a quality supposedly unusual in a Jewish lad. Perhaps this was a reaction against the gloom he noticed in the family at times when business was "bad," though his father was doing quite well in San Francisco. In 1869 Will Mack estimated his assets, including stocks in gold mines, at about $20,000.

But trouble was ahead. That September, the "Black Friday" business panic began. There were bank runs. The bottom fell out of gold mine stocks, and a leading banker drowned himself in San Francisco Bay.

Stocks owned by Will declined sharply in value. "Every lane has a turn & I suppose at some time or another our prospects will look more cheerful than at present—*Nil Desperandum!*" he wrote to his brother. But his stocks never did make a comeback.

At that time, too, Will began to be severely troubled by asthma. He concluded that San Francisco's climate was the cause of it, and made a decision probably reinforced by an especially severe earthquake that shook the city in October, 1869: He would move back to Cincinnati. He had noticed that on his trip east he had been free from his illness. Not even a more handsome business offer from Mr. Swain of the crockery shop could dissuade him from his decision. In July, 1869, the family set out for Cincinnati aboard the transcontinental train "that left every Thursday for the East."

Julian's grandparents stayed on in California. Fanny Tandler lived only a year after the Macks' departure for Cincinnati. When she died, she was honored for her charity work with "the greatest funeral procession which has ever taken place in San Francisco among the Jews here," as Julian's grandfather reported to his sister in Chicago.

Through his remaining years, Abe Tandler enjoyed letters that came from his daughter Beckie and also from his grandsons Julian and Henry in Cincinnati. "They write very nicely to me; they do very well," he wrote to his sister. Once he inquired of Beckie: "Is Julian learning *Musik*—and how is Henry getting along . . . ? I would like to hear them playing & singing." But in 1881 he died, without seeing any of them again.

4. "Gemütlich" Cincinnatian

"Cincinnati is a sort of paradise for Hebrews," the New England chronicler, Henry Howe, wrote in his *Historical Collections of Ohio*. He meant that the Cincinnati Jews in those days were considered as an integral part of the city's general German community, then one of the biggest concentrations of Germans in America. As a result, the German Jews there were perhaps more relaxed than those anywhere else in the world at the time. "Assimilation" flourished among them. And Julian Mack caught that spirit. He grew up almost completely free of any sense of "alienation."

Rabbi Isaac Mayer Wise, by then highly regarded as the leader of Cincinnati's ultra-Reform B'nai Jeshurun Congregation, aggressively encouraged "assimilation." One of his daughters married a quite emancipated Jew, Adolph S. Ochs, also of Bavarian stock, who became publisher of *The New York Times*. Another daughter married a non-Jew. "Be Jews, but also be Americans," Dr. Wise urged. "The race-proud Jew is a fool," he would also say. "The national Jew is a liar, because there is no Jewish nation, and he is not a Jew simply because his mother was a Jewess. . . . The Jew's pride and distinction is exclusively in his religion." Young Julian Mack in Cincinnati was steeped in this view of Judaism.

A sense of *Gemütlichkeit* also characterized the Cincinnati that Julian knew as an adolescent. Miss Henrietta Szold, of Baltimore, for one, sensed that atmosphere when she visited the city in 1883. "The Jews of Cincinnati are much more intelligent than ours. . . . The young men here study up to their twentieth year, even if they are to enter business," she commented. Miss Szold was to know Julian Mack later; indeed, he was to help her greatly in her splendid career in Palestine as founder of Hadassah. But in 1883 she probably did not even know his name, though he might have been one of the young Cincinnati Jews whom she had observed so approvingly during her visit. For Julian had easily adjusted to the ways of Cincinnati.

He was speeded in this by the number of family connections he had in the city. In addition to his father's brother, Max, a number of other well-placed Macks lived in Cincinnati. Some were prominent in dry goods or in related businesses. Contracts for supplying "Infantry pants, Cavalry pants, Infantry jackets, etc., for Ohio volunteers" during the Civil War were awarded to firms organized by the Cincinnati Macks. Some of the family even attained enough status to be defendants in a lawsuit covering a wartime cotton contract, brought by the father of General Grant. One Mack, Henry, was elected State Senator and a director of the Cincinnati and Southern Railway, along with the father of President William Howard Taft.

Rabbi Isaac Mayer Wise himself was something of a family connection. His first wife, Therese, had been a Bloch, a sister of Joseph Bloch, who was the husband of Julian's aunt, Julia Bloch. The stately Rabbi Wise had reason to appreciate his Bloch connection. When he first arrived in America, he had had little money. In his *Reminiscences*, he wrote:

"My wife's brother, Joseph Bloch, now living in San Francisco, and her cousin, Samuel Glueckhauf . . . were young, jolly peddlers. . . . They came to New York and offered my wife as much money as she wanted."

Naturally, Dr. Wise welcomed Julian's parents to affiliation with his congregation. Naturally, too, Julian's mother was immediately made a member of the choir.

In addition to Isaac Mayer Wise, the greatest influence on young Julian Mack in Cincinnati came from his father's brother, Max Mack. This uncle, by the 1870's, was an imposing figure in the Mack clan, not only because of his stocky build and the mutton-chop whiskers that framed his sturdy face. He was a typically successful member of the Cincinnati Jewish community, prominent in the insurance business. Indeed, in Julian's branch of the Mack clan, Max Jacob Mack, though childless, was in effect the *paterfamilias*—the proverbial well-to-do "good uncle."

He boasted many admirable qualities—self-reliance, sociability, and a high sense of morality. Though not brilliant, he had a good education, better than that of many immigrants. "He read English,

French, and Italian," a relative recalled, and "could quote readily [from] any of the plays of Shakespeare."

To a high degree, this uncle had the Mack sense of "family," which was also part of something else—a friendly, concerned attitude toward all people. A strong person on whom others could lean, Max inspired confidence.

It was understood that Max Mack would never permit any suffering in the family from lack of money. This was important, for as it happened, business did not go well in Cincinnati for Julian's father. Will Mack had had optimistic plans for becoming a crockery wholesaler in Cincinnati. He even visited Europe, after settling Beckie and the children temporarily with Max and Jennie, to develop business contacts in Germany. But the Franco-Prussian war spoiled those plans. And then depression once more struck the United States, again hitting Cincinnati hard. As a result Will Mack was forced to settle for the status of a small merchant. He opened a tailor shop near Fifth and Vine Streets, where he made only a modest living. But always there was the assurance that if things should really get bad, "Uncle Max was there"—a help to Julian's sense of emotional security.

These hard times had an important influence on Julian Mack. They determined his later politics. Like most German Jews, his father, Will Mack, had been a Republican. But as Will's chances for establishing a wholesale business became more remote, he turned sour on the rigid "hard money" policies championed by the Republicans. In 1872, he voted Democratic; because of the Panic of 1873, he became permanently a Democrat. After that, Julian considered himself a Democrat also; this came to be a vital factor in his career.

Max Mack had better luck than his brother. Around the time Julian was twelve, Uncle Max rose in both income and prestige. He became a successful agent for the very substantial Northwestern Mutual Life Insurance Company of Milwaukee. He founded a Mack dynasty in this venture in which other sons of Will Mack, particularly Julian's brothers Ralph, Lawrence and Millard also took part, along with a son of Millard's, William J. Mack III.

Not, however, Julian. Business was not for him. Very early he had determined to become a lawyer. "I knew from the time I was four that I would go into the law," he once reminisced.

In 1884, Julian became eighteen years old. It was a dramatic year for him, for on June 17, in Cincinnati's celebrated Music Hall, there occurred what the Mack family was to recall as the "Great Graduation," with Julian unquestionably the star of the joint commencement exercises of the city's two high schools, Hughes and Woodward. As a Hughes graduate who had completed a four-year course in three years he delivered one of the class orations. His subject was "Municipal Reform."

His choice of that topic put the spotlight on him. Cincinnati was still reeling from the "Great Riot" of the preceding spring, an episode that had particularly emphasized the need for municipal reform. Cincinnati also had the general reputation of being led by the corrupt local political machine of "Boss" George B. Cox, who ran things from an office on the same block as Julian's father's tailor shop. Under these circumstances, it was whispered that it was certainly audacious of young Mack, as salutatorian, to talk so pointedly about the need for honesty in public affairs.

At the commencement exercises, Julian was not among the recipients of the usual honor medals. But when the exercises were almost over there came a surprise. Julian received a special medal because, as a three-year student, he "had made such extraordinary progress in his studies and won so much esteem by his good behavior and consideration for others."

Nothing like this honor had ever been awarded in the Cincinnati schools before—a fact elaborately commented upon not only in Isaac Mayer Wise's *American Israelite* but also in the *Cincinnati Enquirer*. This was Julian's first publicity.

There followed a family discussion as to how and where Julian should study law. The custom was still widespread then that young men prepared for legal careers by "reading law" with a lawyer, while working as an office boy. But everyone recognized that the better way was to study at a law school.

The Cincinnati Law School, later part of the University of Cincinnati, was a reputable institution. It had been good enough for young William Howard Taft to attend after graduating from Yale

College only a few years before Julian's own graduation. Uncle Max, however, asserted that Julian should have the benefit of the "best law school in the country."

Naturally, that meant Harvard University.

Max decided the issue with a dramatic announcement: His graduation present to Julian would be the financial underwriting of Julian's attendance at Harvard Law School, if he would be accepted.

Julian was accepted by Harvard. He set off for Cambridge in the fall of 1884. Characteristically, he showed no special pride over what was happening to him, though one conceit related to his new status was that he grew a timid mustache. If anyone had suggested that he was playing a special role in a remarkable phase of the American story—a second-generation Jewish lad going off to Harvard—he probably would have responded with his favorite comment: "Oh, posh!"

But the fact was that in 1884 Julian Mack, son of a family of the most modest means (save for Uncle Max), was on his way to joining a true American elite, a group that already included such Harvard Law School figures as Oliver Wendell Holmes, Jr., Rutherford B. Hayes, Joseph Choate, Owen Wister, Robert Todd Lincoln—and Louis D. Brandeis.

No wonder Uncle Max beamed and sister Hilda was exultant. No wonder, too, that Aunt Emma Kay in San Francisco "let the jelly boil over on the stove" as she read in a letter from her sister Beckie Mack of "the great things" that were happening to Julian. "I think the present of Uncle Max to Julian," Aunt Emma replied, "was a noble one and he may feel proud of having such an uncle."

In later years a Jewish lad going to Harvard Law School would be no great cause for special celebration. But in 1884 Julian Mack was in the vanguard.

5. Harvard '87

Harvard Law School in the 1880's was enjoying one of its several periods of unchallenged superiority. In Julian's later phrase, its faculty included "the legal giants of their day," particularly the great James Barr Ames. Incisive, Socratic, and patient, Ames became Julian's special mentor and friend.

In an address at Harvard in 1956, Felix Frankfurter underscored what a boon Ames had been to Julian Mack. Singling out Ames as one of Harvard's foremost teachers, Frankfurter recalled, "He awakened, stimulated, and fructified the qualities of excellence. . . . He gave his time . . . with almost divine extravagance."

Julian Mack was one of Ames' favorites. He fitted remarkably well into the atmosphere in and around Austin Hall, the then new redstone Harvard Law building. His classmates included sons of the rich and the well-born, but also young men whose economic background was no more affluent than his own. The ability to afford luxuries was not supposed to be prized. Hence John Jay Chapman, the essayist, a colorful descendant of John Jay, first Chief Justice of the United States, could proudly describe his room at Harvard as "a dark, horrid little room"—an apt description also of Julian's quarters there.

Like his fellow students, Julian had to carry water to his room from a basement faucet. He had to tote his own wood and coal for the small grate that heated his room in winter. But neither Julian nor his fellow students felt deprived.

Perhaps his Jewish background caused his circle of friends to be somewhat narrow. Most colleges at the time, Harvard among them, tended to accentuate social snobbery. Yet Professor William James' democratic humanism—"cultural pluralism," in the phrase of Horace M. Kallen—was the professed spirit at Harvard.

A factor in this spirit was Dr. Charles W. Eliot, the president of Harvard. Tall, erect and stately "like a great clock," he had clearly formed views on nearly everything, including the idea that prejudice against Jews was ungentlemanly, un-American and assuredly un-Bostonian. In the 1920's both Dr. Eliot and Julian were to have some part together in helping beat down a flareup of apparent anti-Semitism at Harvard under one of his successors—the "Jewish quota" issue. But in the 1880's, to Julian's comfort, Dr. Eliot's cosmopolitanism largely prevailed. So Julian had as many friends as he could handle, almost all non-Jews.

He was younger than most of his 153 fellow students at the law school, three years younger, for instance, than one fellow San Franciscan, John Henry Wigmore, who was to become an authority on legal evidence and who, like most of the students at the school, already held a degree. But neither his age nor the lack of a degree proved a handicap to Julian Mack. Indeed, in his first year, he placed at the top of his class in his grades: Real Property, 92; Contracts, 90; Torts, 89; Criminal Law, 96; Civil Procedure, 92. In Trusts—taught by Ames—he startled everyone by receiving 95½. His record, indeed, was almost as good as that made by another law student, Louis D. Brandeis, a few years before him.

Julian did not shine in written work, nor was he to do so as a judge. There was little flair in his composition. But students and teachers were fascinated by his ability in oral exposition.

Professor Ames took a special interest in him. Like Felix Frankfurter, who came to the school later, Julian idolized Ames. He once recalled him as ". . . the ideal teacher, courteous and patient. If he led the student to the brink of a precipice, he did not let him fall over; he never failed to indicate the path back to safety. . . . He aimed not so much to impart information, as to develop the analytical powers of the man, to make him think as a lawyer."

Julian would have subscribed to a comment by Professor Joseph Beale: "Under all circumstances, Ames was a gentleman. . . . No man was ever less formal. So long as he was sure he was not infringing upon the rights of others, he was oblivious to their comments. He would go at a dog-trot through the streets of Cambridge, or even Boston, without it ever occurring to him that he might be making people stare. He absolutely lacked self-consciousness about inessentials; but no man could be more punctilious with regard to a thing that might hurt the feelings of another."

These comments could well constitute a description also of Julian himself, later on, as a lawyer and judge, including the mannerisms—the "dog-trot," for example—that made Ames something of a "character" in Cambridge and Boston. For in some ways Julian, too, became "a character."

In 1898, long before he was really financially able to do so, Julian established at the Harvard Law School, in honor of Ames, the esteemed Ames Prize for an outstanding essay or book on a legal subject. "I owe to him," Julian wrote, in announcing the Ames fund, "whatever measure of love for legal science and interest in law that I may have."

To Ames, no doubt, he also owed in large part his own great zeal—a pronounced aspect of his later life—for assisting and encouraging younger lawyers, just as Ames had helped and encouraged him

With several fellow students who "traveled" together, Julian formed, in 1886, a study group called the Langdell Society. Its purpose was to discuss legal problems more seriously than was done in usual "talk sessions." One day the Langdell Society discussed the fact that the students at Columbia Law School were publishing their own journal, *The Columbia Jurist*. Out of this discussion came the landmark legal publication, *The Harvard Law Review*.

Felix Frankfurter, a later editor of *The Harvard Law Review*, wrote that Julian Mack was its "essential founder," its "moving spirit." The initial suggestion, in fact, as Julian himself recalled, had come from John Jay McKelvey. But Julian was very much in on the founding discussions; he was a part of the group that decided to seek Professor Ames' advice. "'If he approves, we'll do it,' was the agreement," Julian recalled. Ames approved. The next step was to get subscriptions, advertising, and other financial support. As one of the editors, and "business manager," Julian took on that task. It was in this capacity that he first met Louis D. Brandeis, class of '77. Then already a big-name Boston lawyer, Brandeis became treasurer of the *Review*—a prologue, as matters turned out, to an even more significant association with Julian later on.

The *Review* made its debut in April, 1887. Julian's name was listed twice on the original masthead: "J.W. Mack, Business Manager" and "Julian W. Mack, member of the editorial board." He thus became an "immortal" of the Harvard Law School, for *Harvard Law Review* men traditionally have been special people—lawyers sought out by large law firms, or otherwise marked for distinction.

McKelvey, for example, was to head a large New York firm and publish numerous books on law. George Nutter became a partner of Brandeis. Beale succeeded Ames as dean of the Harvard Law School. Williston became a professor at Harvard; Wigmore, the dean of Northwestern University Law School. And Julian Mack would acquire his own distinguished title, Judge of the U.S. Circuit Court.

This otherwise exhilarating time in Julian's life was shadowed by distressing news from Cincinnati. His mother, long a sufferer from diabetes, had become seriously ill. Her eleventh child, a boy who did not survive, had been born in 1883, while Julian was still in high school. In May, 1885, William Jacob Mack, Jr., was born; and in February, 1887, came the thirteenth child, Robert. From this last birth complications set in and on March 6, 1887, Beckie Mack died.

In June, 1887, Julian received his law degree, *cum laude*. Again he was class orator: his subject, "The Cutting Case." Actually, his performance was not oratory, but the reading of a research paper on an "international incident" involving the United States and Mexico. The paper, which included voluminous citations from English, Greek, Roman, German, Spanish, Italian and Mexican law, was buttressed by correspondence with an Assistant Secretary of State who signed himself "J. B. Moore," and who later became renowned as Justice John Bassett Moore of the Permanent Court of International Justice at The Hague. Still preserved in the Harvard Law Library, the notes for Mack's paper alone covered 149 pages. The paper was judicious, well organized and, except for specialists, quite boring. But it revealed Julian as an undoubted credit to Harvard. He was then turning twenty-one.

In the "Yard" that day, there were probably some who wondered about the class orator. Where did he come from? Clearly he was—and yet he was not—"typical Harvard." An answer could have been: *Jvlianvs Gvilielmvs Mack*—so the Latin-language commencement brochure listed him—personified a new kind of American, the fully Americanized Jew, no longer "quaint," no longer the "greenhorn" peddler, but an individual as American as Henry Cabot Lodge, or even as the novelist Henry James, who also attended Harvard Law School.

Julian did not become a practicing lawyer immediately after his graduation from law school. He first spent three years abroad. Isaac Mayer Wise's *American Israelite,* on May 20, 1887, published, with some elaboration, the details of an award that had come to Julian with his graduation from Harvard and that made this unexpected interlude possible:

> Mr. Julian W. Mack, in addition to being selected as the class orator of the Harvard Law School . . . has received a scholarship of $750 annually for three years, under which he is to pursue the study of comparative law in Germany.

> Mr. Mack is not only a credit to the public schools of this city, but his success over twenty-six competitors is a gratification beyond measure to his family and friends.

The scholarship was the then much-coveted Parker Fellowship that had been established by John Parker, a wealthy Bostonian.

Mack's "competitors," incidentally, included a Harvard College graduate who was especially formidable—the later art connoisseur Bernard Berenson. A young man of Byronesque mannerisms, and a protegé of *the* Mrs. Jack Gardner of Boston, Berenson had "ardently desired to win the Parker Traveling Fellowship at Harvard," as Louise Hall Tharp, Mrs. Gardner's biographer, was to recall: "His marks were high, especially in language, and he knew that he and only one other student were being considered. The other man won." "The other man" was Julian Mack.

The bequest specified that the fellowship was to go to a student of "eminent natural talents or genius . . . so attested by the President of Harvard to the Governor and Chief Justice of the Commonwealth and the President of the American Academy of Arts and Sciences." So, thus certified as a "genius," Julian sailed for Europe in the summer of 1887 to study at the Universities of Berlin and Leipzig. He probably noted in the press that his fellow Cincinnatian, William Howard Taft, had also just moved up a notch in his career by becoming, at the age of 29, a judge of the Ohio Superior Court, a step in a career that was to culminate in his election to the Presidency of the United States.

In those 1880's the $750-a-year Parker stipend permitted a comfortable, even somewhat luxurious, existence in Europe. Even so, Julian watched his expenditures carefully. In *Vision*, Alexandra Lee Levin's biography of Dr. Harry Friedenwald, the eminent Baltimore ophthalmologist, there is a record of Dr. Friedenwald examining the eyes of "an American student" at Dr. Hirschberg's eye clinic in Berlin. When Hirschberg noticed that Dr. Frieden- wald's patient was "wearing a big overcoat with a large fur collar," suggesting wealth, he came down from his private office "in a fury because the fellow had the audacity to come to the clinic, thereby depriving him of a private patient's fee."

"The fellow" was Julian Mack—an "Innocent," though perhaps not so innocent, "Abroad."

Whether Julian did a great deal of serious studying in Berlin or Leipzig is questionable. He probably did not study much. He attended lectures only when he felt like it. Since he did not seek a degree, he did not have to do any written assignments. He was mainly occupied with sightseeing and other diversions. Nor did he pass up the opportunity of taking in Paris; he enrolled for a period at the new Sorbonne, though there, too, he did more sightseeing than serious studying.

He did "dabble" in some legal research for a paper he planned, but never wrote, and for his Harvard friend Wigmore. Wigmore was then working on the first of his many books that would cause Justice Oliver Wendell Holmes, Jr. to call him "the first law writer in the country."

In Europe, Julian kept up, through the newspapers and journals, with public affairs. There was a good deal going on. Later he had reason to look back upon some of the events in Europe as foreshadowing evil times for the Jews of Germany. Frederick III, the German Emperor, was then being openly criticized as "too friendly" toward Jews. Wilhelm II, the "Kaiser Bill" of World War I, who succeeded Frederick in 1888, frankly disliked Jews and yielded to a group of vociferous anti-Semites who opposed the appointment of a Jew as rector of the University of Halle.

Julian was not greatly disturbed by these reports; neither were many native German Jews. They, and Mack, dismissed the attacks as passing aberrations. Yet, in 1889 some Jewish students at the University of Berlin, mainly from Russia, formed a branch of a society known as the "Lovers of Zion." They argued that Jews would never be free from anti-Semitism except in a homeland of their own, which should be in the ancient Promised Land. In this group there were some noteworthy young men whose names would be celebrated internationally in Zionism—Shmarya Levin, Leo Motzkin, Nachman Syrkin, and, later, Chaim Weizmann. In time, Julian was to know, or know of, them all and to call them colleagues in the movement for which they worked together.

Julian went several times to Munich, where he visited his father's sister, Jette, who had long since left Altenkunstadt and had married a Munich businessman, Leopold Steinberger. With its beer gardens, opera house and pleasant coffee and sweet shops, Munich then seemed to Julian the best of all possible worlds—like Cincinnati. Probably he was strolling jauntily about Munich on April 20, 1889, the day when, in Braunau just across the Austrian border, a boy was born who later became known as Adolf Hitler.

Of course, Julian also visited Altenkunstadt. All his life he had heard romanticized talk about his ancestral village on the River Main. The very name conjured pleasant sights, sounds, and also smells of good German cooking. By 1889 most of the discriminatory laws against Jews were gone from there, but so were most of the Jews: There probably were more Altenkunstadters in Cincinnati than in Altenkunstadt itself.

Julian inspected the house that had been his grandfather's but he felt little kinship with it. More than years or miles separated him from the ancestral Macks who had lived in this village. Indeed, the Julian Mack who stood that day in old Altenkunstadt made ridiculous the habit of people in Cincinnati to refer to him as a "German Jew." He described himself as "a thoroughgoing American," and he looked the part, especially in Europe.

The years in Europe "left less impress on his mind and judicial habits than might have been expected," his future friend, Judge Learned Hand, was to say. There is no doubt, however, that Julian had matured markedly. He never lost a certain guilelessness. He was, as Stephen S. Wise once said, "completely without guile." But he did acquire a worldliness on his European junket that had not been discernible before.

When Julian returned to the United States, it would have been natural for him to pick Cincinnati as the place in which to start his law career. Instead, he chose Chicago. Hilda, his favorite sister, was then living in Chicago, married to Simon Bacharach, son of Abe Tandler's sister Babette. She may have been a factor in Julian's decision. But a greater factor undoubtedly was Julian's inclination to stand on his own feet. He wanted to be away from the shadow of his highly successful uncle.

Furthermore, after the Harvard and the Parker Fellow years, he was somewhat uneasy among the bevy of brothers and sisters in the Cincinnati home. Henry, his older brother, had married a girl from down the block, and was working as a partner in their father's tailor shop. Julian and Henry now had very little in common. To most of the other sisters and brothers Julian returned almost as an uncle rather than as their brother. This was especially so with the two youngest brothers, William J., Jr., age five, and Robert, age three. Despite the closeness he always felt for all Macks, Julian had become, for the time being, something of a stranger in his family circle.

In October, 1890, he went to Chicago for an interview arranged for him by sister Hilda's husband with a lawyer there. He returned to Cincinnati thinking that he had secured a position in the lawyer's office. But the lawyer had a change of heart and the job was off. However, Julian did not change his mind about moving to Chicago.

He liked Chicago. Its vitality appealed to him. It was developing as a city that made and would make dramatic history; witness the Haymarket bomb affair of four years earlier, and the Pullman strike of 1894, which was then brewing. Chicago was also innovative. There, thanks to the social worker, Jane Addams, and her co-workers at Hull House, the juvenile court idea would be pioneered in 1899. That idea promised great social advances. It was in Chicago, too, that Zionism would first take formal root in America, with the pioneering "Knights of Zion" organization formed in 1898. Both ideas were to involve Julian, though neither of them was in his mind in October, 1890, when he first began his law career in Chicago.

"After much hesitation & discussion, I had decided to cast my lot in the Windy City & shall go there Sunday. . . . I am off without knowing what the future, immediate or present, has in store for me," he wrote on October 29, 1890, to a friend in Cambridge.

He was then twenty-four, a slow starter.

6. Puritan in Babylon

Like its new resident, Chicago, by 1890, had also just emerged from adolescence. All the factors that made a great inland metropolis were already in existence in Chicago—the railroads, the stockyards, the expanding factories, the immigrant workers, the bold entrepreneurs, the wide-open spirit. In the words of Lincoln Steffens, analyst of several contemporary "Babylons": "No matter who you are, where you came from, or what you set out to do, Chicago will give you a chance. The sporting spirit is the spirit of Chicago."

So Julian, though not of a "sporting spirit," settled in Chicago at an opportune time. No one had less of the entrepreneur's drive than he. In contrast to the brash, even vaunted wickedness of the city, the brutal clawing and in-fighting that went on, he was quite literally a Puritan in that prairie-land Babylon. Yet he became a true Chicagoan.

One aspect of the city, of special concern to Julian, was the kind of law practiced by the majority of lawyers in the city. Clarence Darrow, then also a new lawyer in Chicago, was once asked: "Can one be a successful lawyer, make a great deal of money, [and] do it without resorting to sharp practice, taking advantage of the technicalities of the law, or injuring the other fellow?"

"No," said Darrow.

Julian shared this view, but he had a higher concept of "success."

Actually, Chicago was no worse in this regard than other cities. Moreover, only recently, in 1886, it had elevated to the bench an exceptional lawyer, John P. Altgeld, who in 1893 was to become governor of Illinois, an exemplar of integrity, Vachel Lindsay's "Eagle Forgotten."

The general reputation of Chicago's bar, however, was in line with the reputation of Chicago itself: acquisitive, ruthless, hard. "In Chicago in 1890," a perceptive student, Ray Ginger, has commented, "one goal threatened to swallow up all others; men would do anything to make money." Conspicuous among the city's symbols,

32

along with the railroads and the stockyards, were the red-light
district called "the Levee" and the slums that stretched endlessly
beyond the new "skyscrapers." Yet this was also the period when
two great institutions took shape—the new University of Chicago
and the pioneer social settlement, Hull House.

The University of Chicago was revived the year after Julian's
arrival in Chicago, under Dr. William Rainey Harper.

Hull House had been established only the year before. In the
words of Robert Morse Lovett of the University, this was perhaps
"as important an event as occurred in the United States between
1865 and 1914."

With the University, and with Hull House under Jane Addams,
Julian was to have important associations.

One of the "most esteemed lawyers in Chicago at that time," as
Julian later described him, was Julius Rosenthal. It was with
Rosenthal that Julian started his Chicago career.

It was no accident that Julian's foothold in Chicago should have
been with a fellow Jew. For he now encountered the conventional
social pattern that called for almost everyone in the professions, as
well as in residences and social clubs, to be segregated along
religious, racial, and nationality lines. It was a pattern for which
neither Harvard nor his personal experience had prepared him.

Not that he felt deprived. On the contrary, he was elated that
Rosenthal was his employer. There were more affluent lawyers in
Chicago but none who cut a more respected figure in the city's
general affairs. Dignified, studious, full-bearded, "with a kindly
face"—so Julian remembered him—Rosenthal was also an acknowledged leader—perhaps *the* leader—of the Chicago Jewish community. He was one of the founding members and moving spirits of
Sinai Congregation, then the city's most prestigious Reform temple.

But there was one important respect in which Rosenthal deviated
from the accepted Sinai Congregation doctrine of radical Reform—the question of a revived Jewish state. That issue had been
stirred up in Chicago, shortly after Julian had settled there, by the
Rev. Dr. William E. Blackstone, a Baptist minister from the suburb
of Oak Park, following a "conference of Jews and Christians" in a
downtown Chicago theater where ministers and rabbis had come

together for a discussion of "areas of agreement between Judaism and Christianity." More specifically, Dr. Blackstone believed that Palestine should again become the Jewish state. In 1891 he circulated nationally the text of a "memorial" addressed to President Benjamin Harrison, calling for an autonomous Jewish state in Palestine as a solution to the problem of the Russian Jews.

> What shall be done for the Russian Jews? . . .

> Why not give Palestine back to them again? According to God's distribution of nations it is their home—an inalienable possession from which they were expelled by force. . . .

> Why shall not the powers, which under the treaty of Berlin, in 1878, gave Bulgaria to the Bulgarians and Serbia to the Serbians now give Palestine back to the Jews? . . .

To this "memorial" Dr. Blackstone succeeded in getting the signatures of several hundred leading Americans. These included John D. Rockefeller, J. P. Morgan, Chauncey M. Depew, Chief Justice Melville W. Fuller, Speaker of the House Thomas B. Reed, William McKinley, Joseph Medill and Cyrus McCormick.

Only a few of the "influential" Jews signed the "memorial." Most of them opposed it, including Rabbi Isaac Mayer Wise, who, in his *American Israelite,* paid his respects to Dr. Blackstone by calling him "naive."

"What we want to impress first and foremost on these noble philanthropists," Wise stated, "is [that] we want no new nationality created, and no old one restored, no sectionalism and no particularism in any temporal affairs; we want the quality and solidarity of mankind. . . ."

Another conspicuous opponent was the rabbi of Chicago's Sinai Congregation, Dr. Emil G. Hirsch, who had come to Sinai from Adath Israel in Louisville. Hirsch was then emerging as the most radical spokesman of Reform Judaism, even more radical than Isaac M. Wise. In addition to withholding his endorsement of the "memorial," he went out of his way to denounce it vehemently as "ill-disguised sentimentality."

"We are not Zionists," Rabbi Hirsch thundered. "As long as I am in this pulpit, Sinai Congregation will be unalterably opposed to Zionism. There is no cause for Zionism in America."

But Julius Rosenthal, though prominent in Sinai Congregation, was among the signers of the Blackstone Memorial, dramatic evidence that even a radical Reform Jew could accept Zionism, a fact which Julian, in time, would also personify and dramatize in his own life and work.

7. Blithe Young Lawyer

At first Julian's work for Rosenthal was limited to examining titles to real estate, mostly a dreary business calling for more eye-power than brain-power; hardly the type of law he had envisioned himself practicing. Fortunately, he had as a companion in this work Rosenthal's handsome son, Lessing, a Johns Hopkins graduate, then a student at the Union College of Law in Chicago. Mack and young Rosenthal formed a congenial pair.

Julian's earnings at first were not much above a clerk's wages, about $10 a week, in striking contrast to the $15,000-a-year starting salaries that were to await young lawyers, especially *Harvard Law Review* men, in a later generation. But he was not dismayed. He knew the saying then current at Harvard: "When you put up your shingle, in your first year you are lucky to earn the price of the shingle." For a time he increased his income, like his Uncle Max, by selling life insurance for Northwestern Mutual of Milwaukee, working together with another young man, Charles D. Norton, who later would become private secretary to President William Howard Taft, and still later, president of the First National Bank of New York.

Before long, Julian graduated to more interesting assignments, including probate work. His ability to speak German helped him along, for some of the Rosenthal clients understood only German.

By his second summer in Chicago, Julian had earned enough to indulge in a vacation.

"Mr. Mack left for Mackinac this evening and will be gone probably ten days," Lessing Rosenthal noted in a memorandum to his father in August, 1892.

When Julian returned, Lessing gave his father a note indicating the good relationship that existed between Julian and the Rosenthals:

"Mr. Mack floated in Monday . . . fat and sassy as ever."

The following spring, 1893, the World's Columbian Exposition opened on Chicago's lake front. It meant increased law business for such firms as Rosenthal's. Yet, on April 1, a month before the great fair was to open, Julian moved out of the Rosenthal office to a nearby office at 84 Washington Street. Friends were shocked. But the understanding had been from the outset that Julian would remain with the elder Rosenthal only until Lessing, the son, would be admitted to the bar. Lessing was admitted that spring, and he and his father formed the firm of Rosenthal & Rosenthal (in later years King, Robin, Gale & Pillinger, with a noteworthy clientele including the clothing firm of Hart, Schaffner & Marx) *sans* Julian Mack.

"I'm occupying rooms jointly with an older lawyer—each having private offices—because he says he has more than he can do & will turn over business to me," Julian wrote to John Wigmore. The "older lawyer" was Zach Hofheimer, a Virginia-born Jew of German descent who "looked like an Irishman." Hofheimer, too, had started out with Julius Rosenthal. A good business-getter, he already had associated with him another interesting young lawyer named Sigmund Zeisler.

Mack, Hofheimer and Zeisler made a distinctive trio of sharply differing personalities. The combination did not portend a long-term arrangement, but in this interlude Julian acquired in Zeisler one of his most interesting Chicago friends. Zeisler, an intellectual Jew who had come to America from Silesia, was married to the prominent concert pianist Fanny Bloomfield-Zeisler and was one of the main defense lawyers in the Haymarket trial of 1886–87.

After a time, Julian, albeit not wholeheartedly, formed a partnership with Zach Hofheimer and Sigmund Zeisler, an arrangement brought about by business resulting from the World's Columbian Exposition. Hofheimer obtained a good share of the business. Several "concessions," including "The Moorish Palace" and "Old Vienna," retained him for legal services. Litigation over such issues as whether or not the voluptuous dancing girl, Little Egypt, wore sufficient clothing would arise from time to time. Julian usually did the "written work"; Zeisler handled the court appearances or conferences with Exposition officials; Hofheimer, being the "good mixer," mainly "handled" the clients.

But more important than these matters was a major case in which

Julian alone was the lawyer—the sensational bankruptcy of Herman Schaffner & Co., the city's leading "Jewish investment house." A relative of Julius Rosenthal and a prominent figure in Jewish charities, Schaffner had handled debentures for Charles T. Yerkes, the traction "magnate," a connection which first gave his firm great prestige, but later led to its downfall. For, as Theodore Dreiser relates in his novel *The Financier,* Yerkes was then deep in questionable transactions that caused his banishment from Chicago.

On July 3, 1893 Herman Schaffner disappeared. A few days later his hat was found floating on Lake Michigan.

SCHAFFNER BANK FAILS
Friends Hint at Suicide and Despair
Herman Disappears—He is Brother-in-Law of Julius Rosenthal

Those headlines in the *Chicago Daily News*—emphasizing Schaffner's connection with Julius Rosenthal—told the essentials of the tragedy that rocked the Jewish world of Chicago. A dozen lawsuits followed, with Julian retained for the key lawsuit, that of Benjamin S. Levy et al. v. Chicago National Bank. Julian Mack had "arrived."

Even before the Schaffner case, Julian had enjoyed the feeling of having attained some prominence. A "Congress of Jurisprudence and Law Reform" was held at the World's Exposition, and Julian was named its coordinator under the chairman, President Henry Wade Rogers of Northwestern University. Thus Julian came to the attention of the leading lawyers not only of the city but of the nation as well. It was he who invited Professor William Roscoe Thayer of Harvard to deliver a paper at the Exposition on "The American Doctrine of Constitutional Law," a paper which Felix Frankfurter, more than sixty years later, was still to view as "a basic guide to lawyers and laymen alike." It was Julian, too, who put his friend, John Henry Wigmore, on the program with a paper on Japanese law—Wigmore's first appearance in the limelight.

At about this time some of Julian's fellow graduates of Harvard reactivated the Harvard Club of Chicago. Julian was first an officer and later president of the club, a salient mark of prestige, especially for a Jew.

Rabbi Hirsch in particular noted Julian's prominence. The ideal Jew, to Emil G. Hirsch, was a self-reliant, respected, cultured man who was fully Americanized, yet "not excessively materialistic," as he often preached at Sinai Temple. Obviously, he saw that ideal in Julian Mack and he set out to draw him into Sinai Congregation. Julian soon joined. Before he had been a member a year, Julian helped Dr. Hirsch organize a "lecture forum" in conjunction with the revived University of Chicago—a model for similar forums around the nation.

Will Mack took great pride in how well his son was doing. By then he had turned over his tailor shop to his son Henry while he himself joined Uncle Max's staff of insurance salesmen. At times he used Julian's office in Chicago as headquarters for soliciting business, with Julian helping to line up prospects. In May, 1894, on stationery of "Hofheimer, Zeisler & Mack," Will wrote to his brother appreciatively of Julian's success. But Will's letter also betrayed worry over his own health: "I have not felt well since my arrival & unless I improve & Business prospects are better, I shall return home soon," he wrote. Within a week, Will Mack was dead of a heart attack.

At the funeral in Cincinnati, Julian, at twenty-eight, was treated as co-head of the family, along with Uncle Max—a recognition of the fact that he seemed well established in what appeared to be a thriving Chicago law partnership, and was a prestigious member of the community there. Actually, a setback was ahead of him.

Hofheimer, Zeisler & Mack was falling apart. The surface cause was the depression of 1893, which lasted until the Spanish-American war in 1898. But aside from this slump, Julian had suffered a personal disappointment in the Schaffner case. As he wrote to Uncle Max, he had won "a splendid legal victory" in the State Supreme Court. But when the fees were apportioned among the various law firms involved, Julian was practically ignored. Then there developed temperamental difficulties with Hofheimer and Julian decided to pull out of the partnership. By his own choice he never had a partner again. Practicing by himself, he was as busy as he liked to be—probably busier. But he still did not make much money. He never would.

During this period, Northwestern University launched its own law school, successor to the Union College of Law. President Rogers, who had been dean of law at the University of Michigan and was later to hold the same position at Yale, took on the deanship of the Northwestern law school and began to recruit a faculty largely to be composed of Harvard-trained men.

Two of Julian's colleagues on the *Harvard Law Review* staff, John Wigmore and Bluett Lee, were immediately appointed. President Rogers subsequently offered an appointment also to Julian Mack but Julian declined.

"I feel I would be doing an injustice to my partners if I were to leave them now, or even in January next, as Rogers suggested," he wrote to Wigmore.

Later, in 1895, when the offer from Northwestern University was renewed, Julian, by then free of his partnership, accepted. He was to enjoy this university connection greatly. In view of his modest earnings from his law practice, he appreciated even the $300-a-year salary—a miserable stipend," to use his own phrase. And he liked being known as "Professor Mack." By that time he felt securely settled in Chicago, though one important personal step still remained: marriage.

Early in 1890, while attending the wedding of his brother Millard in Cincinnati, Julian met the bride's sister, Jessie Fox, who caused him to linger in Cincinnati longer than he had intended. Indeed, he spent considerable time with Jessie at the home of her father, Solomon Fox, a well-to-do jeweler who was prominent in the Cincinnati Jewish community.

Jessie was a vivacious young lady. In truth, some people wondered whether she was precisely the kind of wife Professor-Lawyer Mack should have. But she fascinated him. He liked her irreverent humor, which was sometimes directed at him. He even rode horseback with her; rather, he *sat* on a horse, his coattails flying—which was often the case even when he was not on a horse—and held on.

Julian and Jessie were married on March 9, 1896, at Cincinnati's Phoenix Club. Rabbi Hirsch came from Chicago to perform the ceremony as a gesture of his special esteem for his valued congregant. Also officiating was Rabbi David Philipson, of Cincinnati, who, like Hirsch, was to become a vigorous opponent of Zionism.

In February, 1897, the Macks' only child, Ruth, was born. "[Julian] had badly wanted a son," a brother-in-law said. But Julian showed so much affection toward this daughter—"too much," some relatives said—that no one could feel he was really disappointed. Already as a youngster, Ruth revealed a "keen and ardent mind," as Horace M. Kallen once told Julian. She was to have an outstanding career in psychiatry and a long personal association with Sigmund Freud, with whom she collaborated in his famous "Wolf Man" case. Julian found great pleasure in her brilliance and had an intellectual relationship with her that greatly enriched his life.

The first home of the Macks was a rented house on Drexel Boulevard on Chicago's South Side, in the Kenwood district, then the center of the upper middle-class German-Jewish community, the tone of which was set by the University of Chicago to the south and by Sinai Temple to the north. The Mack home was a comfortable place, made possible in large part by a generous wedding gift, the traditional dowry, from Jessie's parents.

Edgar Lee Masters, in his autobiography, *Across Spoon River,* described Drexel Boulevard as a street of "odious respectability." A slanted view, of course. But there was no doubt about the boulevard's aura of settled respectability.

Yet, Julian and Jessie were not wholly of that aura. Jessie was the first in her set to take up cigarette smoking, and also the fad of bicycling; she was "the prettiest girl that ever rode a Columbia bicycle along the west drive of Grand Boulevard in Chicago," Franklin P. Adams once reminisced in his column, "The Conning Tower," in the *New York World.* Adams had known her when he was a Chicago newspaperman.

Julian also stood out, mainly as more of an intellectual than most in the neighboring households. He was a key figure in the "Book and Play Club," a salon-like group which was the "in" set of wealthy

Chicago Jewry—the Rosenwalds, Loebs, Schaffners, Adlers, Rosenthals, and the like—with Julian frequently acting as chairman. In
the years to come, this club was to invite a wide variety of speakers
ranging from Ben Hecht to Horace M. Kallen, and to feature
performances by such musicians as Fanny Bloomfield-Zeisler, the
wife of Julian's former law partner. Vachel Lindsay read his
poetry—for a fee of $250.00.

Julian also kept up with most of the so-called "highbrow" journals
such as *The Nation, The Century, The North American Review,* as
well as with current books. This in itself made him an oddity among
his neighbors.

Also, he began to develop a reputation for being somewhat
off-beat, like Dean Ames, because of his gourmet interest in food.
Neighbors noticed that he, not Jessie, did much of the family's food
shopping.

Then, too, he and Jessie entered into a somewhat odd household
arrangement, doubling up with another couple, the Eugene
Goldmans. A sister of Max Epstein, founder of the General
American Tank Car Corporation, Mrs. Goldman had been a school
chum of Jessie's in Cincinnati and when Mrs. Goldman moved to
Chicago after her own marriage, she and Jessie resumed their old
friendship. The doubling-up arrangement was Jessie's idea and
Julian went along with it—probably with some ambivalent
feelings—to please her. For several years the Macks and the
Goldmans were looked upon as one family. When Mrs. Goldman's
brother formed the tank car enterprise that was to grow into a
two-billion dollar corporation, he prevailed upon Julian to join it as
a director. But Julian did not remain for long: he still had no
propensity for money-making.

The Mack menage seemed continuously in a state of "open
house," slightly chaotic. A friend described a "normal" day at
Julian's residence as "like the play 'You Can't Take it with You.'
People came in and out, some played cards, [while others] banged
on the piano, sang, or talked; it was a jolly group. Julian would sit at
a desk, reading or writing, apparently not bothered by all the
coming and going."

Even so, Julian and Jessie were integral parts of the genteel

German-Jewish community. Naturally, they attended the Sunday services conducted by Dr. Hirsch at Sinai Temple, then self-styled as "the most liberal congregation in America, and possibly in the world." And happily, at least from Julian's viewpoint, Dr. Hirsch preached very little religion, except when he denounced Zionism, his strong points being social justice and high ethical standards, a fact which at times proved annoying to some of his wealthiest congregants, but pleasing, always, to Julian.

In 1902, the University of Chicago established its law school, the "Harvard of the West," and Julian left Northwestern to join the original faculty of the new school. For this appointment, too, he was indebted to James Barr Ames. Determined to make his law school another Harvard, President Harper of the University of Chicago had persuaded President Eliot of Harvard to authorize Dean Ames to give every help to the new institution. Ames did so, even loaning Joseph Beale, Julian's associate on the *Harvard Law Review,* to serve the University of Chicago Law School as its first dean.

Ames pointed out to Dr. Harper that, if he wanted to create a Harvard-style law school, he could not do better than get three Harvard men who were then at Northwestern—Wigmore, Bluett Lee, and Julian Mack. Wigmore—by then Dean at the Northwestern Law School—decided to stay at Northwestern, but Mack and Lee accepted Harper's offer at once.

Later, Beale tried again to snare Wigmore for the University of Chicago. "With a faculty composed of Wigmore, Mack, Mechem, Whittier, a bright young man [as lecturer] . . . I should feel that I left in Chicago the strongest law faculty in the country, on the average," Beale wrote to Harper.

Unquestionably Julian was happier at the University of Chicago than he had been at Northwestern. For at Chicago he was part of the inner circle that administered the school. His rank was that of full professor. In particular, he was responsible for developing the well-stocked library for which the University of Chicago Law School became known. Though some students later remembered Mack mainly as a "prof who would dash wildly out of class to attend court downtown," he was undoubtedly a star member of the Chicago faculty. Benjamin V. Cohen recalled that Jerome N. Frank, for one, considered Judge Mack as "his favorite teacher at the law school, [who] helped him most and gave the best understanding of the law in practical operation and effect." Harold L. Ickes, who was to serve as Secretary of the Interior under Franklin D. Roosevelt, had similar recollections of Julian Mack.

The University of Chicago from the outset was an institution where Jews felt especially at ease. There was a practical, historical reason for this: Had it not been for financial help from Chicago Jews, the university might not have survived. Back in September, 1892, Rabbi Hirsch, whose grandson, Edward Hirsch Levi, was destined to become president of the university, had noted in his *Reform Advocate*:

> Jews of this city have reason to be proud of this institution. At a time when the whole plan [for its survival] seemed destined to miscarry, it was a social organization of Jews [the Standard Club] that came to the [financial] rescue.

Julian was to be on the University of Chicago Law School faculty for the next 38 years. Probably at some point he might have given up his private practice to become a full-time professor of law at Chicago. However, after his first year in Chicago, he became involved in a new interest that set him on another course.

8. His Brother's Keeper

Julian's new interest was Jewish social work in particular and the "Jewish problem" in general. Indeed, by 1900, the "Jewish problem," which had been merely incidental to Julian in his Harvard years, very nearly became his most absorbing interest. A new migration of Jews to America, a mushrooming influx of East European Jews—chiefly the result of the Russian situation that had inspired Dr. Blackstone's "memorial"—was the spark.

By American standards these newcomers were an odd-looking lot. They were often insulted and mocked as "greenhorns." Many of the men wore beards and traditional sidecurls. Most of them possessed little more than the minimum few dollars required for admission to the country. Thus, unlike the Jews who had come to America from Germany a generation earlier, thousands of them were forced into sweatshop occupations. To make matters worse, their arrival coincided with the effects of the depression of 1893.

Of special concern to Julian Mack was the fact that Chicago caught much of the "overflow" from the new immigration which had resulted in the rise of large ghettoes, primarily in New York, Philadelphia and Boston. Indeed, a ghetto composed of poor Russian, Polish and Rumanian Jews early grew up on Chicago's West Side in the area of Hull House.

The well-established German Jews—Julian's social class—were unhappy about this development. Having themselves attained a comfortable degree of integration in America, many of them saw their own position threatened by these newcomers, who appeared to be poor prospects for assimilation. When the migration started, the first response of the German Jews was to try to limit its flow.

Various Jewish philanthropic agencies in Europe, notably the Baron de Hirsch Fund and the Alliance Israélite Universelle of France, helped the East European Jews in their migration. American Jewish leaders also cooperated, through various charity organizations, as a matter of Jewish brotherhood. But they did so basically with two main guidelines: that only a "reasonable" number should be allowed to come in any given period; and that only "able-bodied, employable" persons should be welcomed. As the *Jewish Messenger* of New York tartly observed in May, 1881:

> It is very philanthropic to desire the Jews of Russia to leave that Empire, now that pogroms have broken out in the Ukraine, but to suggest that three million of them settle in America suggests more enthusiasm than common sense.

In October, 1881, the Russian Emigrant Relief Fund, also in New York, cabled to the Alliance Israélite Universelle of Paris:

> Send no more emigrants. Committee must return incapables.

The "brother's keeper" spirit among established Jews in America still existed, but in this situation it was obviously weakening.

There were exceptions: Emma Lazarus, the poetess; Henrietta Szold, the editor, and later founder of Hadassah; and Michael Heilprin, the encyclopedist, were among the "settled" Jews who were deeply distressed because the newcomers were not more warmly welcomed. They roused activity, individually at first, to foster a new attitude. Others were troubled too, a minority, but a vocal one—eventually including Julian Mack.

By 1891 the German-Jewish leaders in the United States faced up to the fact that there was no halting the flow. "Incapables" as well as "capables" had to be expected from Russian Poland and other East European areas—by the thousands.

In 1891 Jacob H. Schiff, the banker of Kuhn, Loeb & Co., made a statement that signaled the new outlook to his fellow German Jews:

> There is considerable unjustified prejudice against these people, especially on the part of those who know nothing about them. These Russian emigrants are, in the main, a sturdy race, thrifty and anxious to work, and if they are only started in the right manner, they are sure to become successful.

A new strategy was adopted. In an effort to hold down the size of the ghettos in the large cities, the newcomers were encouraged to settle in small inland towns, or to become farmers. Thus Schiff and other leaders of Jewish charities in New York worked out a program with their counterparts in other cities in the United States whereby the other cities each were to "accept" a certain number of immigrants, so relieving the congestion in New York and other eastern centers. Chicago, Cincinnati, Milwaukee and St. Louis were to act in their turn as "distributing points" for the smaller communities in their areas.

A Jewish Agricultural Society, with Rabbi Hirsch as chief sponsor, acted to divert some of the newcomers to farm areas in Texas, Kansas, the Dakotas, and Minnesota. There was great satisfaction over this effort among its sponsors. Some viewed it as an answer to anti-Semitism. If Jews were to become farmers, instead of pawnbrokers, who could hate them? Such was their concept, and for a time this "back to the land" movement seemed promising. But eventually most of the immigrant families in the experiment made their way back to the cities because only a few were fitted for farming in the western hinterlands. There was an additional factor. Where, in the prairies, could Jewish husbands be found for Jewish daughters?

The "dispersal program," as it was called, was carried on nationally through "The American Committee for Ameliorating the Condition of Russian Refugees." The Chicago branch was called "The Society in Aid of the Russian Refugees." Julius Rosenthal was a key member of the executive committee. Meetings were often held in Rosenthal's law office, especially while Julian Mack was still there.

In the beginning, Julian was only an observer. Before long, however, he was drawn into the program as a participant. It was his first experience with Russian Jewry. He developed an important friendship with a radical Russian-born Jew, Dr. Theodore Sachs, an immigrant from Odessa, who, like Julian, was destined to leave a mark on Chicago history, as founder of the city's pioneering municipal tuberculosis sanatorium.

When Dr. Sachs arrived in Chicago in 1891, he came almost at once to the Rosenthal office with a letter of introduction. Some years later Julian recalled:

> I met him the first or second day after he reached Chicago from Russia. He had been a student of law in Odessa and had been compelled to leave the country because he had joined his fellow students in certain liberalizing movements. He knew no English when he came here, he had no money, no friends, no prospects. His sole possessions were health, character, ability and ambition; and the ambition was not for his own advancement, but to serve humanity.

> Julius Rosenthal . . . and I took a deep interest in him from the start. We urged him to study law, in view of his past studies. But he told us that he had decided to study medicine, not for the money there was in it, but because he then believed that he could be of greater service to his fellow man as a physician than in any other capacity. . . .

> For over ten years he gave of his services day and night without a penny of pay in all of the cases referred to him by the Jewish charities, as well as by a number of other, nonsectarian charitable organizations.

> He became particularly interested in tuberculosis because he saw the terrible results of this dread disease among the poorer people. His keen sense of obligation to respond to the call for social service had caused him to become in every way a social worker, as well as a physician. His survey of the housing situation in several of the West Side wards, and the relation between housing and tuberculosis, was one of the first and, probably, the most important study of this kind made.

In short, Dr. Theodore Sachs, whom Jane Addams also praised in *Twenty Years at Hull House,* was an outstanding example of the type of Russian Jew that Jacob Schiff had welcomed. Quite possibly Julian's friendship with Dr. Sachs helped spark all that Julian began to do for the Russian Jews in Chicago. It is certain that Julian's admiration for Dr. Sachs confirmed him in his attitude which, as Julian's granddaughter Matilda Juliana Hosford recalled, caused him to "show indignation and disgust if anyone made disparaging remarks about Russian Jews." "Mack identified with his fellow Jews, whether Russian, Polish or German; they were his people, so he *had* to work with them and for them. He felt responsible." So Benjamin V. Cohen put it.

In March, 1892, Chicago's "Society in Aid of the Russian Refugees" was alerted to a crisis. The Czar's government had begun a strict enforcement of discriminatory laws against Jews. What Russian Jewry faced was described in July, 1893, by Andrew D. White, the founding president of Cornell University, who was then U.S. Ambassador to Russia. In a report to Secretary of State Walter Q. Gresham, White wrote:

> The treatment of the Israelites, whether good or evil, is not based entirely upon any *one* ukase or statute; there are said to be in the vast jungle of the laws of this empire more than one thousand decrees and statutes relating to them, beside innumerable circulars, open or secret, regulations, restrictions, extensions, and temporary arrangements, general, special, and local, forming such a tangled growth that probably no human being can say what the law as a whole is—least of all can a Jew in any province have any certain knowledge of his rights. . . . The restrictions are by no means confined to residence; they extend into every field of activity.

A new wave of Jewish migration to America began. To provide assistance for those going to Chicago, an emergency fund was needed. Julian took part in the formation of the "Young Men's Russian Relief Association" and at a mass meeting gave a speech remarkable for its mature insight into the basic problems faced by the newcomers.

He conceded that many of the Russian Jews "have developed traits much to be deplored." But, he pointed out, this was "a natural result" of conditions forced upon them:

Living among a people, the lowest of all civilized nations, they have been unable at times to rise much above the common level. Lying and bribery have been the means they were compelled to resort to in order to obtain the necessities of life. . . . Usury is charged against them, but it was the only occupation left open to many of them.

Yet, with immigrants like Theodore Sachs in mind, he assured his audience that not all were of that kind.

Among their number you will find hundreds of honest, able and industrious workmen, and in all of them, even in the lowest, despite their bad traits, despite their wants and their misery and their mistreatment, there [are] not wanting those qualities which have ever characterized the Jewish race at all times and in all climes . . .

He was sure, he added, that "within one or two generations," there would emerge from the immigrant ghettoes "a people worthy and fit to take their place as citizens of this great republic."

Be your motives what they may [he concluded], whether you feel the competition of this new mass; whether as Americans you foresee danger to our institutions from this sudden unchecked and enormous immigration; whether as Jews, jealous of the good name which you and your ancestors have acquired in this land; or whether as men, from motives pure and high, because your hearts are wrung with pity and with sympathy for these wretched sufferers—whatever be your motive: I say it is your duty to join with us in this organization, to help us meet this problem face to face, to grapple with it boldly, and, with the help of God, and by earnest and unselfish efforts, find for it a peaceful and a useful solution.

Rabbi Hirsch, for one, was greatly impressed with Julian's speech and published it in full in his *Reform Advocate*. Other leaders in the

Jewish community were also impressed, so much so that a few weeks later, when the board of directors of the United Jewish Charities of Chicago met at Sinai Temple to elect a new secretary, they elected Julian.

Julian Mack thus became, in effect, the directing official of Jewish charities in Chicago, which meant that from then on he was deeply involved with every aspect of the Jewish immigrant problem. It meant also, and officially, that he had clearly surfaced as "his brother's keeper" in line with his family background and his personality, continuing, on a far larger scale, the tradition which his family, especially on the Tandler side, had established in San Francisco. But this development was to have even greater significance in Julian's life. Julian Mack, so markedly an "emancipated" Jew, was from then on to move in the mainstream of Jewish life.

He had expected his duties as secretary of the United Jewish Charities (later styled the Associated Jewish Charities, still later the Jewish Federation of Chicago) to be just a sideline activity. But the office very nearly became his major occupation, for he had become secretary at a time when the amount of work to be done was at its most time-consuming. More and more funds were needed for coping with the influx of immigrants. But the depression of 1893 had dried up sources of support. On top of the Schaffner banking failure, the bank of Lazarus Silverman also collapsed. Silverman, like Schaffner, had been a leading supporter of Jewish charities.

Funds had to be obtained somehow for the Michael Reese Hospital, for emergency relief, for a sheltering home, a home for the aged, an orphanage, an employment agency, and a settlement house on Maxwell Street, as well as for transporting immigrants to other communities in accordance with the "dispersal program." The brunt of this fund-raising was borne by Julian, who found that he had a flair for securing money to help others.

Finances were not Julian's only concern. Friction between the new immigrants and the older Jewish community frequently erupted, and he had to function as mediator. He found, incidentally, that the newcomers' complaints were usually justifi-

able. Not only were they still looked down upon by many German
Jews; they were also exploited in the stores and factories where they
worked.

The socialist Russian-Jewish workers, who formed Yiddish-speak-
ing labor unions, had serious complaints. Almost unanimously the
German Jews, their employers in the clothing factories, were
anti-union. This situation involved Julian directly since it had come
to be the practice in Chicago, as in New York, to threaten strikers
with denial of the services of various Jewish philanthropies. An ugly
example of this occurred in 1891. A strike by a newly-formed
Chicago Cloak Makers Union in 1897 was broken after Joseph
Beifeld, an employer active in Jewish charities, arranged that no
striker's family should receive help of any kind. Julian saw to it that
this outrageous tactic was ended. It was a forecast of the
sympathetic attitude which he was to show toward exploited workers
later, along with Louis D. Brandeis, as a prominent arbitrator of
labor disputes in the garment industries of New York and
Cleveland.

One particular incident between the newcomers and the "settled"
Jews involved the establishment of the Maxwell Street Settlement
for Jews, just down the street from Hull House, and resulted in his
first meeting with Jane Addams. Miss Addams, then in her thirties,
was an attractive woman already showing the qualities which in the
words of her nephew-biographer, James Weber Linn, were to make
her "the first real adventurer in the unexplored country of social
amelioration in America."

She was hostess at a meeting at Hull House to launch a Jewish
settlement. Julian Mack and Lessing Rosenthal were the main
speakers. They outlined a program which had been mapped out for
the settlement by the Young Men's Hebrew Charity Association. To
their astonishment, their audience responded with angry outbursts.
The newcomers resented being asked to accept a program that had
already been laid out. There was also indignation because the
settlement idea looked like an effort—which Rabbi Hirsch later
acknowledged—to "convert" Orthodox newcomers to Reform
Judaism.

But the real reason for the outbursts was the clearly pent-up indignation on the part of the Russian Jews over what they felt to be a supercilious attitude toward them on the part of German Jews, of whom Mack and Lessing Rosenthal seemed to them typical. Julian sought to appease them with a comment that proved more prophetic than he could have realized then, in the year 1893.

"Let's not quarrel," he said, "The wheel of fortune never stops turning. Today the German Jew helps the Russian Jew; tomorrow the Russian Jew will help the German Jew."

He learned an important lesson that evening. Regardless of the good will of the "settled" Jews toward the folk they helped, and regardless, too, of the immigrants' apparent or real need for guidance, the newcomers had to be given a "say" in what was proposed. Miss Addams phrased this point succinctly to Julian at that meeting: "One does good, if at all, *with* people, not *to* people." It was a point he was never to forget. By following that precept, he helped save the Maxwell Street Settlement.

Julian learned still other lessons about the Jewish people, particularly through his supervision, as charities secretary, of the operations of the Michael Reese Hospital.

Established by the Chicago Jewish community—meaning the "German" Jews—the Michael Reese Hospital later became one of the great hospitals of the nation. But during this period it was in financial trouble. It was beset by other problems, too, that were just as annoying. For example, Orthodox Jews raised objections because the medical staff was not exclusively Jewish. They objected particularly to the chief of staff, Dr. Ernst Schmidt, an exceptionally prestigious surgeon and civic leader who had headed the Haymarket Amnesty Association to prevent the execution of the anarchists accused in the Haymarket bomb affair of 1886. Everyone had great respect for Schmidt—but he was not a Jew.

Then, too, objections were raised against the fact that the hospital was located on the lake front, and not in the ghetto area. Another complaint concerned the hospital's kitchen, which did not observe the Jewish dietary laws. This complaint was voiced in such bitter terms as to underscore a comment Miss Addams made to Julian after the Maxwell Street Settlement meeting in 1895. "It seemed to me," she said with astonishment, "that there is more ill feeling between the Reform Jews and Orthodox Jews than between Jews and Gentiles."

These difficulties showed that Julian had taken on an apparently thankless job. Yet he retained the post of charities secretary for the next ten years, becoming, in effect, "Mr. Jewish Charities of Chicago."

In 1904 he also became president of the National Conference of Jewish Charities. By that time, philanthropy had attained greater importance than the synagogues in the Jewish community. So Julian Mack emerged as a major spokesman not only for Chicago Jewry but for American Jewry as a whole. Gone completely from him now was the posture that Jewish affairs were no more than incidental concerns to him.

The Dreyfus case in France, which had been going on since 1894, accentuated the need for involvement. Julian had come to accept anti-Semitism in some form as a fact of life. But he had primarily associated it with "barbaric" Russia. That anti-Semitism could flare up virulently in "civilized" France, home of "the rights of man," was a jolt to him, as to many others, Jews and non-Jews, such as the young journalist from Vienna, Theodor Herzl, the novelist Émile Zola in Paris, and another novelist, Maxim Gorki in Nizhni Novgorod, Russia.

Miss Addams, who happened to be in France in 1900, was also shocked. "The city was full of horror about the Dreyfus case," she recalled. "Many Frenchmen felt that Dreyfus had not had a fair trial, that no one knew whether he was guilty or not, because he had not been tried on the preferred charges, but on his racial affiliation."

Here Jane Addams pointed up the aspect of the Dreyfus case that especially touched Julian as a lawyer: the breakdown of a legal system. Alfred Dreyfus, a captain in the French army, had been accused of selling military secrets to Germany. But as Julian sadly noted: "It was Dreyfus the Jew, not Dreyfus the man, who was accused by bitter anti-Semitic enemies. So the Jewish people all over the world underwent trial."

He began, for the first time, to wonder whether the Jews were really secure, even in America. For implicit in the prosecution of Dreyfus was the old allegation, also made in debates over Zionism, that Jews could not be full citizens in any host country, but would always be considered as aliens.

In the *Chicago Record,* Finley Peter Dunne summed up the attitude of a good many persons when he had "Mr. Hennessy" comment about the Dreyfus case:

"I don't know anything about it, but I think he's guilty. He's a Jew."

To be sure, Julian was not so deeply affected by the Dreyfus case as was Theodor Herzl, for whom the case cinched his resolve to set forth his ideas in a small book, *The Jewish State,* a work that led to the rise of modern political Zionism. Nonetheless, "I was stirred in my soul," he later recalled.

The forge was warming up.

9. Judge Mack

His connection with Jewish charities brought him associations with the leading Jewish businessmen of Chicago. Normally, his law practice should have benefited. But this did not happen. Julian did, however, form close friendships with some businessmen, especially Julius Rosenwald of Sears, Roebuck & Co.

For a considerable period, Julian functioned as Rosenwald's adviser on philanthropies, which amounted eventually to some $60,000,000. "They are the Moses and Aaron of Jewish charities," a newspaper noted. Yet the legal business of Sears, Roebuck went to other lawyers.

Still, Julian's role in Jewish charities brought him a signal reward. It led to his becoming "Judge Mack."

In 1903, the Democratic mayor of Chicago, young Carter Harrison, faced a tough campaign for reelection. It was the period of the rise of "muckraking" in Chicago journalism; William Randolph Hearst had just started a muckraking newspaper, the *American*. Harrison knew the value of seeming to go along with "reform," and also the value of the "Jewish vote."

Earlier, it had been assumed that the "Jewish vote" was solidly Republican. Rabbi Hirsch, for example, had been a Republican elector for William McKinley in the presidential election of 1896. Indeed, the rabbi of Congregation Sinai was capable of delivering, in highly moral tones, highly partisan Republican speeches.

On the national scene, Theodore Roosevelt, as President, also courted the "Jewish vote"; he named a Jew, Oscar Straus of New York, to his Cabinet as Secretary of Commerce and Labor.

To offset this, the Democrats began to cater to the Russian Jews; in 1900 they even put up a Jew, Samuel Alschuler of Aurora, as candidate for Governor of Illinois.

Mayor Harrison was not known for any special friendship toward Jews. But in 1903 he looked for an opportunity to "do something for them," just as Chicago politicians had long been "doing something" for the Irish, the Germans, and the Poles. The opportunity came with the death of a civil service commissioner. Harrison offered the appointment to Julian. In itself, this post was not important; it was a mere sideline to his law practice. But Julian was aware that it might lead to something more significant—a judgeship, for instance. So he accepted.

Beforehand, the mayor incidentally had satisfied himself on two points about Julian. First, that Julian was a Democrat—which he was, thanks to his father's defection to the Democrats back in 1873. Second, that Julian's selection would please the Jewish community. The appointment was highly, even extravagantly, praised.

"We congratulate Mayor Harrison upon having appointed Mr. Mack," the *Chicago Legal News* said. "He is thoroughly educated, strong both in mind and body, and incorruptible." "The city is honored when a man so accomplished and of such high standing accepts a position in the government," said a prominent alderman.

Julian's excellence as a citizen and lawyer, however, was not the major factor. His connection with the Jewish community, particularly his role in Jewish charities, had been taken into account. The mayor, in fact, openly stated that he "really had not known 'Professor Mack' previously," but "the distinguished lawyer had been recommended to me by Rabbi Joseph Stolz."

That Julian's selection would especially please Rabbi Hirsch, despite his Republican affiliation, was also a factor. Indeed, the whole Sinai Congregation "crowd," mainly Republican, was to approve warmly—including Lessing Rosenthal, who was then active in the Municipal Voters' League and the Civil Service Reform League and was one of the mayor's leading critics. Harrison had scored a political ten-strike, so plainly that even Julian, who was usually naive in politics, knew it.

Three months after Julian became civil service commissioner, the Harrison organization slated him as a Democratic candidate for judge of the Circuit Court of Cook County. Julian's willingness, even eagerness—to accept a judgeship at this point in his career reflected his attitude toward the acquisition of personal wealth, for at that time judges were notoriously underpaid. Thus, at least in the large cities—except for venal politicians who expected to get rich from a judicial post—only wealthy lawyers would seek a judgeship as a capstone to a successful career.

Julian Mack then was still in his thirties and commanded only a modest income. His decision to become a judge, therefore, meant that he had permanently given up the idea of becoming a wealthy man. He had chosen a career of intellectual activity and public service over a lucrative law practice which might well have become his even without use of the tactics described by Clarence Darrow.

In his selection for a judgeship, his Jewishness was again an element. For, though he was conventionally wary about admitting it, he did not overlook opportunities of soliciting votes among Jews as such.

Julian needed such help, or so he thought. For his candidacy appeared to suffer a setback in a poll taken by the Chicago Bar Association. He lost the recommendation of the Bar Association by 17 votes. He was too young, it was said. Even so, all the city's leading newspapers supported him. What Chicago needed, said the *Tribune* in particular, was an "absolutely honest and independent Judiciary," and Julian's election, it added, would help achieve that goal.

Significantly for Julian, that was the year of the Kishinev pogroms. During the Easter holiday of 1903, fifty Russian Jews were murdered, hundreds of others were brutally assaulted, and the homes and shops of still others were wrecked by looters while the Czar's police looked on—or openly participated.

The news of Kishinev came just as the judicial election campaign in Chicago was reaching its climax. The reaction resembled that which had been set off by the Mortara case. In Chicago, a protest meeting was held, featuring Clarence Darrow and Jane Addams. Like his grandfather Tandler at the Mortara meeting in San Francisco in 1859, Julian was on the platform at the main Kishinev meeting in Chicago; he was also one of the speakers.

In the subsequent election, the vote in the Jewish districts was practically solid for Julian Mack. As a result, he was at the top of the list of winning candidates.

In later years, it would not be considered exceptional in America for a Jew to become a judge. But at that time, in 1903, it was, even in New York. Chicago had elected only one Jew to the bench before Julian. Consequently, Julian's election was widely celebrated, especially among the Sinai Congregation "crowd"—he was "one of their own."

More important was the reaction of the "ghetto" Jews. They generally viewed public officials, who to them were personified by the police, as an oppressive "enemy," and with good reason. Mistreatment of poor Jews was a common complaint, a situation comparable to the plight of the Negroes in northern cities a generation later. The chief complainants were peddlers with their pushcarts in ghetto markets; they were often victims of police officiousness and petty blackmail.

"America isn't so different from Russia," one Maxwell Street pushcart operator told Louis Wirth, the University of Chicago sociologist. "Here, instead of from the Czar and bureaucrats, we have to buy our right to make a living from the grafters and politicians."

Harassment of Jewish peddlers by hoodlums was common. The police usually looked the other way. Or the police joined, at least vicariously, in the "sport" of beard-pulling, rock-throwing and name-calling.

To be sure, non-Jewish immigrants were the victims of similar abuse. Jane Addams, for one, had "emotional difficulty," as she put it, even in telling about it. She recalled

> . . . the Italians, whose fruit-carts were upset simply because they are "dagoes," or the Russian peddlers, who are stoned, and sometimes badly injured, because it has become a code of honor in a gang of boys to thus express their derision . . . the Greeks, filled with amazement when their very name is flung at them as an opprobrious epithet.

But the Jews suffered the most. Finally, they organized at Hull House a "Jewish Peddlers' Protective Association," which retained as its lawyer Clarence Darrow.

"Organize, organize, so your votes in elections will count,"

Darrow counseled them. But the harassment went on.

The Jews in Chicago were also deeply concerned about police brutality against strikers in labor disputes. Here, too, ghetto Jews had cause for special complaint, for abuse of Jewish workers in strikes was especially rampant. Recalling the day he was broken in by Jacob Riis as a police reporter on New York's East Side, Lincoln Steffens in his autobiography tells of seeing two policemen "half-forcing, half-carrying a poor, broken, bandaged East Side Jew" into the office opposite that of the Superintendent of Police.

"There," he quoted Riis, "you have a daily scene in Inspector Williams' office! That's a prisoner. Maybe he's done something wrong, that miserable Russian Jew; anyway, he's done something the police don't like. But they haven't only arrested him, as you see; they've beaten him up."

The situation in Chicago was no different; at times, it was worse. Since the Haymarket episode, Chicago police commanders had learned that the quickest route to favorable publicity and other emoluments was to be "tough" with labor "agitators," and to create scares about anarchists or other radicals, some of whom were Jews.

One especially disturbing incident occurred in the Chicago ghetto. In a round-up of radicals following the assassination of President McKinley in Buffalo in 1901, numerous Jewish homes in Chicago were raided. Fears reminiscent of Cossack visitations in Russia were naturally felt. Among the "suspects" jailed was the editor of an insignificant anarchist sheet, an intellectual Russian Jew with a doubly Jewish name: Abraham Izaak.

Leon Czolgosz, McKinley's assassin, had in fact once visited Izaak. But Izaak had suspected Czolgosz of being a "spy," shunned him, and warned fellow radicals against any association with him. Accordingly, there was less reason for arresting Izaak than for jailing, say, William Randolph Hearst, whose papers had printed some verse which, by clear implication, called for McKinley's death by "an assassin's bullet."

Izaak and his wife and daughter were held incommunicado for days in a dank sub-basement cell of the City Hall. Jane Addams appealed to Mayor Harrison to permit Izaak to talk with a lawyer. The mayor refused, but he permitted Miss Addams to talk with

Izaak. The result: The press played up her visit, implying an affinity between Hull House and anarchists.

"I at once discovered," Miss Addams recalled, "that whether or not I had helped a brother out of a pit, I had fallen into a deep one myself. A period of sharp public opprobrium followed, traces of which, I suppose, will always remain"—to the dismay of Julian and other admirers of Miss Addams and of Hull House.

For Miss Addams, the Izaak incident was a painful lesson. Some of her major financial supporters, including Mrs. Potter Palmer, dropped away. The incident carried a lesson also for the ghetto Jews. Mistakenly or not, they concluded that, as Jews, they had no rights which officialdom felt required to respect. No wonder, then, that a hopeful thrill ran through Chicago's West Side when Julian Mack, though a "German" Jew, was elevated to the bench. He was "one of their own," too, the ghetto Jews hoped, and he did not disappoint that hope. As with Brandeis in Boston, the more association Julian had with East European Jews, not only with professional men like Dr. Sachs of Odessa, but also with working-class Jews, even socialists or anarchists, the greater became his affinity for them. More and more—to the puzzlement, doubtless, of some neighbors on posh Drexel Boulevard—they became "his people."

Though at thirty-seven he was many years younger than most of his judicial colleagues, Julian took his seat as judge of the Cook County Circuit Court in July, 1903 with an aplomb that caused astonishment.

At the outset he demonstrated a trait that not many persons suspected. In court the usually amiable Julian became something of an authoritarian—not tyrannically or boorishly so, but an authoritarian nonetheless. Certain lawyers disliked this. This was true particularly of lawyers accustomed to have judges look to *them* for enlightenment on the law.

In their view, a judge was just another lawyer, usually one who had been placed on the bench because of politics and not for his legal brilliance. As they viewed matters, it was up to them to guide the judges' thinking and, in the process, to impress their clients.

Julian frustrated such lawyers. More often than not he did the instructing, citing statutes or precedents that the lawyers had omitted. Sophisticated lawyers soon caught on, too, that it would be wise to consult the current issue of the *Harvard Law Review* in their preparations prior to appearing before him. For, whether from personal or other reasons, Julian let it be known that he kept up with "his" *Review*, and that lawyers in his court neglected it at their peril. He could also be disconcerting to a lawyer who reeled off an endless string of cases in support of his pleadings.

"Well, what is your *best* case?" Julian would insist.

But he quickly won esteem for his grasp of the law and for his fairness.

Of certain judges, there was gossip, justified or not, that they were amenable to "fixes." Looking at Chicago, Lincoln Steffens pronounced its alliances between criminals and politicians worse than those in New York. Obviously, some judges were involved in such unsavory dealings. But it went without saying that Judge Mack was above suspicion.

In his early period on the bench, he showed a punctiliousness regarding the letter of the law that laid him open to criticism. Thus, when he ruled, on a technicality, that Chicago's Municipal Court Act, which had set up a "poor man's court" in place of Justice of the Peace "shops," was unconstitutional, he was overruled by the State Supreme Court. He later admitted that this reversal had been right. Still, he had a consistently "good press." Indeed, he became, on the Chicago bench, a symbol of judicial probity.

Street assaults upon Jews came to a crisis very early during his judicial service. An aged Orthodox rabbi, Abram Glick, died of a heart attack after being stoned by hoodlums. At last, the mayor insisted that the police make arrests.

"The stoning of peddlers has become the most abominable nuisance in Chicago," Julian announced when a group of boys involved in such outrages was brought before him. "The Jew-baiter must go—we are not living in Russia. I will stop it if I have to imprison every youngster in the city."

His attitude was summed up in the headlines of the *Chicago Tribune* of March 25, 1905:

PEDDLER BAITERS
TO BE LOCKED UP

Judge Mack Sentences Five
and Warns All "Incipient
Murderers"

Obviously, Judge Mack alone could not end such incidents. But now, for the first time, Jewish peddlers and other similarly tormented foreign-born in Chicago felt that they had a friend in court. They recognized in Julian the first official voice strongly raised in their behalf—a judge who was a Jew with no diffidence about defending his own kind. The situation in Chicago was confirmation, to a degree, of a cogent passage in Herzl's *Jewish State:*

> No one can deny the plight of the Jews. . . . Attacks in parliaments, at meetings, in the press, from pulpits, in the street, on trips. . . .

Though he at least showed proper indignation as an American and as a Jew, Julian did not pretend that he, or any other judge for that matter, was really meeting the problem.

At first he served mainly in the "chancery" division, where business cases formed the bulk of his docket. There was a sameness about these cases that was boring; this was one drawback to his judicial life. But there were saving features—his professorship at the University of Chicago, which he retained, and his continued connection with Jewish charities.

Then he received an assignment that placed him in the forefront of what for him was to be the most personally satisfying judicial activity—service in the new, pioneering Juvenile Court of Chicago.

Here Julian Mack was in his element. More than half a century later, his service in that court would be recalled as trail-blazing.

10. The Child Saver

Ostensibly, Julian's service as juvenile court judge was considered a sideline, the kind of chore that other judges avoided. After all, the Juvenile Court involved neither money, nor questions of property, nor issues of life or death. It "only" dealt with youngsters in trouble, most of whom, according to the common idea, were "worthless" or incorrigibly "bad."

The Juvenile Court, then, was mainly a matter of social work which many judges considered demeaning. Not so Julian. Precisely this assignment, in certain respects, became the most important phase of his long judicial career. Among American men and women known in the social welfare field as "child savers," he emerged as outstanding.

At that time, as later, there was a major misconception in the public mind as to the concept of a juvenile court. It was generally assumed that Chicago's Juvenile Court had been established primarily for dealing with children involved in crimes. But criminality, or "delinquency," was only one phase of the problem which the court had been set up to handle. In the view of the Hull House sponsors of the act that created the Juvenile Court in 1899, the court's main work was with neglected and abused children: school drop-outs, boys or girls who had wandered away from home or who preferred to sleep in alleys or lofts, girls in sexual "trouble," youngsters employed in trades forbidden to them by law, children (and there were many such) who had no homes, and youngsters who took drugs.

The language of the act itself made all this clear: Its title was "An Act to Regulate the Treatment and Control of Dependent, Neglected and Delinquent Children," with the emphasis upon "neglected" and "dependent."

The act's definition of "neglected" and "dependent" children charted the main purpose of the court—to assume jurisdiction over any child

> who for any reason is destitute or homeless or abandoned; or dependent upon the public for support; or who habitually begs or receives alms; or who is found living in any house of ill fame or with any vicious or disreputable person; or whose home, by reason of neglect, cruelty or depravity on the part of its parents, guardian or other person . . . is an unfit place for such a child; and any child under the age of 8 years who is found peddling or selling any article or singing or playing any musical instrument upon the streets, or giving any public entertainment.

The Juvenile Court was, in fact, a social agency. Its function of administering discipline for delinquency, sending youths to reformatories, or placing them under the control of probation officers was supposed to be secondary.

A special building was erected across the street from Hull House for the court. The hearing room was arranged as a parlor rather than a courtroom.

Miriam Van Waters, noted juvenile court worker and author of a standard book on child welfare which Julian publicly commended, perceptively stated in *The Survey:*

> When our first juvenile courts were founded . . . it was supposed that we had discovered a new way of treating the young offender. He was not to be proceeded *against* as under the old criminal laws; but as a minor ward of the state he was entitled to guardianship, protection, and wise parental control. The fact that he had committed an offense would not change his relationship to the state for he was given a special legal status and his offenses were not to be regarded as crimes.

Julian understood that concept. He attempted to implement it more conscientiously than his predecessors—and most of his successors. In that respect, he was the court's real pioneer in Chicago and was recognized as such by the Hull House social workers and others in the field of social welfare. As *The Survey Graphic* once recalled:

> . . . Judge Mack's outgiving smile was gavel enough to bring boys and girls within the warmth and directness of his gorgeous give and take. He drew on new learnings—child health and welfare, probation, psychiatry—and showed what can come of it when chancery powers turn youngsters, hitherto handled as culprits, into wards of the state. Past master in this modern alchemy of adolescence, his precedents have endured. Small wonder his neighbors at Hull House claimed Judge Mack. . . .

To perceptive social workers, the juvenile court movement was a first step, the opening wedge, in a comprehensive program of social welfare. It represented definite recognition of the responsibility of the state for the social welfare of children, then an almost revolutionary concept in America. Child-labor legislation, mothers' pensions, aid to dependent children—such developments, the Hull House folk envisioned, were expected to follow along the trail blazed by the Chicago Juvenile Court.

In later years, after it had been dwarfed by other reforms, and after juvenile courts had generally failed, apparently, to live up to the original expectations, the juvenile court idea seemed scarcely to merit the great importance that the people at Hull House had attached to it. Later social workers were to wonder about the praise showered upon it, and also why it had once been regarded as so controversial.

But in the early 1900's, when public welfare work in the United States was in its infancy, Jane Addams, for one, felt justified in listing the Juvenile Court of Chicago as one of the top achievements of Hull House, and in designating Julian Mack as one of the ablest of the Juvenile Court's judges.

Julian cooperated wholeheartedly with Miss Addams and other Hull House workers. In effect, he became a part of Hull House. It was a mutually helpful relationship, he profiting from the Hull House insights and Hull House benefiting from the prestige of association with him. Especially did his solid status as a judge help to offset suspicion that Hull House was a "radical" institution. Also, when Hull House needed special funds, Miss Addams knew that Julian was the man to see for tapping some person of wealth—usually Julius Rosenwald.

Julian seldom failed her. In her private rooms, until her death, among photographs of persons she especially admired, there was a picture of Julian Mack.

Clear then—and still clearer in times to come—was one significant point that he stressed. The proper working of a juvenile court depended to a large extent upon the judge and how well he was backed by probation officers, case workers, and psychologists. The court had to be properly staffed, and the judge had to be temperamentally and intellectually suited to its goals.

The difficulty was that such judges were not common. Sixty years later, when the basic point of juvenile court procedure was, in effect, ruled out by the Supreme Court, this was the nub of the matter.

Julian actively plumped for a high type of juvenile court judge, one, for example, like the daughter of Rabbi Stephen S. Wise in New York, Judge Justine Wise Polier, to whom Julian was a kind of godfather. He argued against the practice of rotating judges in the court on a monthly basis. What was required, he felt, was long-term assignments so that juvenile court judges could develop professional competence.

A good portrayal of what went on when Julian handled the court was given in an article in a Boston legal publication, "A Day with Judge Mack in the Juvenile Court of Chicago," which stressed Julian's informality. He had picked up the idea of Governor John P. Altgeld that conventional robes worn by judges "add nothing to the stature of a good judge." Thus, Julian wore his ordinary business suit and discarded the conventional "bench," holding his hearings at an ordinary desk, hoping to make the youngsters who were brought before him feel that they were in a sitting room.

The article went on:

> A boy is brought before him and is kindly greeted by him. The
> boy has been in bad company, is out of school, and is charged

with stealing. This is his first appearance before the judge, who seems already to have gained his confidence. The judge talks kindly to him and draws him out. The judge says to him: "I am going to give you a chance to make a man of yourself. I want you to promise me that you will go to school and keep out of the company of bad boys, and stop stealing."

The boy gives him his promise and the judge continues, kindly, but firmly: "If you are brought here again, I will have to punish you. Do you understand this?. . ."

There were special problems; among them, as Julian quickly discovered, was religion, for along with political maneuverings, the Juvenile Court was beset by sectarian pressures. This would happen particularly when he was called upon to decide whether some youngster should be placed in a private foster home or in some denominational institution. Tangles between Protestants and Catholics often resulted. Philip Bregstone commented on this problem in *Chicago and Its Jews:*

Mack's first efforts were to free the court from the sinister influences of creed and dogma. This was no easy task, for it involved a struggle against the clergy of almost all denominations, an opposition powerful enough to be almost invincible. However, he succeeded at last in divorcing the court from religious bigotry and the first move, in the process of juvenile reform, was won.

Boys and girls whom he reluctantly sent to reformatories or industrial schools viewed Judge Mack as a man of fairness. He made a point of visiting the reformatories, something that many other juvenile court judges apparently failed to do. On one visit, as he walked about the institution, a youngster called out:

"Gee, fellows, here's the judge that sent us here!"

Whereupon he was greeted by numerous loud and friendly hellos.

"Three cheers for Judge Mack!" one boy exclaimed.

It was an image that pleased Julian. It meant that the juvenile court idea was working—in 1903–04.

To be sure, there was Judge Benjamin B. Lindsey in Denver. Thanks in large part to Lincoln Steffens' writings about him, a later generation tended to view Judge Lindsey as the leading, perhaps the only, exponent of the juvenile court idea. True, Judge Lindsey was important. Yet, in his quieter way, Julian exceeded the more publicized Denver judge as a champion of the court's philosophy. He expressed admiration for Judge Lindsey's work, and Lindsey, though inclined to consider Mack too timid in criticizing social ills, returned the compliment. Indeed, Lindsey went out of his way to "woo" Julian's favor.

Yet, by a kind of instinct, Julian kept Judge Lindsey at arm's length. He was made wary by Lindsey's penchant for controversy. The Denver judge often created antagonism toward the juvenile court principle simply because he was for it. Julian, on the other hand, seemed to win friends for the court. To a large extent, it was his "baby" and he cherished and defended it with parental zeal. Indeed, what his Uncle Max had been to him and to his brothers and sisters in Cincinnati, he was, in image, to literally hundreds of youngsters. "What service he rendered in the Juvenile Court of Chicago, which his understanding and forward-lookingness did most to create!" Stephen S. Wise once exclaimed.

The juvenile court movement desperately needed such advocates as Julian Mack. Politicians did not like it. They especially resented the concept so vigorously championed by Julian that probation officers and other case workers associated with the court should be professional social workers, not political hacks.

Many lawyers—who eventually, in the 1960's, got their way—objected to the court because its proceedings dispensed with their services. There was opposition, too, from those who professed to see "socialism" in the juvenile courts. As one Illinois State Supreme Court justice incredibly declared:

> There is a general feeling throughout the state that we are building in Chicago, in the Juvenile Court, a great paternalis-

tic system of government which is destroying the influence of
the home. If this is true, it behooves us to be on guard against
any such danger. We must not employ the Juvenile Court to
"save" society.

The court was also accused of "coddling young criminals." Law
was law, crime was crime, and violators should be treated firmly and
punished. Such was the argument constantly presented in editorials
reminiscent of the Elizabethan age, when boys could be hanged for
stealing loaves of bread.

In defending the juvenile court idea, Julian became a crusader—
almost. But not merely for the establishment of juvenile courts. He
also urged social welfare action generally to minimize the causes of
children's dependency and neglect which amounted to a national
scandal.

Unintentionally, because temperamentally he was one of the
least likely persons to be counted among overt crusaders, he found
himself a figure in a major phase of the muckraking movement of
the day. "'Conserve the child' was a leading slogan of the time," as
Louis Filler notes in *Crusaders for American Liberalism.* The
muckraking magazines took up that cry. Edwin Markham, William
Hard, Upton Sinclair and even Theodore Dreiser began to be
prominent in the movement which led to the formation of the
National Child Labor League, forerunner of the Child Welfare
League, the Infants' Welfare Society, and similar child-saving
organizations.

Julian took on a heavy speaking schedule, both in Chicago and
around the country. He hammered away continuously at the
objection that the juvenile court system did not provide for
"adversary proceedings," i.e., attorneys representing the children,
and that there was no provision for verdicts by juries. Such
objections, he pointed out, missed the whole point. Children in the
juvenile courts were not supposed to be "tried." They were not
"defendants" in a legal duel. Rather, they were wards of the state,
with the judge in the role of parent. If this point went unrecognized,
he reiterated, the whole concept would not be understood.

In St. Louis at the time was young Roger N. Baldwin, who later founded the American Civil Liberties Union. He, too, was a crusader for the juvenile court idea. A graduate of Harvard, Baldwin, at the urging of Louis D. Brandeis, a family friend, had entered social service in the early 1900's as a settlement worker in the slums of St. Louis. He later became chief probation officer for the juvenile court there. In 1907, Baldwin organized the National Probation Officers' Association to eliminate politics in the selection of juvenile court workers and to assure the appointment of competent children's judges who went along with Julian's ideas. Naturally, Julian supported Baldwin's activity.

When Baldwin visited Chicago, Julian was one Chicagoan he made a point of looking up. Years later, Baldwin recalled for the Columbia University Oral History Project the Chicagoans who, "full of zeal and good sense, sustained an atmosphere of progressive attacks on social evils that I had never since seen duplicated." He listed Jane Addams, Julia Lathrop, Clarence Darrow, Florence Kelley, Mary McDowell, and Julian Mack.

Julian, in fact, became for young Baldwin a model, "one of my earliest ideals," a man whose personality, as well as his work, "fascinated me."

"What impressed me most about him," Baldwin recalled, was "his breezy, hearty way of dealing with people, quick, energetic, and considerate. He had enthusiasm for what he was doing and the urge to do it better."

To "do it better" required trained professionals. Graham Taylor, of Chicago Commons, a social settlement on Chicago's North Side, came up with an answer to the problem of training case workers by starting "The Chicago School of Civics and Philanthropy," which offered courses in social work, the first of their kind. Julian cooperated by serving on the board of directors; he also gave lectures. Julia Lathrop, close friend of Jane Addams, became the director of research. Thus, "Social Service" as an academic discipline was born in Chicago.

When in 1916 this school faced dissolution because of lack of funds, Julian worked out the plan whereby it was saved. Taken over later by the University of Chicago, it became the university's School of Social Service Administration.

Oddly, or perhaps not so oddly, the Illinois State Supreme Court as a body did not share the social workers' view of Julian's importance in the Juvenile Court. After his first year, it peremptorily entered an order transferring him to the Appellate Court. This was a promotion, but Julian did not want it.

"I feel that my work in the Juvenile Court is unfinished," he wrote to the Justices, asking that they rescind the promotion. "There is so much to be done. The question of [the] handling of the juvenile problem is one of the chief problems of our times."

The Justices at first refused to withdraw their order. But social reform groups of Chicago protested and the Justices were bombarded with letters requesting that Julian should be permitted to continue where he was. The Supreme Court backed down.

His juvenile court service in the following year was especially noteworthy, for it was then that he helped launch the Juvenile Protective League movement, a nationwide citizens' movement, the forerunner of the Child Welfare League of America. It began with the organization of the Juvenile Protective Association, with Julian as chairman, assisted by the energetic Jessie Binford of Hull House, and also by a young social worker, Grace Abbott. The Association was committed to the regulation of such places as dance halls and saloons, in the interest of children; to checking on employers who violated child labor laws; to working for more parks, playgrounds, gymnasiums, free baths, vacation schools, and more social settlements.

Julian sketched the aims of the Association:

> We are getting together all the men and women who are really interested, all religions, all nationalities, black and white, and we are getting them to work together for the good of the children. We are not endeavoring to reform Chicago—that is too big a job. But we are trying to make it possible for a child in any part of the city to lead a decent life.

The ideas he then urged were, in effect, the ideas which Jane Addams had articulated in one of her first books, *The Spirit of Youth and the City Streets.* They boiled down to the view that one main cause of juvenile "delinquency" lay in the failure of the cities to provide wholesome outlets for "the spirit of adventure and play that marks normal young people."

After his second year in the Juvenile Court the Illinois Supreme Court once again ordered Julian's promotion to the Appellate Court. Again there were protests. As the *Tribune* stated, "Those who have had the most to do with the establishment of the Juvenile Court want Judge Mack reappointed." But this time the Supreme Court Justices did not relent.

"The Judges took the view," the *Tribune* reported wryly, "that they did not care to spare Judge Mack to the Juvenile Court because his fine legal mind was needed in a place where more important lawsuits were being decided."

A whispered explanation had it otherwise: another judicial election was coming. The favorable attention that Julian was receiving from his child welfare activity had aroused political jealousy.

But though Julian had to leave the Juvenile Court he continued to function as one of the foremost spokesmen for the juvenile court idea. For years afterward, though many judges—some excellent, some indifferent—were to follow him, Chicago's Juvenile Court remained synonymous with Judge Julian W. Mack.

11. White House Conference

President Theodore Roosevelt in this era also became interested in child welfare. In January, 1909 he sponsored at the White House a "Conference on the Care of Dependent Children," the first White House conference on children. Roosevelt ignored the view that the Federal government should not be involved in social welfare.

The Conference was one of "T.R.'s" last acts before turning over the Presidency to Julian's fellow Cincinnatian, William Howard Taft. Critics from the "right" looked askance at the project. Foreseeing such a reaction, Roosevelt, before calling the Conference, asked leaders in child welfare work to support him by making a formal request for the session. Julian was one of those asked, along with others such as Jane Addams and, incidentally, Theodore Dreiser, then an editor of a family magazine, *The Delineator.*

Julian was one of three vice-chairmen chosen to conduct the Conference. He also served on the committee that drafted resolutions which Roosevelt later sent to Congress, including one calling on Congress to establish a Children's Bureau, an idea first proposed by Lillian Wald, the New York settlement house leader.

As with the juvenile court idea, Miss Wald's suggestion at first met with resistance. The bugaboo of socialism was raised. As Jane Addams wryly recalled, "At three Congressional hearings in its behalf, we constantly encountered the familiar argument of 'states' rights' and the insistence that the states alone were concerned in such matters. It became clear that the federal government could interest itself in agriculture and fisheries, but not in childhood."

In 1912, as the major concrete result of the White House Conference, Congress reluctantly did establish the Children's Bureau. As a consequence, the first "social-insurance laws" in the United States were adopted, along with the New York Workmen's Compensation Statute, and the Illinois Funds to Parents Act, providing payments from county funds to parents who would otherwise be unable to care properly for their children. Within two years, twenty other states were to adopt similar legislation. Other such progressive legislation came later, all thanks to the Children's Bureau.

The White House Conference also recommended the formation of a central organization for coordinating all "child-saving" activity in the United States. Out of this came the Child Welfare League of America. However, not only because of what it accomplished, but also because it was held at all, the 1909 White House Conference deserves more prominence than it has received in histories of social welfare activity in the United States. For it marked the first official American recognition of the principle of national responsibility for underprivileged persons. As Miss Addams recalled, "It gave to social work a dignity and a place in the national life which it had never had before."

Moreover, leaders of the Conference managed to turn the spotlight on the need for governmental action to establish minimum working hours and wages, to regulate or abolish child labor, to impose safety standards in factories and mines, and for similar "advanced" measures, all at an opportune time, for the U.S. Supreme Court just then had before it the celebrated "Brandeis brief" in the case of Muller vs. Oregon. In that brief, Brandeis presented sociological data that supported the right of the State of Oregon to adopt a maximum-hours law for women in industry. Previously, in case after case, the Supreme Court had barred such legislation as unconstitutional. The coincidence of Julian's interest in child welfare and Brandeis' concern over social issues under-scored the similarity of their outlooks, a fact destined to ensure their work in tandem, especially in Jewish affairs.

Along with Miss Addams and Judge Lindsey, Julian was especially vocal at the Conference in pointing up the connection between dependency and neglect of children and the social problems which the Oregon-type of legislation tried to alleviate. Children were being neglected, he pointed out, because mothers were forced to work, often for such long stretches that they had neither the time nor the energy to care for them. Thousands of children were being orphaned annually because of industrial accidents resulting from lax safety measures; low wages accounted for conditions of neglect. State laws and court decisions deprived wage earners almost entirely of decent compensation in case of injury, thus making for more wretchedness among children in poor families.

It was Julian who struck a basic theme in his closing address of the Conference at a dinner. "Preventive work—that is the significant thing of this conference," he told his audience, which included President Roosevelt. "Not what we shall do for the dependent child of today, not whether he shall go into an institution, or into a family home, but how shall we stop dependency. Let us get at the causes and eradicate them. Let us get together with all those working for a social betterment. Study the causes. See that in each community the opportunity to work and to work at a living wage be given so that the workingman may be enabled, not through charity, but through justice, through his own earnings, to keep his family together."

He also raised another question, which almost no one had wanted to mention: Should needy unmarried mothers be given public assistance that would enable them to bring up their children, or should these children be taken from them arbitrarily and placed into institutions? Julian said that unwed mothers should be treated like other mothers; even—or perhaps especially—illegitimate children deserved justice.

Thus, in the context of that era, Julian emerged as a liberal spokesman—a prototype of the American-Jewish liberal before this had become a type—on the national scene.

In August, 1909, the American Bar Association invited him to address its convention on the juvenile court idea. He delivered an address which he later re-worked into an article published in the *Harvard Law Review*. The following October, the then progressive *American Magazine* featured him in an article about national leaders of the Jewish world. "Judge Mack," the article said, "is one of the ablest of the younger generation of American Jews." He even attracted attention abroad. An article in a 1909 issue of the London *Times* referred to him as "one of the four greatest Jews in the United States."

In 1911, the National Conference of Charities and Correction (later styled the National Conference of Social Work) elected Julian president as successor to Jane Addams. His presidency of the Conference was noteworthy for being in tune with the Progressive movement climaxed in 1912 by the LaFollette-Roosevelt political eruption and the rise of Woodrow Wilson. For it was then that American social workers went all-out for the social program which ultimately emerged as the New Deal of the 1930's.

Julian advocated that program. "This country will surely lose its supremacy if the hands of the present generation are to be so effectively tied by a dead past that it cannot at the proper time emulate European countries in their social legislation," he told the Cleveland Conference of Social Workers in his presidential address.

Nor did he, like so many other reformers of the period, overlook the plight of the Negroes, who at the time were practically forgotten, even by most of the liberals. Thus, Julian presided at an early meeting of the National Association for the Advancement of Colored People in Chicago, which was addressed by the militant intellectual W.E.B. Dubois. Along with Julius Rosenwald, who was to give millions for the uplift of Negroes, Julian recognized that the black people of America needed advocates for their cause no less than the immigrant Jews from Russia. He was among a number of leading Jews who helped the Blacks, a fact which not all Blacks were subsequently to remember.

Miss Addams, for one, noted that Julian's leadership was crucial for liberal social welfare policies in general. His prestige offset constant right-wing carping that professional social workers of the National Conference were "fuzzy, dreamy do-gooders." This was not so easily said of Mr. Justice Julian W. Mack of the Appellate Court of Illinois.

12. *Immigrants' Champion*

Meanwhile, the immigration problem—especially the Jewish immigration problem—was boiling. Along with his active interest in child welfare, Julian continued to be greatly concerned with the needs of the immigrants. Indeed, he saw more clearly than most that the problems of children in trouble and those of immigrants in need of help, or at least of understanding, were related crises, since the majority of children in trouble were the children of immigrants.

Later, welfare work in the United States would center largely around the Blacks who "migrated" to the Northern cities. But in the early 1900's its sphere was mainly among the foreign-born, though the problems were the same in the case of both these newcomer elements: both had to be absorbed decently into the established community, helped to "adjust," and made to feel wanted.

In the 1900's the problem became even more critical than in the 1890's. The number of immigrants of all kinds kept on increasing. Especially the Jewish ghettos, including that of Chicago, grew larger and seamier.

The year 1905 was crucial. That year Russia went through an attempt at revolution as a result of her defeat in the war with Japan. The Czar presumably yielded to the clamor for reforms, including the calling of a popularly elected parliament, the Duma. There were hopes that, among other reforms, a liberal policy toward the Jews would result. But the opposite happened. "The Duma," as Israel Zangwill told a London gathering in August, 1908, "is even more anti-Semitic than the autocracy or the bureaucracy."

Czar Nicholas II, though portrayed in the movies as a tenderhearted man because of his great love for his hemophiliac son, openly encouraged organizations specifically formed to persecute Jews. The circumstance that Jews had been among the supporters of the revolution served as a convenient excuse for terror and murder. And the Czar, "that stupid little man," as Theodore Roosevelt once called him, rewarded the murderers of Jews with decorations.

Pogrom followed pogrom. In Bialystok, in Gomel, in Odessa, in

Kiev; in Vilna, Lodz and Yekaterinoslav; again in Kishinev and in a hundred other Russian cities and villages, especially during the Easter holidays, there was the shouted refrain: "Death to the *zhyds!* Beat the *zhyds!*"

At Easter time a leaflet was distributed in Pinsk which read:

> Brothers, Workers, Orthodox and Catholics: Christ has risen. Let us embrace, kiss, and go kill Jews.
>
> (signed) THE MONARCHIAL SOCIETY

Of the pogrom in Bialystok in July, 1905, Julian read in the *Chicago Tribune:*

> Young girls were frightfully violated under the eyes of their mothers. One Jew had both legs cut off. Numerous corpses had nails driven into their limbs and heads. A doctor at the Jewish Hospital was thrown from the top of the hospital into the street at the moment he was dressing wounds. . . .

To this account the newspaper added:

> There is now no shadow of doubt that the whole affair was carefully planned and organized, and that the Jews were deliberately consigned to their doom by Russian officials.

Moreover, in this Bialystok pogrom, the Czar's soldiers had been active participants, not merely onlookers as they had been in Kishinev in 1903. One refugee from Bialystok was the singer Rosa Raisa, whom Julian later came to know. She left Bialystok in 1906 as a girl of thirteen, her mind forever seared, she once said, by the horrors she had witnessed there. One day, after she had become a celebrated star of Chicago's grand opera company, she exclaimed to a friend:

> . . . Do you know what a pogrom is? Do you know what it is to see a drunken peasant take a Jewish baby by its legs and crush its skull against the wall of a house as though it were a club? I wondered if a song could live after that. . .

That was Russia in 1905.

As American Jews set about to celebrate the 250th anniversary of their settlement in the New World, reports came of new pogroms—this time in Orel, Vyazma, Kherson, Rostov on the Don, Kishinev, Ismaila in Bessarabia, in Mohilev, Yekaterinoslav, and again Bialystok, Koseletz and Uman.

"What the death toll amounts to will never be known," the *London Jewish Chronicle* reported. "One account places the number of Jews killed at 15,000, and the number wounded and permanently injured at 100,000."

Again, there were protest meetings. Jacob H. Schiff, for one, was so greatly disturbed that he threw all his prestige as one of the nation's leading bankers behind a request to President Roosevelt for military intervention by the United States. Quixotic? Schiff did not think so. On December 8, 1905 he wrote to Roosevelt:

> If the United States were justified in 1898, as they doubtless were for the sake of humanity, to intervene in Cuba . . . is it not, in the face of the horrors now occurring in Russia . . . the duty of the civilized world to intervene. . .?

But Roosevelt was discouraged by Elihu Root, his Secretary of State, from doing even so little as publicly voicing moral condemnation of the Russian outrages. The first President to have a Jew in his Cabinet, Roosevelt himself would have liked at least to criticize the Czar. But Root persuaded him that an open American protest would only "irritate" the Czar, "increase the anti-Jewish feeling, and . . . make further massacres more probable."

To Secretary Root, the protests voiced earlier over the Kishinev pogroms by his predecessor, John Hay, represented "demagogic cleverness" inspired by Roosevelt's wooing of "the American Jewish vote for his reelection in 1904." In this case Secretary Root, urbane and cultivated, representing the "best people" in politics, adopted a stance that other American State Department officials were to continue where Jews were involved—even into the period of Hitler and beyond. It was an attitude that helped turn toward Zionism many American Jews who, like Julian Mack, had been brought up to oppose the establishment of a Jewish state.

Roosevelt instructed George von Lengerke Meyer, then the American Ambassador to Russia, to "obtain the facts"—in effect, to lodge a protest with the Czarist government against the outrages. However, the Ambassador's private papers reveal that Meyer's chief contribution was to assure the Czar's Foreign Minister that he, Meyer, did not wish to be "inquisitorial." His concern, he told the Minister, was "merely to put his government, if Russia desired it, in such a position as to prevent public opinion from becoming incensed through the exaggerated accounts of the press."

The press reports were not exaggerated. The diary of a British diplomat, Colonel Richard Meinertzhagen, cites a report from the British consul general in Odessa concerning the 1905 pogrom there:

> . . . When the Russian Revolution was in full swing, it was decided to have a pogrom in Odessa. Many Jews were warned of their impending danger and succeeded in bribing the revolutionary leaders not to molest them, but some 400 Jews were nevertheless killed. The pogrom lasted three days *and was organized by the Minister of the Interior in order to demonstrate to the Tsar that the people were not yet fitted for self-government.*

Even without pogroms, life for Jews in Russia remained incredibly hard. If the Czar's troops did not participate in assaults or condone them, they continued, as they had since the 1880's, to seize Jewish boys for lengthy military service, mainly in order to "de-Judaize" them. Russian Jews once more began to leave Russia. Some went to Palestine, where small Zionist colonies had already been established. In the ranks of these emigrants there were pioneers of the future State of Israel, notably a young lad from Plonsk, David Green, later known as David Ben-Gurion.

Others, such as Dr. Chaim Weizmann, the scientist from Motol and Pinsk, eventually went to England. But relatively few followed suit, because England had just adopted legislation severely restricting such immigration.* Germany also put up new bars against the Jews, as did France.

Most of the Jews who left Russia went to the United States. The names of the interesting people—some famous, some not—in this group make a long list. Those destined for fame included a girl from Kiev, Golda Mabovitch, who lived first in Milwaukee and then in Denver, before going as a Labor Zionist pioneer to Palestine. There, she would become known as Golda Meir, and eventually, like her co-worker David Ben-Gurion, she would become Prime Minister of Israel.

By this time the established American Jewish community no longer thought of resisting the flow of refugees. The new disasters to Russian Jewry were too appalling. Julian was no longer the exception when he urged that the immigrants should be welcomed.

In 1906, top leaders of American Jewry, prompted by the wave of immigration from Eastern Europe, formed the American Jewish Committee. An American version of the French Alliance Israélite Universelle, the Committee was founded to assist Jews everywhere, though there was, and would be, controversy as to whom the Committee actually represented. By design it sought no mass constituency. Nearly all its leaders, for one reason or another, feared a "popular" organization. But there was no doubt that at the time the American Jewish Committee spoke for established American Jewry. The "big names" were represented: Jacob H. Schiff, Louis Marshall, the Lewisohns, the Sulzbergers, Cyrus Adler, the Strauses—and Julian Mack.

The formation of the American Jewish Committee represented a revolution. Most of the leaders had previously reflected the attitude that in America Jews should not be considered, in public affairs, as different from the general American public. They had abhorred any kind of "separatism." The formation of the American Jewish Committee signaled that the time had come for this policy to be altered. The very men who earlier had wanted no part of any Jewish "bloc" had come around, of necessity, to forming one. Representing

---

*By an historic quirk this legislation, aimed mainly at Jews, was largely sponsored by Arthur James Balfour, who was later to be honored as a friend of the Jews for the Balfour Declaration on behalf of the Jewish National Home in Palestine.

Chicago among the founders of the American Jewish Committee were Julius Rosenwald and Julian Mack.

Originally, Julian's attitude toward the Committee had been ambivalent. His rabbi, Dr. Hirsch, was opposed to the formation of the group, arguing that rabbis, not laymen, should speak for Jewry. Adolf Kraus of the B'nai B'rith also opposed the Committee, arguing that his organization alone was sufficient. Simon Wolf, an influential Washington lawyer, prominently associated with the B'nai B'rith, was also opposed. Representing in Washington the "Board of Delegates" of the Union of American Hebrew Congregations, Wolf was looked upon as *the* Jewish lobbyist; he felt that his activity was sufficient, and the argument was strongly advanced that to establish any group which presumed to speak for all Jews was "dangerous."

At first, Julian tended to agree, but he changed his mind and helped work out a formula to satisfy some, if not all, of the objectors. He was chosen First Vice-President of the Committee. The American Jewish Committee became, as it has remained, a strong voice against anti-Semitism and against anti-alien sentiment in general.

"We have at last come together, united by a common grief, the Bialystok pogroms," Julian told the National Conference of Jewish Charities.

A strong voice was needed. The rising tide of immigration produced a mounting sentiment for sharply restricting immigration, or cutting it off altogether. Congress established the U.S. Immigration Commission, representing both Houses, to consider a revision of immigration laws. The motive, clearly, was to impose new restrictions in order to keep out "undesirables."

The chairman of the Commission, Senator William Dillingham from the State of Washington, was openly an "anti-foreigner." He was the original sponsor of a formula for restricting the admission of immigrants from any one country to a small percentage of the number of natives from that country already living in the United States.

This formula was to result in the "quota" laws of the 1920's; its purpose was especially to limit the immigration of Jews.

Popular magazines began to feature anti-Semitic articles. The January, 1907 issue of *McClure's* led off with one by Burton J. Hendrick, the historian. It was headlined "The Great Jewish Invasion."

In 1908 Henry James, the novelist, sniped snobbishly at the Jewish immigrants in a highly-touted book, *The American Scene*.

A New York newspaper article about the Russian Jews included this incredible comment: "A look at them, so dirty, so vicious appearing, would explain, if not justify, the pogroms in Kishinev and Bialystok."

Such vileness might have been passed over. But not so the article, "Foreign Criminals," by General Theodore Bingham, Police Commissioner of the City of New York, in a 1908 issue of the elitist *North American Review*. Bingham asserted that more than half of all crimes in New York City were committed by Jews. This was clearly a falsehood. When confronted with facts, or rather, his lack of facts, the general apologized. But his original statement was often quoted by anti-Semites.

Certain university scholars and even some social workers collaborated in this vile campaign. As Professor Oscar Handlin of Harvard noted in his book *The Uprooted,* scholars in the then new field of sociology tended to look with a jaundiced eye upon the immigrants and so lent academic sanction to prejudice. Thus, a "succession of books purported to show that flaws in the biological constitution of various groups of immigrants were responsible for every evil that beset the country."

Against this revived American Know-Nothingism, reinforced by Russian-financed propaganda to the effect that most Jews were revolutionaries and anarchists, Julian, among other Jewish leaders, spoke out boldly. He specifically expressed resentment over the attacks on Jews as "undesirables."

We Jews, who settled here for two hundred and fifty years [he said as a principal speaker at Chicago's observance of the 250th anniversary of Jewish settlement in America] need not bow our heads, nor crawl before any man in America. We stand here the equal of all, with as much right as does the descendant of the Puritan and the Cavalier.

We must unitedly rise up in this country and say to our fellow citizens that the doors of the United States, which have been opened for centuries to the oppressed of all lands, shall not now be closed to the poor Jews coming here. The doors of the United States shall never be closed to any decent, honest man coming here to settle, to found a home in our country, wanting to become an American citizen.

Obviously he had not changed his views since his speech at the Chicago mass meeting in 1892. "How," he asked, "can we, who have tasted the fruits of liberty and unrestricted freedom, raise our voices to bar anyone wishing American citizenship?"

Then he added: "We must welcome the people persecuted by the rulers of monarchies and teach them to be American and to uphold Judaism. This is true philanthropy, and it is in this field that all true Jews must meet as one."

He was still his "brother's keeper."

Again and again incidents occurred which pointed up the plight of the immigrants. In 1908, in Chicago, 19-year-old Lazarus Averbuch, who had recently arrived from Russia, was shot and killed by Chicago's Commissioner of Police, George Shippey, at the Commissioner's home. One of Shippey's sons was also shot dead, and Shippey himself suffered knife wounds. No one ever found out what had really happened. The Police Commissioner declared that Averbuch had probably been an anarchist. He claimed that the attack upon him and the shooting of his son had been part of a plot to assassinate him and that he had killed Averbuch in self-defense. As in the earlier case of Abraham Izaak, the Chicago police then went on a rampage of "raids" in the ghetto in search of anarchists.

This police activity was so shocking that Jane Addams devoted considerable space to it in *Twenty Years at Hull House*. According to her account, acts of the police included raiding "a restaurant which they regarded as suspicious because it had been supplying food at cost to the unemployed," and "ransacking private homes for papers and photographs of revolutionaries," in connection with which they triumphantly carried off to the City Hall a number of "suspicious" books—including works by Shakespeare and Herbert Spencer.

Shippey, who a few years later ended his career in an insane asylum, gave out numerous statements on the theme that Russian Jews were "dangerous radicals." At the same time lurid and irrelevant stories were printed about the self-proclaimed anarchist, Emma Goldman. "Anti-Semitism spread over the City. . . . Jewish school children were hooted at and stoned; one young man was forced to leave a dental college because of persecution by his fellow students."

Averbuch became a symbol of the fears and antipathies of native-born Americans, on the one hand, and of the agonies of the immigrants, on the other. Mainly, as Julian Mack soon perceived, the case was being distorted to give extra support to the elements behind the U.S. Immigration Commision.

What, precisely, was behind the incident at the home of Police Commissioner Shippey? Did young Averbuch, unemployed and apparently not overly bright, really knife the Commissioner and kill his son? Why had he come to the Commissioner's home? The whole matter was obfuscated by the "anarchist scare," and by attacks on Hull House and other welfare workers.

"Social settlements are first cousins to the anarchists," Police Commissioner Shippey asserted. Thus the attacks included, by inference, Julian Mack, who protested the police tactics against Hull House.

Bernard Horwich, later Julian's colleague in Zionism, set down a noteworthy account of the incident. As chairman of a committee to investigate the case, Horwich had been able to accomplish what the police had failed to do—persuade Averbuch's terrorized sister, Olga, to talk.

She and her brother [Horwich wrote] were born and reared in Kishinev. There they lived through the bloody pogroms that took place in the year 1903. Soon after this calamity . . . they left Russia and came to Chicago. . . .

During his search for a job, [Averbuch] became acquainted with a boy, who advised him to go to California, as living was much cheaper there and it would be easier for him to get work. He did not have the fare to California, however, and his friend thought that if he would go to someone with political influence and tell him of his predicament, he might obtain free transportation to Los Angeles.

[Averbuch] accordingly made inquiries as to who would be the most influential person for him to see, and was advised by someone to see Chief of Police Shippey. Instead of going to the latter's office, where he would be busy and would not be able to talk to him, [Averbuch] went straight to the Chief's house, arriving early in the morning, before Mr. Shippey left for downtown. There he was killed.

His sister insisted that he was not an anarchist, that he knew nothing about political matters, that he did not have any weapon with him at the time, and that he was a frail, nineteen-year-old boy who would not harm a fly.

Our committee, with the aid of many persons interested in social justice, made further investigation and found that what the sister had told us was true—that the boy had been killed through a terrible error.

In contrast to some Jewish leaders who preferred to have nothing to do with a "Jewish radical," Julian attended Averbuch's funeral. This was his way, as a judge of the Appellate Court, of showing solidarity with the ghetto immigrants. It was another step in what increasingly became his role: to serve as a bridge between the ghetto Jews and the established, "respectable" community at large.

The Averbuch affair had one good result. It inspired an organization expressly dedicated to the defense of immigrants.

Organizations aplenty, working with the basic charitable agencies, already existed to help immigrants find jobs and develop skills. But there was none expressly concerned with the political and related problems of the immigrants, and in particular to offset the propaganda fostered by the U.S. Immigration Commission and its supporting "Know-Nothing" organizations. This need was now met in Chicago with the formation at Hull House of the League for the Protection of Immigrants, later known as the Immigrants' Protective League.

As in the case of the Juvenile Protective League, Julian was chosen as the first president also of this organization, heading a board that included Professors Ernst Freund, George Mead of the University of Chicago philosophy department, James R. Angell, later President of Yale University, and, naturally, Jane Addams and Julia Lathrop.

For Julian, the Immigrants' Protective League became a second crusade. Two young women students at the Chicago law school, Sophonisba P. Breckinridge and Grace Abbott, started their social work careers with him, as directors of the league. Both women were to become deans of the School of Social Service Administration of the University of Chicago.

The problems faced by the League literally filled a book—Grace Abbott's *The Immigrant and the Community,* for which Julian wrote the introduction. It was a recital, in large part, of the peculiar hardships which the immigrants faced not only in Chicago but all over America. It was a record also of shocking situations to which the immigrants were subjected—mean tenement life, disgraceful sweatshops, and unlawful conditions that produced incidents like the tragic Triangle Shirtwaist fire in New York.

But these troubles were only part of the story. Not only were immigrants as a class the victims of police brutality, callousness, and exploitation; they also became the dupes of confidence men. They were tricked out of their savings by fraudulent "immigrant" banks, cheated by unscrupulous employment agencies, and, in the case of girls, seduced by organized "white slavers."

They were, in truth, the exploited Blacks of a later era.

Some Jewish immigrants—more numerous than once was

acknowledged—found conditions in America so contrary to their expectations that they returned to Russia. Not a few, it may be assumed, regretted that they had not gone to Palestine, despite all the hardships there; some, in fact, did leave the United States for the older Promised Land, preferring labor in the deserts to life in the city ghettos.

Most, however, stayed in America, accommodating themselves to the squalor of the ghettos. Many eventually worked themselves up from the ghetto, often with the help of settled Jews like Julian, or simply by their own perseverance.

To aid the newcomers, the League, of which Julian was president, not only opposed legislation attempting to restrict immigration but also worked to expose and counter the exploitation of immigrants. There were few clear victories. But Julian found the effort "deeper and heartier than any other public work." To fellow members of the League who were not Jews, he once candidly said, "Perhaps I feel more deeply on this subject than some of you because I am a Jew."

The need to checkmate the "white slave" traffic with immigrant girls was especially acute. In the Juvenile Court Julian had already received a shock with respect to both prostitution and pandering. He had started out with the conventional notion that Jewish girls were never involved in any such activity. According to all sociological studies, the incidence of prostitution among Jewish girls was lower than in other ethnic groups. Yet to find *any* Jewish girls in "the life" appalled him—just as similar conditions in New York had shocked Jacob H. Schiff.

Through the League, Julian made a distressing discovery. Procurers were making a practice of routinely waiting at Chicago railroad stations to meet immigrant girls in order to entice or literally force them into prostitution. Case after case turned up of girls who had innocently accepted help at a station from "kindly" strangers, only to be drugged or plied with liquor during a meal, then assaulted sexually, after which, feeling that they had been "ruined," they agreed to become prostitutes. Writeups of such instances read like potboiler plays, yet they were factual.

As a witness before the U.S. Immigration Commission, Julian

placed on record considerable data about that situation. His purpose was to persuade the Federal immigration authorities to take action.

> We found in Chicago [he told the Commission] that thousands of girls come through as immigrants, either destined for Chicago or the West and Northwest. They come on immigrant trains, sometimes early in the morning. They do not go out to the West until late at night. So they are stranded in Chicago during the day—sometimes for nearly twenty-four hours or longer. They do not speak the language and they are subject to all sorts of dangers . . . subject to rascality, to the importunities of agents of brothels, and a good many of them are picked up before they get off the train, before they reach Chicago, for lack of efficient supervision on the way.

He urged a remedy:

> If it is legally possible—and we think it is—it would be a measure of justice and wisdom for the U.S. government not to let its hands off the immigrant when he leaves Ellis Island . . . until he reaches his ultimate destination. . . .

Not until 1916, however, did the government act to provide "immigration stations" in Chicago and other inland cities, where immigrants were sheltered until officials made certain they were in good hands. In the meantime, the Immigrants' Protective League in Chicago assumed the task of checkmating the "scoundrels"—Julian's word. A "caretaker" service to insure each immigrant's safe arrival at his destination was set up by volunteers. Young lawyers were enlisted in this service, including Julian's brother, William, also a graduate of Harvard Law School, who at that time had begun a law practice in Chicago along with the youngest brother, Robert.

All the while the Immigrants' Protective League published reports, put out releases, and sponsored meetings, many of which Julian addressed, to counteract anti-immigration propaganda.

The League scored one clear and important victory—in a landmark legal fight known as the Rudovitz case.

Christian Rudovitz, who had taken part in the Russian revolution of 1905, had come to Chicago as a refugee. As Edith Abbott recalled, "The old imperial Russian government was always reaching out its strong arm to bring back for trial at home the political refugees who had started abortive revolutions," and Rudovitz was selected as an example.

Not surprisingly, the U.S. Department of State cooperated with the Czar's government. It had Rudovitz arrested, to be extradited on the charge that he had participated in Lithuania in a crime involving robbery, arson, and the murder of a man. The case turned on the question of whether Rudovitz was to be considered a common criminal, and hence extraditable, or whether he was a revolutionary who, in the American tradition, was entitled to political asylum in the United States. A compliant U.S. Commissioner ignored Rudovitz's role as a revolutionary and ruled that he was simply a common criminal.

At this point, only Root, the Secretary of State, could reverse the ruling, and Root, whose State Department still consistently avoided giving offense to the Czar's government, stubbornly declined to intervene. Supporting the Department in its refusal was one of America's most prestigious "international" law firms, Coudert Brothers, the lawyers of the Russian government in the United States.

It was then that the League took up the case, aware that if Rudovitz were to be deported, many other immigrants from Russia, including a number of Jews involved in the aborted 1905 Russian revolution, would also face arrest and deportation at the mere request of the Russian government.

After losing a plea for a re-hearing, the League sponsored public meetings to bring pressure on the Department of State. Among the participants were Rabbi Emil G. Hirsch, Clarence Darrow, Jane Addams, and Julian Mack, a familiar line-up.

"It is impossible for anyone unacquainted with the Russian colony to realize the consternation produced by this attempted extradition," Miss Addams recalled.

She was especially moved by one old man who, "tearing his hair and beard as he spoke, declared that all his sons and grandsons might thus be sent back to Russia." In fact, she added, "all of the younger men in the colony might be extradited, for every high-spirited young Russian was, in a sense, a revolutionist."

In the end, it was Julian who turned the scales in favor of a reversal of the Rudovitz ruling. In connection with a more formal appeal to Secretary Root, he arranged for his old Harvard classmate, Dean Wigmore, who did not usually join in liberal causes, to prepare a comprehensive analysis of the case based on the evidence against Rudovitz. Wigmore, whose specialty was "evidence," held that the crime alleged against Rudovitz was political. To extradite Rudovitz for offenses committed in connection with the Russian revolution of 1905 would be tantamount to arguing, he wrote, "that when Paul Revere, before starting his midnight ride to Concord in 1775, took a horse from the stable of a Tory neighbor, he was therefore a common robber in that act, though a political hero in making his ride."

Mack's enlistment of Wigmore's opinion against extradition was, of course, a master stroke which apparently impressed Secretary Root.

Julian also used his prestige to enlist the aid of William J. Calhoun, a prominent "downstate" Illinois lawyer who had especially potent connections in the State Department. Calhoun, who later became U.S. Ambassador to China, argued the case before Secretary Root. On the last day of his tenure as Secretary of State, Root finally overruled the Commissioner so that the Russian request for the extradition of Rudovitz was refused.

How many immigrants were saved from extradition to Russia by this victory for the principle of political asylum is not known. But clearly, hundreds were saved, including Jan Pouren, who was involved in a similar *cause célèbre* in New York. "It was," Philip Bregstone noted, "one of the great moments in the life of the Russian Jews in America."

13. What Is a Jew?

How long would America maintain an open door for Jews? This question troubled Jewish leaders, including Julian, in those early years of the new century. For obviously many of the attacks made upon Jews during that period were calculated to persuade Congress to adopt a new immigration policy, closing the doors to Jews seeking a haven in the new world.

The signal event in the revision of American policy toward immigrants, especially Jews, began to unfold in Washington in December, 1909. It was a series of hearings held by the U.S. Immigration Commission which had been established by Congress, mainly at the behest of elements opposed to further immigration except from the so-called Nordic or Anglo-Saxon countries.

Julian was invited to give his views to the Commission, appearing as head of the Immigrants' Protective League and as a vice-president of the American Jewish Committee. By inference, he also represented the enlightened social workers of America; as such, he was a major spokesman for the pro-immigration side.

He made no bones about his views. "I am strongly liberal on the immigration question," he candidly told the Commission in his opening statement. "I have not any doubt," he added, "that I am influenced in my view because I am a Jew. But I am equally certain that I would have the same view if I were not a Jew." An open-door policy on immigration was, he observed, "good for America."

He emerged, indeed, as a star witness principally because he engaged Senator Henry Cabot Lodge in a debate over the touchy question: What is a Jew?

Most Reform Jews professed to believe, as Julian also did at the time, that this question had been settled long ago. Jews were individuals who adhered to the Jewish religion.

"I do not recognize the Jewish race," Julian told the Commission, echoing sermons of Rabbi Isaac Mayer Wise in Cincinnati, Rabbi Elkan Cohn in San Francisco, and Rabbi Emil G. Hirsch in Chicago. "There are Jews who do. I do not."

But the question was really not settled; it never would be, despite the declarations of the Reform rabbinate or the position of anthropologists who challenged, in essence, the whole conventional structure of racial classifications.

Besides, the Zionists, who were already gathering strength, were agitating on behalf of the idea that Jews definitely formed a national and racial, or ethnic, group. This was the basis for the Zionist goal of a revived Jewish state. Regardless of anthropology, the Zionists had on their side a fact: Jews who ceased to practice Judaism as a religion were still considered to be Jewish. Even Jews who converted to Christianity were still regarded as Jews by others, if not in their own view.

So it was all a complicated matter. Nor was it merely academic. There were practical considerations even then, before the Nazi Nuremberg laws of twenty years later. In fact, it was a practical consideration that caused this question to be raised at the Immigration Commission hearings. For some time the immigration authorities had been dividing immigrants from Russia into *two* categories: "Russians," and "Russian *Jews*." Julian protested against this classification. Listing immigrants as Jews rather than as Russians or Rumaniàns or Englishmen, he argued, needlessly gave ammunition to anti-Semites. The immigration reports did not list how many Catholics or Protestants entered this country. Why, then, he asked, single out Jews in that regard? Thus, he was consistent in his view that Jewishness was a matter of religion only.

Henry Cabot Lodge, on the other hand, sided with the immigration authorities. Priding himself on being "a scholar in politics," Lodge obviously had studied "the Jewish question," and was convinced that the Jews constituted a race. He pointed out, incidentally, that even the Orientalist, Cyrus Adler, vice-president of the American Jewish Committee, who was not a Zionist, had referred to "the Jewish race," in his introduction to *The Jewish Encyclopedia* of 1903. So usage, if not anthropology, certainly was on his side, Lodge argued; thus, wittingly or not, Lodge presented the Zionist position.

Lodge also felt that too many Jews from Russia were being admitted to the United States. In several published letters to his close friend, President Theodore Roosevelt, Lodge urged a stricter enforcement of immigration regulations. He was disturbed because Roosevelt's Secretary of Commerce and Labor, Oscar Straus, was a Jew, and the Immigration Bureau was under Straus' department.

"That Mr. Straus is adverse to the laws which affect the entry of poor Jews, and especially to the 'poor physique' clause, I believe to be true. If it is true, it is unfortunate in the head of that Department," Lodge wrote to Roosevelt in July, 1908.

The debate between Lodge and Julian, both Harvard alumni, revealed the chasm that separated the two men. Their exchange resulted from an earlier colloquy between Lodge and Simon Wolf, in which Lodge had brought up the name of Benjamin Disraeli. He had cited Disraeli as an example of a Jew who believed in the idea that the Jews constituted a race, "something of which Disraeli was proud."

Previously, Julian had stressed his view that religion was the prime factor in a person's Jewishness. He had made this point in order to discount the distorted view then current as to why Jews were leaving Russia for America; they were leaving, it was said, not because they were being persecuted as Jews, but only in order to improve their economic position. This argument was calculated to deprive the Russian Jews of the welcome traditionally given by America to refugees from religious persecution, including Lodge's own Puritan ancestors. This position, incidentally, accorded with the propaganda that was being spread in the United States by the Russian government. If Jews were persecuted, the Russian line suggested, it was not because of their religion, but because of "disagreeable traits not connected with religion."

"I say that is not true," Julian said. "It is the Jew in religion who is oppressed in Russia. Many of them would escape that oppression . . . if they converted. The Russian Jews who come to America—nine-tenths of them, ninety-nine one hundredths of them—would infinitely rather stay right in Russia. . . . They would rather stay where they are, and practice their customs, which have existed for generations, than to come here. It is only the miserable religious oppression that drives them out."

He expanded that theme with a discussion of the motivation

behind the Jewish charities program in the United States. "The Jews in this country take pride in preventing a Jew from becoming a charge on the rest of the people," he pointed out. "They do that perhaps in part for a selfish reason—for fear that if a Jew becomes a public charge, that situation may cause a greater anti-Semitic feeling. But most of them feel it a matter of duty to those who, as they know, are the victims of purely religious oppression."

Both Julian and Simon Wolf also stressed that the anti-Semitism that resulted from classifying immigrants as Jews (rather than as citizens of their native country) was not something abstract. Both men cited instance after instance of particular rigidity on the part of immigration officials in enforcing regulations against an immigrant because that immigrant happened to be a Jew.

Then Julian got into the revealing part of his debate with Senator Lodge. The records of the Commission, worth reading verbatim for the light they throw on attitudes held then—and later—toward Jews, contain this exchange:

> *Mack:* Permit me to say a word. If Disraeli had come to this country, he certainly would have said that he was an Englishman.
>
> *Lodge:* He would have been classed racially as a Jew.
>
> *Mack:* If you adhered logically to what you are saying, you would classify me, because my father was born in Germany, as an American-born child of the Jewish race. I would disclaim that. I do not recognize the Jewish race. There are Jews who do. I do not.
>
> *Lodge:* There is some division on this question.
>
> *Mack:* Yes. The newer element of Jews in this country who largely are not yet American citizens, recognize that division, and claim there is a Jewish race; that is, historically. They want to re-create it as a nation. They really claim the Jewish nation rather than the Jewish race. A Jewish nation, nonexistent at present, they would like to reestablish as one of the great

political nations of the world. . . . If I said my father was a
Jew, born in Germany, you would put me down as a Jew in
race.

Immigration Official: You would be put down as a native born
of a "Hebrew" father. The Commission uses the term
"Hebrew" instead of "Jew."

Mack: You would amaze me, if you did it. . . . There is one
practical reason to be interposed against this classification,
particularly in dealing with people who are here. To stir up
race feeling is, we all know, highly injurious. There is no
question as to the existence in this country of anti-Semitism
among some people, just as there is in Germany and in other
countries.

Rep. Wheeler: There is no question of the existence, among
some narrow-minded people, of a feeling which may be called
anti-Romanism.

Mack: Not the slightest. But you do not classify Christians as
Protestants or Roman Catholics.

Lodge: In the census—

Mack: I am talking about your work here now. You are not
classifying the Protestants and the Catholics in any manner
racially. But you are classifying the Jews.

Now, when the Jews disclaim that racial feeling—those who
are Americans—and the ones you are classifying are largely
American citizens—you classify them as Jews and you
immediately raise the feeling that they are of a foreign race;
that they are foreign to us; that they are not Americans the
same as we are. Therefore, they are strangers.

We all know that prejudice, as such, is based largely and
fundamentally, whatever it may be aggravated by, on the idea
of the stranger.

There always was prejudice against the stranger, and you

emphasize the fact that the Jew here is a stranger to our land. That is the thing we resent. . . .

The reaction of the U.S. Immigration Commission was an eye-opener to Julian. He saw then, if he had not seen it before, that men of "breeding," senators and the like, even Harvard graduates, could be as narrow in their attitude toward Jews as men and women of little education. The Commission totally rejected his views. Here was a milestone in Julian's education in the realities of the "Jewish problem," even in the United States. The report of the Commission, issued in 1912, declared:

"While appreciating the motive which actuated the protest against the designation of the Hebrew as a race or people, the Commission is convinced that such usage is entirely justified."

Worse still, the Commission recommended even stiffer restrictions on immigration, including an unreasonable literacy test and more rigid health requirements.

In a report to board members of the Immigrants' Protective League, Julian pinpointed the unreasonableness of the views held by the Commission:

> The commission has come to some very unwise conclusions. In setting up an educational test, they have set up a totally false test for future inhabitants of this country. Education is desirable, highly desirable as a prerequisite of citizenship. But as a test for admission to this country it is a totally false one. It is no indication of character. . . .
>
> Then again, they talk of resorting to some physical test—the ability to pass an examination as would admit a man into the American army. . . . The very idea of shutting out the man of high character and high ideals because . . . he cannot pass a test that would admit him into the American army!

There was more to come. When the recommendations of the Commission emerged in the form of the Dillingham Bill, Elihu Root, then a member of the U.S. Senate, tacked on an amendment even more reprehensible than any of the provisions contained in the bill. Root's amendment called for the deportation of any alien "who shall take advantage of his residence in the United States to conspire for the violent overthrow of *a foreign government recognized by the United States*"; i.e., Russia. This meant, the *New York Post* commented, "that this country is no longer to be a refuge for the victims of tyranny in other lands."

The Immigrants' Protective League mounted a campaign to oppose Congressional adoption of the recommendations made by the Commission. Other agencies also entered the fight. But it was clear that the era of an open United States was ending. When the almost complete shut-off came in the 1920's it meant, in effect, a death sentence for countless numbers of European Jews who might otherwise have come to the United States.

All this was clear—especially to the Zionists, who remembered, if others did not, that seven years earlier, England, too, had set up a "Royal Commission for Alien Immigration," primarily for the same purpose as the Commission in the United States: to restrict the immigration of Jews.

Julian's appearance before the Immigration Commission had a personal, rather freakish and unexpected consequence. He came under bitter attack from a prominent Zionist spokesman, the journalist Bernard G. Richards. Richards represented the views of most Zionists when, in an article, "Jewish Leaders and the Jews," in the January 10, 1910 issue of *The Jewish Advocate* of Boston, he denounced Reform Jewry for "the arrogant and impertinent" claim that the Jews were not a race. Julian's testimony, along with that of Simon Wolf, was called "bungling blundering":

> Poor Judge Mack and poor old Mr. Wolf! . . . To try to cast off their identity and to deny a living fact, out of fear that the knowledge of our numbers will bring enmity against us, is both cowardly and disgraceful.

A tempest was stirred up—a forecast of later, even stormier, conflicts between Zionist-oriented Jews and non-Zionists. The turmoil caused the American Jewish Committee to retreat and to issue a statement implying that, in this controversy, Julian was representing only himself.

Ironically, the very men who assailed Julian then were later to become his colleagues in Zionism. Even Richards, to cite one example, was to work especially closely with him a decade hence. They even became friends. Richards was to praise Julian highly for his service to Judaism. But "he treated me very coldly in 1909," Richards recalled.

There was more irony. Senator Lodge eventually turned out to be one of the strongest advocates of the Jewish homeland. In 1922 he was to sponsor the resolution by the United States Senate that pledged American support for Jewish aspirations in Palestine. It was Lodge who steered the resolution to unanimous passage, emphasizing that "the Jewish people in all portions of the world should desire to have a national home for such members of their *race* as wished to return to the country which was the cradle of their *race*. . . ."

14. Incipient Zionist

At the very time he was so vigorously disavowing the thesis that the Jews were a "race" or could be called a "nationality," Julian was already moving toward a Zionist position. Subconscious as well as practical pulls were taking him there—a shift not unlike the experience of Ludwig Lewisohn in moving from non-Zionism, even anti-Zionism, to ardent Zionism.

> When the hearts of men begin to be troubled [Lewisohn wrote] the crumbling of their defenses has begun and the walls they have built against the light begin to be undermined from within. They may and often do still furiously, or stubbornly, deny the great change on the edge of which they stand. But . . . the change, when it comes, has all the appearance of a conversion, a sudden turning, and is yet, in fact, but *the last link* in a chain woven perhaps through months and years. . . .

It was so, apparently, with Julian, one "link" in his case being his reaction to the Immigration Commission.

He came away from that hearing with the depressing conviction that the political cards were stacked against the immigrants, especially against Russian Jews. If America closed its doors to them, where would they go?

Zionism was obviously a sensible answer—if the goal of a homeland for Jews in Palestine could be achieved. But in 1909 Julian was not yet ready to say "yes" to that question. Neither, however, could he now say "no." That in itself was progress toward Zionism, great progress at the time for a Reform Jew.

Another "link" was his long-simmering reaction to some painful observations he had made while in the Juvenile Court. Jews, as a whole, still had a very low crime rate. Yet, there was no denying that Jewish names were showing up more and more in crime reports. At the time, an interesting notion was being advanced on this point:

101

Many Jews seemed to be suffering from a lack of self-respect. If they had a land of their own, their self-esteem would be increased and there would be no more criminality among them.

That was an unprovable notion, of course, for there was much crime also among ethnic groups in the United States (the Irish, the Italians, and so on) who were not "stateless." But thoughtful Jews, among them Louis D. Brandeis, did see something in the notion.

Julian Mack began to think along the same lines.

Ironically, one factor in his growing sympathy for Zionism was the American Jewish Committee. From its outset, the Committee conveyed the image of opposition to any notion that Jews formed a "race" or even a separate "people." Schiff, Louis Marshall and Cyrus Adler at the time were anti-Zionists, or distrustful of Zionism—though Schiff and Marshall were to change their stand later on. It was these men who gave the Committee its tone.

Yet, to assume that the Committee was entirely anti-Zionist, even then, was error. Even Schiff, Marshall, and Adler already felt a warm "Jewish sympathy," as it would be termed, for the Jewish settlements developing in Palestine, and they favored helping these settlements. Though they said that they favored such help no more than they favored helping Jews in say, Algeria, Brazil, or Russia, the fact remains that, to the extent that they gave support to the Palestinian settlements, those leaders of the American Jewish Committee were helping Zionism.

Julian himself, up to the time he became a member of the Committee, had paid little attention to the settlements in Palestine. But at meetings of the American Jewish Committee there were reports about them which conveyed a kind of romantic excitement. Places like Petach Tikvah, Rishon LeZion and Zikhron Ya'akov began to take on meaning for him.

Moreover, the American Jewish Committee included some out-and-out Zionists, among them a handsome young New York rabbi, Judah L. Magnes. When Julian first met him, Magnes was secretary of the Federation of American Zionists, a leader who, had it not been for his marked inability to work for long in harness with others, might have emerged as *the* leader of world Zionism. This charismatic rabbi, a brother-in-law of Louis Marshall, would go through phases that even his admirers were to label as quixotic with respect to his Zionism, all of which were eventually to involve Julian. In the late 1920's Magnes was to break with most Zionists by advocating an Arab-Jewish "bi-national" state, rather than a Jewish state, in Palestine. But, even so, Magnes was destined to head the Hebrew University in Jerusalem, and some of his original zeal for Zionism inevitably rubbed off on Julian.

Also on the American Jewish Committee was the public-spirited, gentle philanthropist, Nathan Straus. Brother of Oscar Straus, he was almost as highly respected for his philanthropies as Jacob Schiff. He, too, was a Zionist, and he had Julian's warm admiration. Likewise, there was Dr. Harry Friedenwald of Baltimore, the ophthalmologist who had examined Julian's eyes at the Berlin clinic some two decades before. He and Julian became close friends as fellow members of the Committee, and often discussed Zionism, of which Dr. Friedenwald was an ardent advocate.

During this period, also, Julian came to know Henrietta Szold. Like Emma Lazarus, whom she resembled in her sensitivity to Jewish matters, Miss Szold was openly an ardent Zionist; she was destined to found Hadassah, the American women's Zionist organization. Julian developed a great admiration for her. Later he was to arrange an annuity for her, to which Julius Rosenwald, Brandeis, Judge Irving Lehman, and Mary Fels contributed, to enable her to carry on her work with Hadassah free from financial worry.

For the first time, Julian thus found himself associating congenially with Jews that were, for him, a new type—fully Americanized Jews like himself, yet pro-Zionist. To his surprise, he found their Zionist views not at all abhorrent, but fascinating—if not yet convincing.

Magnes made Zionism seem like poetry. Straus infused it with a down-to-earth philanthropy. Miss Szold clothed it in a style that reminded him of Jane Addams, and he was impressed by the fact that Solomon Schechter, who in 1902 became president of the Jewish Theological Seminary of America under the personal sponsorship, no less, of Jacob H. Schiff, had proclaimed himself a Zionist.

Julian's mental barriers against the Zionist idea, going back to his San Francisco and Cincinnati days, were crumbling. Tentatively, he began to reexamine the entire Zionist picture, sensing that his earlier attitudes had been too simplistic. It became clear to him that there were various kinds of Zionism, not just the bugbear against which many Reform rabbis like Emil G. Hirsch were railing.

He learned, for example, about Ahad Ha'Am, a philosopher and businessman, who stood, in essence, for "cultural Zionism" and had developed a large following for the concept of reestablishing in Palestine not a Jewish state but a Jewish community, holding that first priority should go to the re-establishment of Jewish culture as a living organism. Only then, Ahad Ha'Am felt, would a Jewish state be viable.

There were other Zionists who would have been satisfied with a Jewish "homeland" in Palestine that would be a protectorate of some European power or powers. Still others, the "Territorialists," such as the Jewish Territorial Organization led by Israel Zangwill, would even have foregone Palestine altogether. They had been prepared in 1903–4 to accept from Britain's Colonial Secretary Joseph Chamberlain an offer of part of Uganda in East Africa, and had sought to persuade Theodor Herzl to go along with the "Uganda Scheme." Later, they were to opt for territory in Mexico, or even in Russia.

Within these divisions, there were yet other divisions: Labor Zionists, notably the Po'ale Zion Movement, bourgeois Zionists, religious Zionists, secular Zionists, and so forth. It was all most intriguing to Julian. More important, he grasped the point that the eclectic nature of Zionism invalidated the usual objections to the idea. Even if Jews of his background found the idea of a Jewish *state* repugnant, why should they object to a Jewish *homeland* or to a Jewish *cultural community* in Palestine?

In 1907, there entered into Julian's circle Dr. Shmarya Levin. Witty, handsome, a dazzling orator in Yiddish, English and Hebrew, Dr. Levin was a striking example of the Russian Jewish intellectual. One of the students in Berlin who had formed the "Lovers of Zion" chapter when Julian was there in the 1880's, Levin had become a government supervisor of an educational program for

Jews in Russia but resigned when he learned that the Czar's program called not for true education but for the "Russification" of Jews in order to eliminate Judaism. He also participated in the attempted revolution of 1905.

Later, he was a Jewish representative in the Duma, Czarist Russia's short-lived Parliament, and a leader of the "League for the Attainment of Equal Rights for the Jewish People in Russia." As a member of the Duma, Levin joined in "The Vyborg Manifesto," a remonstrance to Czar Nicholas II for his failure to punish subordinates responsible for the Bialystok pogrom of 1906. He was ordered arrested. Escaping to Germany, he became a member of the Zionist Executive, the central guiding body of the World Zionist movement and probably its leading platform propagandist before the rise of Chaim Weizmann.

Levin first visited the United States in 1907 to lecture on the pogroms in Russia after the 1905 revolution. Since Jacob Schiff was his sponsor, all doors were opened to him. In Chicago he spoke at the exclusive German Jewish Standard Club. "His winning ways disarm all criticism," said even Rabbi Hirsch's *Reform Advocate*.

Jacob Schiff presented Levin at a meeting. To emphasize that he, Schiff, was not a Zionist, Schiff said, "I want you all to know that I consist of three parts. I am an American, I am a German, and I am a Jew." Levin's response became a classic. He wondered, he said, how Schiff divided himself—horizontally or perpendicularly? If horizontally, which part did Schiff assign to his fellow Jews—his buttocks?

That was Shmarya Levin. Julian was fascinated by him, and came to love him, even when on occasion he violently disagreed with him over Zionist affairs.

In 1909, Levin came to the United States again, this time in the interest of a "Technikum," a technological institute in Palestine, which was to become known as the Haifa Technion. His goal was to enlist American financial support and to organize an American board of directors. Schiff and Louis Marshall agreed to be members, and encouraged Julius Rosenwald to join.

"This institution is not Zionistic," Marshall assured Rosenwald. "It is wedded to no 'ism' save Judaism."

When Levin came to Chicago to meet with Rosenwald, who, like

Schiff, agreed to contribute $100,000, Julian sat in on the conference. As a result, he decided to become a member of the "Technikum" board along with Rosenwald.

For Rosenwald this was merely another philanthropic venture, like his support of Booker T. Washington's Tuskegee Institute for Negroes in Alabama. But to Julian, the connection with the "Technikum" meant something more. It helped forge a chain of connections between himself and the Jewish institutions of Palestine.

Shmarya Levin's great hope was to convert Julius Rosenwald to Zionism. For he was mindful of the benefits the Jewish settlements in Palestine would reap from the Sears, Roebuck millions. Though fascinated by Shmarya Levin's wit and exquisite Yiddish, Rosenwald held aloof.

But Levin was to make a great catch, in good time, in the person of Rosenwald's closest friend, Julian Mack. Indeed, the effect of Shmarya Levin on Julian was quite like the influence of Mordecai Cohen on the hero of George Eliot's pro-Zionist novel *Daniel Deronda*. Levin made him appreciate, more than before, the "glory side" of being a Jew. "Shmarya Levin was my Zionist teacher," Julian later recalled.

15. The Friend from Palestine

Also at this time there entered into Julian's life Aaron Aaronsohn, a young agronomist of Zikhron Ya'akov and Athlit, Palestine. Blue-eyed, fair-skinned, with the sturdy physique and open countenance of a Hellenic athlete, this attractive Jewish figure was a Renaissance man in his intellect and interests.

He had a crucial influence on Julian Mack. He also influenced Brandeis, among others, and though he was deemed controversial by some—as are all such "natural" men or women—he was truly a figure to be revered by world Jewry.

His parents were Rumanian Jews, members of a group of "Lovers of Zion" who had emigrated to Palestine in 1881, when Aaron was a boy. They had helped establish Zikhron Ya'akov, north of Haifa, not far from the Mediterranean shore. To this day, there is in Zikhron Ya'akov an Aaronsohn Museum, a memorial to the entire Aaronsohn family.

The Aaronsohns, including Aaron's sister, the legendary Sarah, had had good reason for leaving Rumania. One of Aaron's grandfathers had been murdered in a pogrom—hanged from a tree. Against him had been raised the old accusation that he had helped "kill a Christian child to get Christian blood for matzoth"—the medieval "ritual murder" charge that later was to figure also in the notorious Beilis case.

In Palestine, young Aaron displayed a keen interest in agriculture. He zealously believed that the soil of Palestine—untended or left eroded by the Arabs—could once more become fertile and green as in Biblical days. When he was seventeen, he was sent by the Rothschild Fund to study scientific agriculture in France. On his return to Zikhron Ya'akov as an agronomist, he set up a laboratory for experimenting with plants that would thrive in desert soils.

About 1907 Aaronsohn made what was considered a major discovery. He had found in the upper Galilee specimens of a type of wild wheat obviously indigenous to that area. This discovery was of particular interest to horticulturists of the U.S. Department of Agriculture. For years they had sought ways to improve wheat-growing on millions of acres of land in the western plains and in California, where some soils were not much better than that of Palestine. Aaron's discovery and his methods seemed to provide the answer they sought.

From David Fairchild, chief of the Foreign Horticulture Bureau of the U.S. Department of Agriculture and son-in-law of Alexander Graham Bell, came an invitation to Aaron to visit the United States for conferences and lectures.

Fairchild's autobiography, *The World Was My Garden*, includes interesting recollections of Aaron's arrival in the United States in 1909.

> I soon discovered that I was in the presence of an extraordinary man. Although Aaronsohn had never been there, his knowledge of California almost equalled his knowledge of Palestine. No foreigner had ever been in my office who had so keen an understanding of the soils, climates, and adaptability of plants to their environment. . . .
>
> The speed with which Aaronsohn picked up English was amazing. In a week's time I heard him carrying on technical conversations, comparing the flora of Palestine and California. His store of information proved so unusual that he was requested to write a bulletin on the cultivated plants of Palestine. His was one of those rare pioneer minds which quickly leap to the essentials, and he sat down and in short order drafted an article covering a wide range of useful plants which, in his opinion, should find a congenial home in America. I remember that his opening paragraph contained the expression *"ex Oriente lux"*—light comes from the Orient.

Fairchild arranged a trip to the West Coast for Aaronsohn. On his return Aaronsohn told Fairchild that he had one important personal request. "I want you," he said, "to introduce me to some of the wealthy Jews in this country." At Fairchild's request, Dr. Cyrus

Adler then gave Aaron a letter of introduction to Julian Mack, asking Julian to introduce Aaronsohn to Julius Rosenwald.

Julian arranged the meeting with the desired result. Rosenwald agreed to put up funds for a laboratory for Aaronsohn in Palestine. Jacob H. Schiff made a similar pledge. In 1910 there was formed the Jewish Agricultural Experiment Station at Athlit, an American-supported enterprise. The board of directors included Rosenwald, Schiff, Judah L. Magnes, Louis Marshall, Morris Loeb (Rosenwald's brother-in-law), Cyrus Adler, Henrietta Szold, and Julian Mack.

Had they foreseen what was in store for the station, some of the incorporators, perhaps even Julian, probably would not have joined in the venture. For aside from its scientific work, Aaronsohn's laboratory at Athlit was to play an important, dramatic, and illegal, role in the subsequent history of Palestine.

During World War I this laboratory was to become the headquarters, or the "blind," of "Nili,"* the first modern underground movement of Palestine's Jews, which gave vital intelligence to General Allenby's forces for the British conquest of Ottoman Palestine.

Aaronsohn headed "Nili." He was its brain. This dramatic story is told in part in Anita Engle's factual account, *The Nili Spies;* in Michael Blankfort's novel, *Behold the Fire;* and in Meyer Levin's *The Settlers.*

There was also tragedy in the story. Aaron's sister, the beautiful, extraordinarily intelligent Sarah Aaronsohn—whom some sources, doubtless in error, have linked romantically with Lawrence of Arabia—was captured by the Turks during her work with "Nili." Under cruel torture, rather than betray the group's plans, she, at twenty-seven, shot and killed herself. In 1923, recalling Sarah's act and Aaron's work, General Allenby was to write of the conquest of Palestine:

> The name of Aaronsohn will through the ages be remembered
> as that of a family who, with the entire disregard of self,

---

*The name of the organization was taken from the Hebrew initials of *Netzah Yisrael Lo Y'shaker*—"The glory of Israel will not fail" (I Samuel 15:29).

endured all—even to martyrdom—in the cause of Civilization
and Humanity, and whose courage and devotion were largely
instrumental in carrying that cause to final success.

Aaronsohn's conviction that Palestine could once again be made
a fertile land did not convince men like Julius Rosenwald, who
insisted that a homeland in Palestine was not economically sound
"and never would be."

Julian Mack, however, was impressed. He became Aaron's closest
friend in America. "I never felt as close to any man as I did to Aaron
from the time I first met him on his original visit to America,"
Julian later confided. Aaron himself once wrote to Julian: "We have
always understood each other, at a hint, or a word."

That Aaron should have made such a striking impression on
Julian at their first meeting was not surprising. In 1930 William C.
Bullitt, the American diplomat and confidant of Presidents, who
met Aaron at the Paris Peace Conference in 1919, was to recall him
as "the greatest man I have ever known. . . . He was the
quintessence of life, of life when it runs torrential, prodigal and
joyous."

Aaron's personality had the impact of that of Winston Churchill,
Felix Frankfurter was to tell Henrietta Szold's niece, Alexandra Lee
Levin. "I do not need the fingers of my two hands to include him
among the most memorable persons I have encountered in life,"
Frankfurter said.

On Julian, however, the impact of Aaron Aaronsohn was more
than personal. That such a man lived in Palestine made a profound
difference in Julian's attitude toward Palestine as a homeland for the
Jews. He contrasted Aaron's image with that of the ordinary Jewish
immigrant in America and found himself thinking that *the land*
made the difference. He began to see Palestine as a land capable of
producing many such men. The Isaac Mayer Wises, Emil G.
Hirsches, and Cyrus Adlers might keep railing against the idea of a
revived Jewish homeland in Palestine. Julius Rosenwald might
persist in questioning the economic viability of Palestine. But there
was Aaron Aaronsohn—symbol of a new kind of Jew, a vital answer
to the doubters and critics of Zionism.

16. Taft's Choice

The year 1909, when he first met Aaron Aaronsohn, was significant also in other ways for Julian Mack. Both his Uncle Max and his mentor James Barr Ames died. And Julian, then forty-three years old, came up for election to a second term as judge of the Circuit Court of Cook County.

In view of his devotion to social welfare causes and his closeness to Hull House, opposition from the trade union movement to his reelection was unexpected, even shocking.

Samuel Gompers, head of the American Federation of Labor, had evolved the political policy for the American trade union: "Reward our friends, defeat our enemies." But this policy was at times perversely implemented. In 1909 labor unions were especially fretful over court injunctions. Julian had issued only one such decree. That case had involved not wages or working hours, but the support by the Building Trades Council at Chicago of one union of stone cutters against another. In his decision, he had carefully pointed out that if the stone cutters' strike had been for better wages, or union recognition, he would not have issued the injunction. Nor would he have done so if the union members, individually, had refused to work on struck jobs. But for leaders of one union to strike against a rival union, he ruled, was a boycott which, according to court decisions of long standing, was unlawful. He felt that he had no choice but to grant the injunction.

Martin "Skinny" Madden, who was later exposed as having engaged in extortion, was then the notorious head of the Chicago Building Trades Council. Determined to make an example of Judge Mack, he prevailed upon the Chicago Federation of Labor to adopt a resolution demanding his defeat; Gompers, with whom Julian in later years was to have some pleasant association, was present at the meeting but remained silent.

One delegate from the Carpenters' Union did protest. "Judge Brentano issued twenty-four injunctions in one year," he said. "Judge Mack in six years issued only one, and in that case he gave labor plenty of time to come into court to give him an excuse not to issue it."

A plea against the resolution was also made by Margaret Dreiser Robins, president of the Women's Trade Union League, a friend of Jane Addams and member of the Federation board. "Judge Mack is a friend of the trade union movement!" she almost wept. But the resolution was not retracted.

Julian had, however, much support to counter the Federation action. Hull House as a whole rallied its following behind Julian in the election campaign. Colleagues at the University of Chicago took to the stump in his behalf.

"Judge Mack is one of the best judges Chicago ever had," Professor Freund declared, adding, "When unions oppose Judge Mack, they oppose a man who has done much for the workingman."

Julian's law school students, including Harold L. Ickes, also campaigned for him. Probably more important, the United Societies for Local Self-Government, led by Anton J. Cermak, a rising Bohemian Democratic leader, and later mayor of Chicago, supported Julian because it was known that he disliked "dry" laws. This support lined up saloonkeepers in his camp, making up somewhat for the lukewarm attitude toward him on the part of the Democratic party machine, deriving from the fact that Julian had never shown any disposition to decide cases to please the party leadership.

Then too, even though insisting that there should be no "Jewish vote," Rabbi Hirsch nevertheless energetically rallied Jewish voters behind Julian: "We do not go to the polls as Jews. Yet when one of our number has reflected honor upon the office which he held, shall we not see to it that his capacity and integrity be not forgotten?" he wrote in the *Reform Advocate.*

Julian came through the election handsomely, running especially well in the "Jewish wards," the only Democrat on the judicial slate to be victorious there.

His victory despite labor opposition gave him enhanced status. There was talk almost at once that he might be slated for the Illinois

Supreme Court. Some admirers asked, "Why not even the Supreme Court of the United States?"

That fall there was a vacancy in the Federal District Court in Chicago. Julian's name was suggested to fill it. But the appointment went to a "blue-blooded" Republican, Judge George Carpenter, who, as a colleague of Julian on the Circuit Court, had issued numerous injunctions against labor unions. He would be chiefly remembered, if at all, for the enthusiasm with which he denied citizenship to Rosika Schwimmer, the pacifist Jewess who had given Henry Ford the idea for his "peace ship" in 1915.

Julian would have liked that Federal appointment then. He was not happy on the Illinois Appellate Court. For one thing, his colleagues were oldsters who constantly complained that he was devoting too much time to "outside activities."

"The fact is, I hold up more than my end of the work," Julian said disgustedly to his law clerk, Charles P. Schwartz. Yet this was the time when he added to his other interests his concern for the Negroes, participating with Roger Baldwin, Stephen S. Wise, and Jane Addams in meetings that finally led to the formation of the National Association for the Advancement of Colored People. Later, he also joined Baldwin as a sponsor of the American Civil Liberties Union, ignoring allegations that it was "Red." "He was not frightened," Baldwin remembered.

No one doubted that Julian Mack deserved elevation to the Federal judiciary, on which, supposedly, there sat only the highest type of judges, with lifetime tenure. Law scholars in particular agreed that he was extraordinarily brilliant as a "motions" judge, at making oral decisions. He did not like, nor shine in, opinion-writing. "He suffered from pen paralysis," Frankfurter would say, but added, "No judge outshone him on the bench. In England, his oral ability would have made him the peer of the greatest common law jurists."

But since all such appointments were in some degree "political," not even Julian was so naive as not to realize that in 1909 his chances of being promoted to the Federal bench were slim.

The next year, the political situation changed at the very time that Congress authorized the appointment of additional Federal judges. These were to include five jurists who would hold the rank of justice of the Circuit Court of Appeals and would serve on a new court, the United States Commerce Court.

This new court was to have a status only a notch below that of the Supreme Court of the United States and was to deal with appeals from rulings of the Interstate Commerce Commission. Ostensibly its purpose was to relieve the U.S. Supreme Court from the burden of appellate jurisdiction over district court decisions involving regulation of the railroads. Actually, however, the new Commerce Court was established for political-economic reasons.

There had been widespread dissatisfaction with Federal court rulings in railroad cases, a discontent which had been fanned by Progressive Republicans and which came to a head in the 1912 "Bull Moose" split. Moreover, a tug-of-war had been going on for some time between the Interstate Commerce Commission and the courts. Conservatives felt that the Commission was too zealous in controlling the railroads, notably with respect to freight rates, and had often won reversals in the Supreme Court. So the progressives supported the idea of the Commerce Court to "curb" the Supreme Court while conservatives favored it as a possible device to "curb" the Commerce Commission.

As it turned out, this mixed parentage doomed the court to a short life. But at its birth the judicial posts that went with it were considered especially desirable.

Since Chicago was the railroad capital of the nation, it was assumed that at least one of the new justices would be from Illinois. On October 11, 1910, the *Chicago Tribune* listed some "prominent prospects": Walter W.L. Fisher; William J. Calhoun, of the Rudovitz case; Horace Kent Tenney, member of a prominent Chicago law firm; Kenesaw Mountain Landis, who had won fame as a district judge in 1907 by his imposition of a fine of $29,240,000 on the Standard Oil Company—and Julian Mack.

Taft pondered his choices cautiously. The Taft-Roosevelt split was in the offing. In Illinois especially there was division among the Republicans, with even the traditionally Republican *Tribune* siding with the Progressives and "T.R." For Taft to name a Republican—

any Republican—to the U.S. Commerce Court would have meant offending one of the factions. His "out" was to select a Democrat.

Thus Julian's Democratic affiliation worked in his favor. So also did his Jewishness. Like Mayor Harrison back in 1903, Taft in 1910 wanted to appeal to "the Jewish vote." For Taft was in trouble with Jewish organizations, including the American Jewish Committee, the B'nai B'rith, and the Union of American Hebrew Congregations, over a treaty that had been signed in 1832 between the United States and Russia.

This treaty provided that the nationals of both countries had reciprocal travel rights. But since the 1890's, when Russia first began rigidly enforcing her regulations forbidding Jews to travel beyond "the Pale of Settlement," Russia had been refusing visas to Americans who were Jewish.

To support these regulations, Russian consuls in the United States were requiring every applicant for a visa to state whether he was a Jew. The Czarist government also refused to recognize the American citizenship of former Russian subjects unless it had given official permission for their original departure from Russia. Thus many American citizens who had been born in Russia and had emigrated to the United States without an official Russian exit permit were subject to prosecution as criminals if they returned to Russia, although they carried an American passport.

Even "moderate" Jews, including Adolph Ochs of *The New York Times*, began to feel that this situation was intolerable. Ochs intended to "give the subject some publicity, for the purpose of creating public opinion," he told Louis Marshall of the American Jewish Committee.

In the 1908 election campaign, the Republican platform had promised the abrogation of the treaty if the Czar's government would not cease discriminating against American citizens. Yet Taft did not wish to honor that pledge, and he was candid about his reasons. Abrogation of the treaty, he felt, would jeopardize investments made in Russia by American firms, notably the International Harvester Company and the Singer Sewing Machine Company. He hoped to persuade the Russian government by negotiation to lift its ban on American visitors who were Jews. But the Czar's government made it plain that it would not negotiate on the matter.

Indignation among Jewish leaders built up against Taft. Indeed, almost from its inception, the American Jewish Committee made the abrogation of the Russian treaty one of its top-priority projects. In this goal, Julian was at one with his colleagues on the Committee. He believed that it would be easy to arouse favorable American public opinion on the Committee's position because America's honor was involved. All intelligent non-Jews would be interested, he felt, emphasizing that the matter should be presented not as a Jewish issue, but as an American problem.

But Taft held to a do-nothing policy on the Russian treaty. Obviously, then, it was in the interest of his administration to offer as compensation the conspicuous appointment of a prominent Jew to a high position. Julian fitted that bill.

A story has persisted that Julius Rosenwald had "put Mack over with President Taft," a myth with a credible ring because of a later friendship between Rosenwald and Taft, in part personal, in part because Taft had supported legislation that added hugely to Sears, Roebuck profits by providing cheap postage rates for mail order parcels. Indeed, Rosenwald became the largest contributor to the 1912 Taft campaign fund. But at the time of the Commerce Court appointment, Rosenwald did not yet know Taft. It was Mack who was to bring them together later on.

There were other important Jews, however, who let Taft know that Julian's appointment would please them. Most significant was the endorsement that came from Max Pam. Through one client alone, John W. "Bet-You-A-Million" Gates, Pam had an enviable law practice. Another client of Pam's was Charles M. Schwab of Bethlehem Steel; so was the International Harvester Company. Pam also "did the legal work" in the formation of the United States Steel Corporation. In short, Pam was exactly the kind of lawyer apt to be highly admired by William Howard Taft. Moreover, he functioned as Taft's personal "scout" on Chicago affairs and on Jewish matters. As Julian once commented to Brandeis, on certain matters the proper "contact" with Taft was Max Pam. "He can do it, if anyone can."

Max Pam was not a particularly "Jewish" Jew, though one of his brothers, Hugo, was an ardent Zionist. He did give some help to Jewish Palestine.* But when he became a major philanthropist, his gifts were mainly to non-Jewish institutions, such as the University of Notre Dame, whose school of journalism he endowed. However, Max Pam did allow his Jewishness to motivate him in Julian's behalf. It is known that Pam visited Taft at the White House to discuss the Russian treaty—and Julian Mack.

Meanwhile, the press, too, had begun to boost Julian. In September, 1910, the *Cincinnati Times-Star,* reporting "information of a reliable character," indicated that Taft had determined upon Julian Mack as one of the judges of the new U.S. Commerce Court. "This information will be especially pleasing in Cincinnati," the paper said. The *Chicago Tribune* chimed in: "Judge Mack is a progressive-minded judge and that is what the country needs today."

But the two Republican senators from Illinois, Shelby Cullom and William Lorimer, were not pleased. Both raised a fuss over the possibility of Julian Mack's appointment, and insisted that the appointment should go to a Republican instead. This caused the *Chicago Evening Post* to state:

"The Commerce Court, for the sake of the whole idea it represents, must be free from politics in every one of its momentous decisions. That politics should creep into its very beginnings is unthinkable. Senator Cullom would better keep his hands off."

Jewish support behind Julian was highly influential with Taft. "The President has been deluged with letters," the *Tribune* reported, "from prominent Jews and Jewish organizations in all parts of the country urging the selection of Mack. Several newspapers with which Jews have large influence also have been enlisted in the campaign."

Also there was the influence of Charles D. Norton, the friend of Julian from his early days in Chicago when the two of them had sold

---

*Max Pam's will, drawn up in the 1930's, set aside $50,000, with Julian Mack as a trustee, to be used for the industrial development of Palestine, with the provision, however, that "Palestine be under the active control and mandate . . . of Great Britain."

insurance for Northwestern Mutual. By 1910, Norton had become so influential as Taft's private secretary that Mrs. Taft complained, "Will approves everything that Norton hands him."

Norton saw to it that Julian's name was kept at the top of the list on Taft's desk. He was the source, too, of "the reliable information" given to the press. "Dear Charlie," Julian wrote to him later, "I know full well how much all of this is due to your feelings of friendship and genuine interest in me."

On December 11, 1910, Taft sent to the Senate, all in one batch, the names of nine appointees to various judicial posts. These included Associate Justice Edward D. White for Chief Justice of the Supreme Court to succeed Melville Fuller—and Julian Mack for U.S. Circuit Judge, assigned to the U.S. Commerce Court.

There was a tense period of delay in the confirmations. Some Progressive senators, notably Robert M. LaFollette and William E. Borah, were not happy with all the selections. The Progressives were satisfied with Julian but they objected particularly to one appointee to the Commerce Court—U.S. District Judge Robert W. Archbald of Scranton, Pennsylvania, a protege of the Republican "boss," Senator Penrose—hardly a recommendation to the Progressives.

There were angry explosions from some conservatives also. But on December 30, 1910, Julian felt able to tell Dean Wigmore: "I have every assurance . . . that there is no opposition of any kind from any source to my confirmation."

Confirmation came on January 31, 1911. Five days later Julian was sworn in as a judge of the U.S. Circuit Court assigned to the Commerce Court, becoming the highest ranking Jew in the American judiciary up to that time.

17. Manhattan "Macher"

Julian thought that his base as Commerce Court judge would be Washington exclusively. This caused him some regret, he told Jane Addams, who had just published her *Twenty Years at Hull House,* so much of which was concerned with events and causes in which he had played a role. "Leaving the activities that you describe and . . . ceasing, even for a time, to share with you the tasks that are still ahead . . . make me hesitate at times as to the wisdom of the acceptance of the new duties," he wrote her.

To Wigmore, however, he admitted that "the thought of life in Washington is attractive."

It was, at first. But as matters turned out, after the first period of congratulations, he was no happier on the Commerce Court than he had been on the Appellate Court. The truth was, he was unhappier, largely because of the political atmosphere in Washington.

Fortunately, he was not based there exclusively, for the court held some sessions in Chicago as well. Also, during slack periods after the new court had become organized, he made a point of serving voluntarily as a "relief" Federal judge in Chicago. He liked these intervals "at home" and contrived to get them often enough so that he had permanent chambers in the newly-erected "Chicago Greek style" Federal Building in Chicago.

From time to time, also to help relieve the perpetual docket congestion there, he began to sit with Learned Hand and his colleagues on the Second Circuit in New York City.

In that period, until he and Jessie were able to arrange for a permanent apartment atop the Fifth Avenue Hotel, their New York residence was the Ansonia Hotel on Broadway. The Ansonia—Jessie's choice—was a rather flashy place whose tenants included the actress Billie Burke and her husband, the theatrical producer Florenz Ziegfeld, another transplanted Chicagoan. Julian soon became a familiar Ansonian, especially conspicuous for his habitual

119

dash from the lobby to get to the Woolworth Building where he and Learned and Augustus Hand had their private law offices.

New York lawyers soon looked forward to Julian's appearances. For, with his "Chicago ways," as his mannerisms were described, he managed to introduce a special freshness into usually staid New York court proceedings. For example, as in his juvenile court days, he refrained from wearing a judicial robe, still agreeing with Altgeld's observation back in the 1890's that "a robe used as an insignia of office is a relic of barbarism."

As Jerome Frank wrote in a sequel to his *Law and the Modern Mind,* for which Julian had written the introduction, Julian

> . . . went even further. He frequently held trials in his chambers, where he sat at his desk on a level with the witnesses and lawyers. With the formal trappings absent, he found that he could more quickly and easily get at the facts.

Obviously, for a judge, he was "a character"—or so he was called by New Yorkers.

JUDGE, TIRING
OF LONG TRIAL,
HOLDS COURT
ON A TRAIN

Lawyers Match Coins
to See Who Shall
Pay for Special

Thus, the *New York World,* on its front page on May 16, 1913, headlined a story that made New Yorkers especially aware of "the Chicago judge." The story concerned an ordinary lawsuit in the Federal District Court in Foley Square, which had dragged on for six weeks before the Federal judge and a jury. The judge, his "patience worn to the ragged edge," had admonished the lawyers that they must "hurry the trial," the story said. Much of the dispute, in which the Amsterdam Building Company had sued the R. V.

Delaphane Company for $31,000, was over the supposedly complicated nature of the work done by the building company on a warehouse in Poughkeepsie.

"If I thought the judge would agree, I would take this court and jury up to Poughkeepsie and let them see the work for themselves," one lawyer finally said. According to the newspaper account, "the judge had no objection, if both sides agreed, especially as both sides promised to charter a special train for the legal excursion." He had the lawyers match coins to see which side should foot the bill.

> At 8:30 A.M., the special left Grand Central Station with the full court. It was in session, at the rate of fifty miles an hour, when the train went through Tarrytown. . . . Time passed so quickly that they were surprised when they reached Pough-keepsie. There the judge, jurors, and lawyers inspected the building . . . then sat down to an elaborate lunch ordered by the judge. The "court on wheels" returned to New York last night. The decision will come today.

The "judge," of course, was Julian Mack.

He was immediately lionized by the New Yorkers. Dining and speaking invitations poured in on him. The city's "Our Crowd" Jewry—the Schiffs, Lewisohns, Strauses, Morgenthaus and Wertheims, who already knew him as a member of the American Jewish Committee—took him up socially.

Overnight he was drawn also into New York civic affairs. Aside from the splash he made on the Federal bench, his work in social welfare in Chicago attracted a ready-made circle in New York, including Homer Folks, a leading New York charity worker; Lillian Wald, of the Henry Street settlement; Florence Kelley, who had transferred her headquarters from Hull House to Miss Wald's settlement; and both Paul U. Kellogg and Edward T. Devine of the *Survey*—all persons active in New York civic movements of various kinds, all eager to draw Julian into their causes.

Thus, when the New York State Constitutional Convention was planned, he was called in as adviser on New York's juvenile and family laws. Thus, too, when the Foreign Policy Association was formed, he was invited to serve on its first board of directors. When Survey Associates was organized to support the *Survey* magazine, he was drafted to be its chairman. And he was part of the group around Herbert Croly, Randolph Bourne, Walter Lippmann and Felix Frankfurter that launched the liberal magazine, *The New Republic*.

When his old admirer, Roger Baldwin, started the predecessor organization of the American Civil Liberties Union, Julian was in that group also, and he became a member of the liberal National Lawyers' Guild—connections which in the 1930's would get him listed in Mrs. Elizabeth Dilling's *The Red Network* among such "subversives" (in the Dilling view) as Eleanor Roosevelt, Jane Addams, Robert Maynard Hutchins and Felix Frankfurter.

There were also significant associations with Jewish figures of quite a different cast from "Our Crowd." One such figure was Felix Frankfurter, then a young lawyer on the staff of Secretary of War Henry L. Stimson. Frankfurter frequently showed up in New York City, his home base.

In all but appearance, Frankfurter was another Aaron Aaronsohn—brilliant, loquacious, gregarious, full of the joy of living. And, as had happened with Aaron Aaronsohn, Julian and he immediately became friends, a friendship of special value to Frankfurter when on more than one occasion his later connection with Harvard University would be in jeopardy.

Through Julian, Frankfurter, too, became an intimate of Aaronsohn's. The two younger men and Julian made a buoyant trio, future collaborators in Zionism. An entry in Aaronsohn's diary for 1913, concerning a visit to the Armory Art Show in New York, reflects the relationship of the three men:

Saturday, March 15, 1913. N.Y.

Call on Mack at 15 past 9. Go together to the Exhibit of American Painters which closes today.

Work of Cubists & Futurists looks crazy to the normal average man. . . . Felix Frankfurter left the Exhibit and Mack takes me to *The Outlook* at a 1/4 to one. Frankfurter arrives at one. . . .

T.R. [Theodore Roosevelt] drops in. Fat gentleman. His excess of flesh disappoints me. Fail to see on his face the energetic look his picture so strongly shows. Has deep scars on his neck, especially so on his right hand. His projection of the chin and his shaking his fist to his son T.R. Jr. lack real distinction. . . .

T.R. has me seated to his right. Start with story of wild wheat & going back to the origins of our Colonization movement. In saying "We" T.R. stops me, asking, whom do you mean by "we"—Jewish farmers, etc. . . .

My talk lasted for one hour and forty minutes. All who know the Colonel are surprised; From now on my reputation will be: the man who had made the Colonel shut up for 101 minutes. . . .

A match, almost, for Frankfurter, was another Zionist, Stephen S. Wise, rabbi of New York's Free Synagogue.

When Julian began to sit in New York, Wise, then in his thirties, was moving forward rapidly to becoming the nation's foremost rabbi. He was already a factor in New York's civic affairs, as he had been earlier in public affairs in Oregon. He first began to cultivate Julian in April, 1911, when his Free Synagogue, which then met in Carnegie Hall, celebrated its fourth anniversary and Julian was a speaker for the occasion.

It took a fair amount of audacity on Julian's part to be close to Stephen S. Wise. For then, as later, Wise was a top *bête noire* in many circles. In the politics of the general New York establishment, in Reform Judaism, in the "Our Crowd" circle generally, and particularly with the leaders of the American Jewish Committee, Stephen S. Wise was *persona non grata*, a "rebel" who took seriously the social-minded prophetic traditions of Judaism. As a friend of Senators LaFollette and Borah, Wise was in the forefront of every crusade for social reform. Consequently, he stepped on many toes and was frequently the center of stormy episodes—beginning in New York when he declined appointment as rabbi of Temple Emanu-El, "the Cathedral synagogue of American Judaism," on being informed that its trustees reserved the right to censor his utterances. Then, too, though as radically Reform as Emil G. Hirsch, Wise had been an active Zionist since the days of Herzl; he had attended the First Zionist Congress in Basle in 1897 and had helped found the Federation of American Zionists.

Julian, though fully aware both of Wise's "radicalism" and his Zionism, took an instant liking to him. They were soon comrades in numerous activities. Later, in 1922, when Wise organized the Jewish Institute of Religion in New York—a rival of the Hebrew Union College, founded by Isaac Mayer Wise in Cincinnati—Julian became its chairman. He did so, as he once wrote Frankfurter, notwithstanding "my real lack of religious feeling and belief—strong prejudice against active participation in religious matters."

It was Julian, too, who at the time undertook for Wise the difficult assignment of presenting to the Hebrew Union College Wise's proposal that the two schools should merge, with Wise choosing the president of the combined institution. Wise's Zionism was the main stumbling block* and Julian, to his embarrassment, was "practically thrown out of the meeting," as he recalled it, even though his brother Ralph was a trustee of the Cincinnati seminary.

Other leaders of the New York Jewish community, especially Felix M. Warburg, Jacob Schiff's son-in-law, also sought out Julian. In 1913, when Warburg was considering a national organization of Young Men's Hebrew Associations, Julian functioned as the link between the Jews of New York and those of Chicago. Julian presided over a national conference in New York of Y.M.H.A. representatives who formed "The Council of Young Men's Hebrew and Kindred Associations."

In World War I this organization became the Jewish Welfare

---

*The Jewish Institute of Religion differed from the Hebrew Union College in that it inclined to Zionism from the start as opposed to the non- and even anti-Zionist attitudes that prevailed at the Cincinnati institution in those early days. It was not until 1950 that the two schools merged to form an institution known as Hebrew Union College-Jewish Institute of Religion (HUC-JIR).

Board, serving the religious needs of Jews in the Armed Forces. Still later, it became the core of the nationwide Jewish Community Center movement.

Julian pressed a significant suggestion for the Y.M.H.A. movement on Warburg.

"Energetic young Russian Jews should be brought in," he urged, thus beginning to play in New York, as he had in Chicago, the role of mediating link between "German" and "East European" Jews, and also between anti-Zionists and pro-Zionists.

He played a similar role in the relations between the Jewish community as a whole and the rest of the city. Perhaps no other Jew developed so many cordial friendships with non-Jews. To many non-Jews of the New York "establishment" Julian Mack was the first personal correction of a warped image of "the Jew."

Especially was this so in the legal world. He and the Hands, Judge Learned and Judge Augustus, the two leading members of the Federal bench in New York City, became the closest of friends, "brother judges" in fact as well as by convention. Young lawyers, Jewish and non-Jewish, idolized him. A list of them would include Charles C. Burlingham, the lawyer credited with having obtained for Benjamin Cardozo and the two Hands their elevation to the bench; John M. Harlan, later appointed by Dwight D. Eisenhower as Justice of the Supreme Court; Emory Buckner, later head of one of New York's great law firms; and Robert P. Patterson, later Secretary of War—to name only a few. Julian's fresh approach intrigued such young people, as did the fact that he went out of his way to be helpful to them because they were young. He made it a habit, for one thing, when appointing receivers or attorneys for receivers, or when disposing of property in his jurisdiction, to pick young men for such plums.

One such beneficiary was J. M. Kaplan, the later developer of the Welch grape juice enterprise, although he was not a lawyer. He appeared in his court one day to offer a bid for a bankrupt sugar refinery. Julian had never met Kaplan before but, liking the young man's looks, sensing his special ability, and admiring his spunk, Julian passed over the objections of leading New York law firms to give Kaplan the right to take over the refinery. In later years Kaplan was to become a noted New York civic leader and philanthropist.

For young Jewish lawyers, especially those of Russian Jewish origin, it was a new experience to find on the Federal bench a judge so friendly toward them. Though he gave no hint of favoritism toward them merely because they were Jewish, he was keenly aware of the need to strike a balance because of the actions of a number of non-Jewish judges in the opposite direction.

He selected his law clerks in accordance with their abilities. Law clerks to Federal judges of his rank, along with those associated with Supreme Court Justices, later became lawyers of favored status with prestigious non-Jewish firms. But until Julian was named to the Circuit Court of Appeals, few such opportunities had come to Jewish law graduates in any of the major cities.

Julian suffered real distress over this situation. At a Harvard Law School reunion, Roscoe Pound, then dean, confided to him that he, Pound, was also disturbed by the discrimination against Jewish graduates on the part of the big New York law firms. Even *Law Review* editors who were Jews had trouble being placed. Because of this situation Julian instituted a system that had greater significance than either he or Pound realized at the time.

Every year, Roscoe Pound recommended a Jewish graduate of the Harvard Law School to be Julian's law clerk. Later, Frankfurter, on becoming professor of law at Harvard, took over the selection of Julian's clerks. Still later, Brandeis, on becoming Associate Justice of the Supreme Court, adopted Julian's system of having Frankfurter select his assistants. After a time, this system was further elaborated. Clerks chosen for Julian would go on to become clerks to Brandeis. It was understood that their service with Julian was preparation for the higher-level work with the Supreme Court Justice. Thus Nathaniel Nathanson, who later became professor of law at Northwestern University, was clerk first to Mack and then to Brandeis.

Among other young lawyers who attained distinction in their careers after serving as Julian's law clerks were Max Lowenthal, Benjamin V. Cohen, Murray Gurfein, Abram Chayes, Lawrence Berenson, Charles P. Schwartz and Sydney Krause.

Julian's interest in his law clerks and other rising young men, such as Robert Szold, who became a top leader in American Zionism, added a new dimension to his life, as it did to theirs. As several of them have said, he "fussed over us like a mother hen, advising on our diets, our clothing, our love lives." He took the greatest delight in being the medium through which these brilliant young men made good professional connections. These friendships, together with the pleasure he got from vibrant New York as a whole, with its glamour and centrality in large affairs, including Jewish life, all combined to make the New York phase of his Federal Court service highly pleasing to him and to his wife, Jessie.

18. A Joseph in Egypt

But the Washington aspect of his career was quite different. Washington, even for a judge, meant mainly politics, and no one could have been less suited for the Washington political whirl than Julian Mack. Yet he was almost immediately drawn into it when he was on the U.S. Commerce Court, especially because of his ready access to Charles D. Norton and, through Norton, to President Taft himself.

To his surprise, the White House adopted him as a special consultant on Jewish matters, particularly on the problem of Jewish discrimination practiced by Russian officials in their implementation of the Russian treaty of 1832.

Julian was not so naive as to fail to understand the role expected of him, a role so clear that shortly after he was named to the court he raised the point at a meeting of the American Jewish Committee. He sensed that his position might bring embarrassment to the Committee or to himself, and suggested that he should resign from the Committee. But exactly because of the treaty matter, Louis Marshall persuaded him not to resign. For one thing, Marshall was concerned just then over reports that Simon Wolf had been supplying Taft with answers to demands that he abrogate the Russian treaty. Wolf had made the point that to cancel the treaty "would make the lives of Jews in Russia more intolerable."

At first, Julian liked being a White House confidant. It was pleasant to be able to escort Jessie to a state reception at the White House, as he did in January, 1912. There they mingled with V.I.P.'s and were "received," as the papers noted, not only by Mrs. Taft, but also by the widow of Marshall Field, then the Tafts' house guest, while the Marine Band played. It was nice, too, for Julian to have the President express an interest in his work and to get his views on various issues.

There was obvious satisfaction in being listened to, even heeded at times, in the matter of Presidential appointments for this or that public office. Julian played a major role in getting Taft to name Julia Lathrop as the first director of the Children's Bureau; otherwise a hack, or someone unsympathetic, might have been appointed, for Taft really did not like the idea of the Bureau, which he considered a step toward socialism. But at the request of Jane Addams, Julian prodded Taft into appointing Miss Lathrop.

Mack was aware, too, of something that could have been tremendously important—though it was not to be talked about. Intimacy between a judge and a President, any President, can be the path leading to a post every lawyer naturally thinks about—that of Justice of the Supreme Court. The advanced age of several incumbents at the time made it likely that Taft would have to appoint several new Justices. As it happened, Justice John Marshall Harlan, who had been appointed to the Court by President Rutherford B. Hayes in 1877 (he was the grandfather of the later Justice by the same name), was 78 in 1911, when Julian came to Washington. That very year, Harlan died. "Everybody knew that Julian's great desire was to be appointed to the Supreme Court," one of Julian's kin said. This was only a guess, but it may have been correct.

However, in the maneuverings over the Harlan vacancy, Julian made no move in his own behalf. Instead, he joined Schiff and other Jewish leaders in urging that Louis Marshall be considered for the post. In the end, the appointment went to Mahlon Pitney of New Jersey. The elevation of a Jew to the highest court of the land had to wait.

Even so, it was plain that Julian, in view of the universal esteem in which he was held, was definitely a possibility for the Supreme Court should Taft remain in office. He would have been less than human had he not recognized that possibility, especially with Charles Norton watching over his interests. Clearly, this was a factor in his going along with the White House concept of his role in Washington—a kind of "Joseph in Egypt."

Then the issue of the Russian treaty of 1832 became acute. By 1911, the American Jewish Committee and B'nai B'rith were determined to force the public showdown which Julian had previously urged. It came in connection with the convention of the Union of American Hebrew Congregations at Albany, N.Y. in January, 1911. The plan was for Louis Marshall to deliver a summary of the situation, then have the convention adopt a resolution openly calling for the abrogation of the treaty—the first public airing of the question.

Now ambivalent, Julian tried to prevent that direct showdown. In truth, he had allowed himself to be seduced by his closeness to Taft into an uncharacteristic—and clumsy—attempt to play the role of politician. "After full inquiry, I believe [the] cause best served by not speaking on passport [question] at present gathering," he telegraphed Marshall at Albany on the eve of the convention.

Fortunately, his advice was rejected. The convention of the Union called upon Taft to honor his party's election pledge for the abrogation of the treaty, and Jacob Schiff requested Taft to receive a delegation of Jewish leaders at the White House on the question.

Julian met beforehand with the delegation that called on Taft on February 15, 1911. By then he, too, believed in a strategy of firmness. But he asked to be excused from attending the actual meeting with the President. Unquestionably he felt that being in a sense a member of the Taft administration placed him in an embarrassing position.

Taft used the meeting to make it known with shocking candor that, out of concern for American investments, he would not abrogate the treaty with Russia. He then made a serious and stupid error. Impressed by a report on the subject from his latest ambassador to Russia, W. W. Rockhill, a career diplomat, he foolishly expected his guests to be equally impressed. He therefore read to the gathering a part of the report, which was filled with aspersions on Russia's Jews—quotations from Russian officials that Ambassador Rockhill had gratuitously passed along. The delegation was properly appalled.

To make matters worse, Taft suggested that Julian's friend, Charles Norton, Taft's private secretary, read the ambassador's full report to the delegation.

"I beg you, Mr. Norton!" Schiff exploded. "Do not insult us by reading that again!" When the meeting broke up, Schiff declined to shake Taft's hand. "We are still in *golus* [exile]!" one delegate, Bernhard Bettmann of Cincinnati, exclaimed to Schiff as the chagrined group left the White House.

"Yes," replied Schiff. "This means war!"

The "war," directed at Taft, was climaxed by a mass meeting at Carnegie Hall in New York, masterminded by George Kennan, the Russian expert, whom Schiff had retained as public relations expert for the fight. One speaker, significantly, was Woodrow Wilson, then Governor of New Jersey.

A footnote here about Wilson's speech is interesting—if it is true. Julius Haber, a Zionist historian, recalls that

> . . . a spontanous movement was born, right then in the gallery, to boom [Wilson] as the next President of the United States. . . .

Be that as it may, Democrats everywhere, especially in Congress, caught the signal of Wilson's participation. Resolutions were introduced in the House and the Senate calling on Taft to abrogate the treaty. Still, Taft did not yield easily. Egged on by Henry Cabot Lodge, Theodore Roosevelt, perhaps innocently, offered Taft an escape hatch by urging, in the October, 1911, issue of *The Outlook*, that the issue be submitted to the International Court of Justice in The Hague for arbitration. Louis Marshall was indignant.

"Do nations 'arbitrate' on whether or not they keep their word?" he asked.

"I agree entirely with you," Julian wrote to Marshall, beginning to understand a comment that Frankfurter had made about Taft:

"You couldn't get any happiness out of Taft as President."

In November, 1911, another delegation of Jewish leaders called on Taft. This time Julian Mack was with them. So, too, was Julius Rosenwald. "The strong personal friendship said to be felt by President Taft toward Mr. Rosenwald and Judge Mack, it is believed, will bear great weight on the President's attitude," the Associated Press reported concerning that meeting. But Taft remained adamant. He tried to head off Congressional action with a special message to Congress on the subject in December, after a resolution for the abrogation of the treaty had been introduced in the House by a young congressman from Texas, John Nance Garner, along with three congressmen from New York.

Congress took action. The resolution passed in the House, 301 to 1. Only then did Taft reluctantly advise the Russian Foreign Ministry that the treaty was being denounced.

Julian was pleased but, aside from his disillusionment over Taft's placing commercial considerations over civil rights for Jews there remained his regret at having permitted himself to play a see-saw role.

Politics, obviously, was not for him. The less time he spent in Washington the better he felt.

The incident had one good effect on Julian. It helped open his eyes to what at least later on he came to recognize as a fact of life: that such well-meaning non-Jews as William Howard Taft could not be counted upon to defend justice for Jews in a showdown. As Herzl had argued so forcefully, Jews would have to get their rights by standing on their own feet.

There were other political matters that troubled him. One concerned a Protestant-Catholic problem that arose around President Taft: the question whether or not Taft should reappoint the incumbent judge of the Juvenile Court of the District of Columbia, William H. DeLacey, a prominent Catholic. Selection of the district juvenile judge ordinarily was a trivial matter, but the DeLacey case had all the makings of a *cause célèbre,* and it was perilously close to the Presidential election of 1912.

One charge against Judge DeLacey was that he "took too great an interest in the sex life of girls brought before him." It was alleged that he insisted on quizzing them about their sexual experiences even when nothing of the kind was involved in their case. More serious were allegations that he permitted "Catholic power" to influence his decisions. What particularly angered Protestants was Judge DeLacey's practice of having all foundlings baptized in the Catholic Church, a kind of variation on the Mortara affair.

Julia Lathrop, head of the Children's Bureau, was among those who called for Judge DeLacey's dismissal. At the least, she believed, DeLacey ought not to be reappointed. Important Roman Catholics then rallied to the judge's defense. Among them were Chief Justice Edward D. White and James Cardinal Gibbons of the Diocese of

Maryland, then the most powerful and popular figure in the American Catholic hierarchy.

Taft, understandably, had no stomach for tangling with the Cardinal. But his Attorney General, George W. Wickersham, had submitted a report calling Judge DeLacey unfit. For Taft this was a dilemma, from which he hoped Julian Mack would be able to extricate him. He therefore asked Julian to study the case and submit his recommendation.

It was a most unpleasant assignment. Julian had known and liked Judge DeLacey since their cordial association. at the 1909 White House Conference on Children, when Judge DeLacey had supported the policies advocated by Julian. But Julian also had the highest regard for the views of Julia Lathrop.

He spent a good deal of time on the DeLacey case, and then submitted a long memorandum to the President. In it, he defended DeLacey against the sexual allegations. All juvenile court judges, he observed, were subject to occasional misrepresentation in this area. It had happened to him, too, he recalled. In effect, he also cleared the judge on the religious issue. As president of the Children's Council of Washington, he observed, he had heard that Judge DeLacey was "a bigot." But he had personally questioned DeLacey and was satisfied that he was "really broadminded in these matters," and was probably the victim of "suspicion that frequently existed between religious groups."

Yet, citing Miss Lathrop's feeling that this was the "most serious aspect of the case," he wrote that Judge DeLacey had obviously lost the confidence of social workers at various Protestant institutions. He therefore concluded: "While I personally have confidence in Judge DeLacey's good intentions and in his character, I fear that his reappointment would not be for the best advantage of the community."

That formula saved the day. DeLacey was not to be officially found "guilty," but neither was he to be reappointed. President Taft and Attorney General Wickersham were grateful. Julian had pulled them out of a bad hole in time to prevent the DeLacey case from becoming an election issue. But Julian felt soiled.

A still more bitter taste of politics was in store for him. For the three-cornered 1912 election contest—Taft *vs.* Theodore Roosevelt *vs.* Wilson—confronted him with an especially trying dilemma.

As a Democrat, Julian was highly satisfied with Woodrow Wilson ever since he had shared the speakers' platform with Wilson at the fourth anniversary celebration of Rabbi Wise's Free Synagogue in New York. He had been impressed, too, with the notably progressive tenor of Wilson's address. Moreover, Julian noted that Brandeis, though originally a LaFollette Republican, was by then emerging as one of Wilson's leading supporters and advisers —recommendation enough in itself for Julian to support Wilson.

Still, against the pull toward Wilson, there was Julian's personal relationship with Taft. Even within the limited political participation permitted to a judge, could he come out for Wilson against Taft, despite his faults, in the campaign? He decided that he could not.

And what of "Teddy" Roosevelt? The former President's entry into the Presidential race added to Julian's dilemma. For Roosevelt, as a third-party candidate, had presented a platform that included almost all of the social welfare goals which had been adopted by the National Conference of Charities and Correction, of which Julian was president. Added to this aspect of "T.R."'s campaign was the fact that he had the enthusiastic support of Jane Addams.

As it happened, "T.R." himself took Julian off the hook by coming out for a proposal that few judges could have supported—the recall of judicial decisions by popular referendum. Appalled by "T.R."'s proposal, Julian concluded that Roosevelt had become "a false guide . . . a danger to the country."

Yet the dilemma remained. Although he really favored Wilson, Julian still could not bring himself to cast a vote against Taft. His "feelings of personal gratitude toward, and genuine affection for, the President made it impossible" for him to vote at all, he later recalled. So he "purposely refrained from even registering to vote," as he later said.

He did not, however, refrain from some political participation in the campaign through "private conversation." Though he held back from urging anyone to vote for Wilson, he did "urge many to vote for one or the other against T.R." Thus his curiously ambiguous "neutrality" added up to a strong opposition to Roosevelt.

All this he had occasion to explain in a letter—really meant for Taft—to Taft's national campaign chairman, Charles N. Hilles, revealing, into the bargain, some "secret history" of the 1912 election:

> Prior to the Progressive Convention [he wrote to Hilles] Julius Rosenwald and I, and subsequently I alone, when consulted, strongly, though vainly, urged one who has become perhaps the most prominent of Roosevelt's followers not to join his cause, both because of our personal views as to the unreliability of his leadership and personality and because of the causes that this leader has most at heart. I refrain from giving the name lest it might possibly violate a confidence.

The name of "this leader," as the Rosenwald papers at the University of Chicago reveal, was Jane Addams.

Even so, Julian discovered that he was being incorrectly and unjustly pictured at the White House as a "traitor to Taft." "Max Pam tells me," he wrote to Hilles on December 9, 1912, "that you and the President have been told by Mr. Simon Wolf and others that I have actively advocated the cause of T.R. as against the President."

"I cannot conceive how such a false rumor could have originated," he went on, "unless it be because I have some very close friends who are strong followers of the Colonel [i.e., Roosevelt]."

This could have been the explanation. Most of Julian's associates in the National Conference of Charities and Correction were Roosevelt supporters, as were several members of Julian's circle, such as Rabbi Hirsch's son-in-law, young Rabbi Gerson B. Levi, who ran for local office as a "Bull Mooser."

Not merely close friends of Julian's were in the Bull Moose movement. His own brother William was active for a "T.R."-Bull Moose candidate—one of Julian's former law clerks, Charles Schwartz—who was running for the State Legislature, representing the Hull House district. That situation could have been especially embarrassing to Julian, had Simon Wolf known about it.

Wolf had, in fact, made some remarks about Julian to Taft. On receiving a copy of Julian's letter from Chairman Hilles, Wolf denied that he had said "under any circumstances, surely never to you," that Julian had supported "T.R." but he conceded to Hilles that he had "discussed in a negative way with Taft" the "political value" of Julian's appointment to the Commerce Court, adding:

> I said frankly to the President that it would not bring him a single delegate, and would disgruntle the leaders, and the rank and file of the party. This has no reference whatsoever to any personal objections, as I esteem and honor Judge Mack highly, as he so eminently deserves. I further stated that Judge Mack was a Democrat, which he had of course a right to be, and naturally would not be in favor of the President's reelection. To that extent I am guilty, but in no other. . . .

Thus, between the lines, it was clear that regardless of his intentions Simon Wolf had, in fact, subtly "knifed" Julian. It was one more instance of Julian's Joseph-in-Egypt role turning sour.

The Commerce Court experience was, on the whole, an unpleasant one for Julian. At the very outset the court itself was caught up in back-biting Bull Moose politics, which called for a skeptical attitude toward all courts, particularly one established under Taft. When the Commerce Court began making decisions favorable to the railroads as against the shippers, with Julian usually dissenting, it became the whipping boy of hostile Bull Moose Progressives, who charged that it was a minion of the railroads. Julian's dissents inadvertently gave credence to the charge.

Then, in February, 1912, the court received a shattering blow. *Collier's* magazine, whose editors were Norman Hapgood and Mark Sullivan, devoted its main article on February 24 to an exposé of maladministration in Federal courts in general, but with much of the article aimed specifically at the Commerce Court. The article was cruel:

We have a court, established within the last two years, the members of which have been appointed by the President who has been most urgent in his demands for judicial reform, which has exhibited a policy of obstruction more barefaced than that of any other court in the country.

It is comparable only to the Supreme Court of California when that body was literally owned by the Southern Pacific Railroad.

Since it was *Collier's* that had broken the Ballinger land scandal during the Taft administration, that article had a tremendous impact. Immediately after its appearance, Congress moved to abolish the U.S. Commerce Court.

That July, Julian, Jessie and their daughter Ruth were at The Antlers in Colorado Springs, presumably resting. But the news from Washington was not conducive to rest. To Felix Warburg, who had written asking Julian to attend a meeting on the Y.M.H.A. in New York in the fall, Julian wrote that he could not give a positive response "until after Congress has decided what to do with our court."

A bill for the abolition of the court was, in fact, passed by both Houses. This was the first major blow of the Bull Moose insurgents against Taft, a prelude to the Bull Moose split in the Republican party. Taft vetoed this bill, and also a similar measure a week later. But the handwriting was on the wall.

Then a scandal broke. It involved Judge Archbald of the Commerce Court. "There is a suspicion that a judge of the Commerce Court was too commercial," quipped the *Philadelphia Record* in May, 1912, after numerous illicit financial dealings engaged in by Archbald had been brought to light by George W. Norris, then a young Congressman. There was no doubt about Archbald's guilt. Senator Norris later filled a whole chapter in his memoirs with the judge's incredible cupidities. In July, Archbald was impeached by the House of Representatives; the following January, he was convicted.

That was the last straw. Action to abolish the Court—with a proposal also to "abolish" its judges—became the first order of business for the Democratic-controlled Congress after Wilson became President in March, 1913.

That summer, in the leisurely, comfortable style typical of genteel people of that pre-World War I era, Julian was vacationing in the Adirondacks. There, with Jessie and Ruth, he shared a spacious lodge at Blue Mountain Lake, New York, with his sister Fannie, her husband Frederick Mack, and their two daughters, of whom one later married Max Lowenthal and the other, James Gutmann, a professor of philosophy at Columbia University.

From time to time the Macks received visits from other congenial favorites, including Stephen and Louise Wise and Felix Frankfurter, who would bring with him a vivacious, brilliant young girl, Marion Denman, daughter of a Christian minister and Ruth Mack's pre-college tutor. Marion later became Frankfurter's wife, a romance encouraged by Julian. Aaron Aaronsohn also came.

Outwardly it was a typically pleasant Mackian summer—lively conversation, good food, hilarious outings including mountain climbing in which, despite his paunchiness, Julian insisted on taking part, with many rest periods on the way. On one climbing expedition, Ruth got off a comment to her father that was destined for familial lore: "You say *I* am tired, but it's *you* who are tired!" He did, however, get to the top of Blue Mountain, as he made a point of reporting in a subsequent letter to Aaron Aaronsohn: "I have been ashamed to write to you until I could say that Blue Mountain has been conquered."

But another letter from Julian to Aaron, in September, 1913, was less pleasant. It betrayed the fact that the whole period had been for him a time of anxiety because of the Commerce Court situation.

> My court will surely be abolished on Jan. 1st. The House has voted, however, to end our judgeships as well: the whole matter will be in the Senate within a week or 10 days. Whether they will concur, & if they do, whether the Pres. will veto it—we do not know. If it passes, I am legislated out of office. In that case there are 2 possibilities. The vacancy in Chicago

caused by [Federal Judge Peter G.] Grosscup's resignation has not been filled. I may be appointed to it; it is the same position, U.S. Circuit Judge. But that is not at all sure. If not, then I begin again to practice law.

The Senate did come to Julian's rescue, but not to that of the Court. It refused to abolish the judgeships of Julian Mack and Judge Knapp. Some Senators whimsically toyed with the preposterous idea of letting the judges remain but without appropriations for their salaries. But this proposal, too, was rejected by the Senate.

In the end, the Senate amended the measure to provide that the appellate-rank judges on the Commerce Court should continue as "additional Circuit Court judges for assignment to crowded dockets." The House concurred and so, in the words of Mark Sullivan, the brief, hectic, and unhappy existence of the Commerce Court came to an end on December 31, 1913.

No one was more relieved than Julian. In view of his capacity for dissembling, close friends never knew how unhappy he had been all along. To Aaron Aaronsohn, however, he confided that his three years on the Commerce Court had been, for the most part, "wretchedly miserable." As 1914 opened, he felt like a freed man—free in particular to engage wholeheartedly in perhaps the most important phase of his career, the phase of Zionism.

THE ZIONIST

19. Second Life

Julian was then approaching fifty. Certainly he would have had no cause to feel guilty if, in view of his record, he had chosen to settle henceforth for the relatively calm and sedentary role of "just" a Federal judge, the more so since he was a particularly conspicuous Federal judge, of the Circuit Court of Appeals, unattached to any district—"ambulatory," in Frankfurter's description, beholden for his assignments only to the Chief Justice of the United States. That he did not choose to be less active made some of his colleagues, including Learned Hand, rather nervous and at times vaguely unhappy about him.

"That damn Zionism of his!" Learned Hand once barked, affectionately disgusted because Julian had become so involved in that movement. It was not that Hand objected to Zionism; he felt that Julian ought to concentrate, as he himself did, on "the law."

But no such comfortable groove could contain Julian. He did not shirk his judicial duties. Still ahead was remarkably active service as a member of the Federal judiciary in a regular sense, as opposed to the specialized Commerce Court field—almost thirty years of Federal service, as it turned out. That service was to make him outstanding among all the judges in American history for the length and scope of his work. Nor did his standing depend, as in the case of some judges, merely on participation in one or two especially sensational cases, as with Kenesaw Mountain Landis, for example, who then became renowned almost solely for the fine he had imposed on the Standard Oil Company.

Julian was to have his share of publicized cases: the trials of Marcus Garvey and Attorney General Harry M. Daugherty; a lawsuit involving Lillian Gish; an early case involving the legality of abortions; the bankruptcy of the New York subway; the reorganization of the Fox Theatres; the Public Utilities Holding Company Act of the Franklin D. Roosevelt administration; the bootleg case of "Big Bill" Dwyer; and more. But mainly it was his expert handling of the literally hundreds of routine cases that made him a jurist greatly honored by other judges and the legal profession as a whole. Withal, there was ahead for him what amounted to a second life—even more active participation in public life, particularly Jewish affairs.

Then, too, Julian continued to involve himself in other people's lives. Young men whom he met casually still found him an active benefactor. One example was the lawyer Robert Szold. Born in Kewanee, Illinois, a distant cousin of Henrietta Szold, he was a close friend of Julian's brothers William and Robert. Szold visited them in Chicago, and on his graduation from the Harvard Law School returned to work in the legal department of the International Harvester Company. Julian took a great and lasting liking to young Szold who, with William Mack, did volunteer work at Hull House after hours.

Early in 1913, while the Taft administration was still in office, Julian learned that Secretary of War Henry L. Stimson was to appoint a lawyer to be stationed in Puerto Rico as assistant attorney general. Through Frankfurter, then Stimson's main legal assistant, Julian obtained the post for Szold. Later, during World War I, Szold was named Assistant to the U.S. Solicitor General. Thus was nourished an outstanding legal career, one that included much active association in Zionism with Brandeis and also with Julian Mack.

Then there was a young Jewish immigrant from Austryn, Russia, who in 1913 was a graduate student in philosophy at Harvard—and in financial trouble. From George Foote Moore, Harvard's professor of Semitic Literature, Julian, at a Harvard reunion, learned that this student was something of a genius—his paper on Hasdai Crescas was a "masterpiece," Moore said. Yet if he was to continue at Harvard to obtain his Ph.D. the young man needed at least $300—a big sum at the time.

"I will get it for him," said Julian. He did so by describing the student to Felix M. Warburg, who sent along his check. Thus was assured the career of Professor Harry Austryn Wolfson, later the noted Nathan Littauer Professor of Jewish Literature and Philosophy at Harvard, author of distinguished works not only on Crescas, but also on Philo, Spinoza, and others.

In the 1920's, Harry Sheffer, Harvard's mathematical genius—
"the greatest American mathematician," according to Alfred North
Whitehead—faced the loss of his instructorship. Ostensibly the
reason was that his stipend "could not be budgeted." But in
Frankfurter's version of the matter, it was because President A.
Lawrence Lowell of Harvard had been offended by Sheffer's "Jewish
appearance" and other personal matters that had nothing to do with
Sheffer's extraordinary capacity as a mathematician-philosopher.
Julian raised contributions—from the Schiffs, Warburgs, and
others—that saved Sheffer's job.

At the City College of New York, Morris Raphael Cohen, a friend
of Frankfurter's, hoped to concentrate on his great treatise, "Reason
and Nature," but he was earning barely enough to support himself
and his family, and at times not even enough for that. Mack, as
Cohen relates in his autobiography, *A Dreamer's Journey,* raised the
funds that "helped me over a period of vast discouragement and
financial difficulty by subsidizing a sabbatical year."

Perhaps Julian's most significant gesture in this field came soon
after World War I. The then newly-launched New School for Social
Research in New York wanted to add Horace M. Kallen to its
faculty but the money was lacking. Once again, Julian passed the
hat, creating in effect a chair for Kallen, who became, as he was to
remain for half a century, one of the most prestigious faculty
members of the New School. And in the 1930's, when the
"University in Exile" movement was started to bring to the United
States scholars who were refugees from Hitler's Germany, Julian
again was a key "spark."

Together with the Flexners, Julian was also a factor in the
creation of the Institute of Advanced Study at Princeton, which was
formed mainly around Albert Einstein.

All these concerns involved countless meetings, letters and
telephone calls. No wonder he once exclaimed to his law clerk, "I'm
overwhelmed! I'm overwhelmed!" No wonder, too, his desk was
always a "mess." His secretaries and friends tried to get him to be
more orderly and to slow down, but they never succeeded.

His activities in helping students were finally "institutionalized" sometime around 1916, after Julius Rosenwald had had a talk with him about his fiftieth birthday. Felix Frankfurter gave his version of that conversation:

> . . . Julius Rosenwald came to him and said, "Julian, I want to give you a present, something for you personally. . . . The sky's the limit, but I want it to be something for you personally . . . you as a human being, not some cause, but you."
>
> Judge Mack said, "When you said, 'The sky's the limit,' do you mean that?"
>
> "Yes, anything."
>
> I think if he would have said, "I wish you'd buy me J. P. Morgan's *Corsair*," Rosenwald would have said, "All right. I'll see whether J. P. Morgan will sell it. I'll buy it."
>
> At that time I don't know what Mr. Rosenwald was worth—two hundred million, three hundred million, it's all the same to me—vast amounts. And so when Judge Mack questioned him, "Do you really mean this—the sky's the limit?" and Mr. Rosenwald said that he did, what do you suppose Judge Mack said? "Will you put up two hundred and fifty thousand dollars to establish a fund to be distributed by me, and anybody else I associate with me, to worthy or highly talented boys and girls who have shown special talent in some direction, but haven't the means of pursuing it?"
>
> Mr. Rosenwald said, "That isn't what I mean. I want something personal for you!" . . . Well . . . Mr. Rosenwald put up two hundred and fifty thousand dollars.
>
> It may have been more, but I know it was that much, and that gave Judge Mack the kind of immediacy of pleasure, of inner satisfaction, of glow, of something to be happy over which for most people, or ninety-eight percent of mankind, only derives from a good meal, or a mink coat, or a fin-tailed car, a

compact hi-fi, etc. I think that central to all his activities as a human being. . . .

This, substantially, was how the Julian W. Mack Students' Fund was formed. Rosenwald was not the sole contributor. Led by Lessing Rosenthal, the donors also included Dr. Otto Schmidt and some fifty other friends of Julian's, among them a number of non-Jews in Chicago and New York. The total amount raised was less than $250,000, but it was enough for loans made over the years to several hundred young men and women.

The fund had a board of directors, including Bernard Flexner. It also had a "staff," which consisted mostly of Ethel Kawin, a Hull House worker, who later became prominent in social welfare activities.

But for the most part the fund was run by Julian himself. He carefully studied, usually between court hearings, the "summaries" on each candidate. He himself interviewed prospective beneficiaries and also engaged in much ·correspondence with them on their progress, helping them get jobs after they graduated. Those who got into trouble, as some did, he helped to extricate. For those who became ill, he found doctors.

Many of the fund's beneficiaries were to give a good accounting of themselves, thanks to Julian's help. One such young man was Marvin Lowenthal, who became a noted author; his books included *The Jews of Germany*, a splendid translation of Herzl's diaries, and a sensitive biography of Henrietta Szold, which was dedicated to Julian.

Jessie and Julian's friends constantly urged him not to become "so involved." His concern for his "young folk" inevitably took its toll. The phone calls, the letter-writing, the worry, the interviewing—all this alone would have taxed not one, but several persons. He drove himself continuously, displaying stamina that amazed his friends. Yet, had his personal comfort been a major consideration with him, he should have slowed down then, for he had begun to suffer from eye trouble, a skin irritation, and a slight limp.

Yet, instead of slowing down, Julian Mack continued to function as a kind of one-man social agency, all this aside from his organizational activity and his judicial career. "He was the most golden-hearted man I knew," Frankfurter recalled. "He was almost wholly selfless," commented Stephen Wise, And Jacob Billikopf, the Philadelphia social worker, thought that Julian, through his various activities, probably touched the lives of more individuals, personally and directly, than anyone else in his generation.

"Dear Judge, do you never sleep?" Jacob Schiff once asked Julian, marveling, but also worrying, over the numerous activities in which he was constantly engaged. No wonder that during this period Julian began to suffer from "middle-age" physical complaints and that every once in a while he felt over-tired. This puzzled him, but his fatigue was no surprise to his friends or his doctors. As his nephew by marriage, Max Lowenthal, once said, "He did 48 hours to the day." His clerks literally had to hop to keep up with him, or even to keep track of his engagements. Roger Demuth on one occasion resorted to extraordinary means to get a conference with him. "I sent him a telegram—from the next office," Demuth recalled.

In the summer of 1914, while he was vacationing in Maine, Julian was laid low by an especially deep carbuncle on his neck. Rushed to Mount Sinai Hospital in New York, he was subjected to an operation that left a large scar on the back of his neck. In the hospital it was discovered that he was suffering from diabetes—the illness that had striken both his mother and his grandmother Tandler in San Francisco, and which, in 1915, was to cause the death of his brother Henry.

Because of his diabetes, there was fear that the operation might prove fatal. He went through a long convalescence, finally going to Florida, under orders not to do anything at all for a while. This in itself was an ordeal for him.

He also had to accept permanently a rigidly limited diet, "'murder' for him," a friend commented. But he emerged just as active, mentally and physically, as ever, the same blithe, seemingly casual, usually well-tempered person who, in the 1890's, with Lessing Rosenthal and Sigmund Zeisler, had made the rounds of Schlogl's and other top eating places in Chicago. If anything, he was even more so in New York. To be sure, he was no Otto Kahn or Diamond Jim Brady. But he was nonetheless almost as recognizable as those two in New York City or Chicago—still something of the "character" that he had been when he and Jessie had set up their first home on Drexel Boulevard.

As more than one of his friends recalled, he could, and not infrequently did, bellow or belch in public. He could conspicuously munch an apple while walking up Fifth Avenue. Sometimes he would show up at formal affairs such as Harvard reunions in baggy trousers or in a dinner jacket that, to Jessie's dismay, somehow always seemed all awry. Often he went home from a day in court carrying not only legal tomes but also a bag filled with pungently aromatic cheeses he had acquired on the way at a fancy grocer's. It was said of him that one day, going home on a crowded subway train, he found every seat taken. But after standing for a while, he obtained a seat: the passengers seated near where he was standing got up to escape the fumes of the cheese he was carrying in his bag.

He was notoriously given to sprinting breathlessly through railroad stations to catch a train—usually on the split second—leaving his companions in a state of near-collapse. Even in court, though celebrated for his judicial bearing, he could stage something of a show. A lie told by a lawyer or a witness would enrage him.

Nevertheless, he managed to convey a dignity that caused onlookers to be more attracted than shocked, more admiring than startled. No doubt he had a special kind of charisma. He was also blessed with an inborn optimism. It was this quality that, after his first year of freedom from the Commerce Court, caused him to welcome the year 1914. As to so many others in Europe, as well as in the United States, the world at the start of 1914 seemed to him especially good and stable, a comfortable time, relatively—even for Jews.

20. The Eastern Man

He celebrated New Year's Eve, 1914, with special enthusiasm. As a judge, he had received precisely the assignment he had wanted from the very beginning of his Federal service—to function as a "regular Federal judge." He continued to "sit" in Chicago much of the time. But from about 1914 on, his main base of operation increasingly became New York.

New York, among other things, meant family associations which pleased him. True, his two youngest brothers, William and Robert, were in Chicago. But they were so much younger as to be almost of another generation. In New York he had his brother Lawrence, who was closer to his age, and also his sister Fannie and her husband, with whom he had a fine brotherly relationship.

Being in New York also meant living closer to his daughter Ruth, who was then at Radcliffe. He doted on Ruth, excessively so, some of his friends felt. He took special pride in her marked intellectual bent and encouraged her independent, pioneering "feminist" streak. He "valued her opinion on all subjects," one friend noted, "and more so than he did his wife's." He was always loyal to Jessie. But Ruth, from her teens on, gave him what Jessie did not—sparkling intellectual companionship. Her plans for a career in medicine delighted him. He was also glad to be near Harvard University, retaining in full measure the loyal "old grad" spirit—he eventually became an Overseer at Harvard—and enjoyed revisiting the campus, a regular participant in class reunions.

He still retained most of his Chicago friends. But in subtle ways he grew away from some of them. For example, there was Julius Rosenwald. Julian was no longer Rosenwald's adviser on philanthropy, nor did the two men visit each other so frequently as before. "I haven't seen J.R. this summer," Julian had mentioned to Aaron Aaronsohn in September, 1913—a new note, considering how nearly inseparable he and Rosenwald had been for years. Later, the change in the relationship between them would be even more apparent when they found that they had sharply divergent attitudes toward Zionism.

There were other changes, too, affecting Julian's status in Chicago. The Jewish charities organization in Chicago, with which he had been so closely identified since the 1890's, had become institutionalized along the lines of the "federation" principle that he had championed. As a result, neither he nor any other individual remained a dominant figure.

Indeed, by 1914 his crucial role in the Chicago charities setup took on the aspect of "history," like something to be recalled along with the Chicago Fire. This was the case also with the Juvenile Court, the Juvenile Protective Association and the Immigrants' Protective League, which were now "running themselves," with the help of the Abbotts, Sophonisba P. Breckinridge, and other social workers whom Julian had coached.

In 1916 a sad incident occurred which, in a tangential way, pointed up how loose his Chicago ties had become. Theodore Sachs, the Russian Jewish immigrant whose career in combating tuberculosis Julian had helped to start, had come into conflict with the execrable Mayor William Hale Thompson—"Big Bill the Builder." On being elected mayor to succeed Harrison, Thompson set out cynically to politicize the city's Municipal Tuberculosis Sanitarium, the institution that had symbolized Dr. Sachs' life work.

At first Dr. Sachs fought back. "Dr. Sachs had the quaint idea," Lloyd Wendt and Herman Kogan commented in *Big Bill of Chicago*, "that the sanitarium should not become a dumping ground for Thompson payrollers."

Social welfare leaders wrote strong letters of protest to the mayor; so did Julian. But Thompson persisted, using methods reminiscent of those that Julian had once criticized in his high school oration, "Municipal Reform." The situation became so gross that Dr. Sachs resigned from the board of the sanitarium. One day in April, 1916, he was found dead, a suicide. He left the following note:

Unscrupulous politicians should be thwarted. The institution

should remain . . . unsoiled by graft and politics. . . . In
the course of time, every man and woman will know how Dr.
Sachs loved Chicago. . . .

Julian immediately left for Chicago. As Dr. Sachs' oldest friend,
he made the main remarks at the funeral.

Every part of the service was superbly done [William C.
Graves reported to Rosenwald, whom he served as "charities
secretary," replacing Julian] but to me, the "heart" utterances
came from Judge Mack. . . . When Judge Mack appeared
first—he was the Master of Ceremonies, introducing the
others—he looked sad. But when he approached the railing to
speak, the corners of his mouth dropped, his face was drawn,
and he was the picture of distress, almost of anguish. Often
during his remarks there was a sob in his voice, as if he was
almost overcome by his emotion. In speaking of the "attacks"
upon Dr. Sachs which led up to his death, Judge Mack raised
his voice and hurled several adjectives, like shots from a gun,
straight at the City Hall crowd; and the one adjective on which
he put most stress was "damnable!" . . .

There was additional poignancy, from a personal standpoint, in
the attitude of the other mourners toward Julian. It was plain that
many of those who attended that funeral looked upon him as a mere
"visitor" to Chicago, no longer as "one of them." Some Chicago
press notices even referred to him as "Judge Mack of Washington";
others, as "Judge Mack of New York." No wonder old Chicago
acquaintances seemed to greet him as though he were an outsider.

Did they sense that the tragic passing of Dr. Sachs in some
curious way symbolized the end of Julian's career in Chicago? If so,
they were perhaps not wrong. Frankfurter once quipped, "Like
Homer, a number of cities claimed Judge Mack," New York in
particular. By then, indeed, Julian was becoming wholly a New
Yorker, certainly a continental American.

In New York Julian's life-style underwent an interesting change.
Or, more accurately put, his intellectual bent which, at least since

his Harvard days, had made him the natural leader of the "Book and Play Club" set in Chicago, came into fuller expression.

Probably he himself was surprised to find that he, a Federal judge, would often be in the company of rather *avant garde* individualists, including even some Greenwich Village personalities. "No one," as Stephen S. Wise once said, "had a wider range of acquaintance among, and of fellowship with, the intelligentsia." Moreover, the *avant garde* liked him—though some were a bit patronizing of him. Julian liked them, too, without, to be sure, always agreeing with their "advanced" views.

One thing was certain: he was tolerant of every view expressed on any subject, even sex, though, as his granddaughter later commented, he was in his own conduct "very puritanical on sex." Ruth presented him with a real test in that area with some case studies she prepared in her work with Sigmund Freud. "My God!" he once exclaimed. "This is pornography!" But he disciplined himself to accept Ruth's work and staunchly defended her—and also Freud—against allegations of salacious activity, precisely as he defended "leftish" liberals against allegations of "subversion."

Wise's allusion to Julian's association with "the intelligentsia" referred particularly to the highly articulate intellectuals who in 1914 had established *The New Republic*, "A Journal of Opinion Which Seeks to Meet the Challenge of a New Time." This group was quite influential in the nation during that period. According to the Princeton historian, Eric F. Goldman, a widely-held notion at the time was that if one wished some advance light on President Wilson's policies, "one subscribed to *The New Republic*."

The intellectuals exerted influence also on Julian—and he, in turn, on them. In him they had, literally as well as symbolically, "a friend in court." His personal prestige, his presence in their circle was in itself an encouragement, giving a sense of security to the anti-Establishment "Young Turks" of that era—the kind of shielding function Julian had also served with the Hull House people in Chicago. Herbert Croly, author of *The Promise of American Life*, had started it all, but Frankfurter, being, as he himself had once said, "a kind of a godfather" to *The New Republic*, was also important in the group. Through him, Julian became a marginal if not a full-fledged member of that effervescent set.

In 1919, members of this group were to help spark the establishment of the New School for Social Research in New York, a high-level institution of learning dedicated to academic freedom. Julian cooperated in this project also, helping with the planning and active in raising the needed funds.

In addition, as a principal backer of *The Survey* and *Survey Graphic* magazines, he was involved in collaboration with other intellectuals of various shades: Paul Kellogg, Helen Hall, Freda Kirchwey, John Palmer Gavit, Beulah Amidon, and other social idealists who, in Frankfurter's phrase, occupied "the crow's nest of American society." Their magazines were the "bibles" of the social workers. Naturally, many of their writers were considered "far out" and "radical." They, too, found in Julian a sympathetic protector. But he also played a practical role. When Freda Kirchwey, later editor of *The Nation*, once was asked how the *Survey Graphic* intended to finance its beginnings, she replied: "Judge Mack will raise the money." To a large extent, he did.

He himself perhaps did not realize how "liberal" he was in his own thinking. For he was always sensitive to a certain prudence that he felt his judicial office required. "As you know," he once told Stephen S. Wise, "I have felt the tying-down effect of my judicial office keenly, particularly during the war, but also at other times." This was to be especially true during the Sacco-Vanzetti case of the 1920's.

In *Opinion,* Wise in 1932 said of Julian Mack's liberalism:

> It is as real as everything about this genuine being. . . . There are more vocal liberals, but there lives no more effective and truer liberal than he—that is, if the liberal be a man who is open-minded, believes in the reality of human advance, and welcomes every adventure of the human spirit in the direction of truer equality and larger human liberties. . . .

It was not strange, therefore, that Mack became comfortably acquainted with Croly, the Willard Straights, Charles A. Beard, Walter Weyl, William C. Bullitt, John Reed, Walter Lippmann,

Randolph Bourne, Robert Little, Alvin Johnson, and other major literary and academic figures of the era. They were among the main shakers and movers of the time—and Julian, to an extent, among them. What some of his colleagues on the Federal bench would have said of him in this regard, had they known how involved he was, probably would have been unprintable.

He represented, indeed, a type. That is, he was an example of the decent, literate, humanistic, Establishment-connected American who saw no need to defend the Establishment in all its aspects, but rather saw its faults along with its virtues. He was also a good representative of another "type": the American Jewish liberal whose humanist ideology was a fusion of both Americanism and Judaism. Or, to put it another way, he was the product, in his thinking on social problems, of both American and Jewish history, between which, as Justice Brandeis was fond of emphasizing, there was a natural affinity, making Judaism and American democracy synonymous in vital aspects.

Among Julian's new liberal, even radical, associates two men were particularly close to him. One was Harold J. Laski, the British socialist, who was then writing reviews for *The New Republic* while he taught at Harvard College. At the time—before Hitler changed his views in that regard—Laski was aggressively indifferent to Jewish matters. Yet Laski developed the warmest affection for Julian Mack. Particularly in 1919 he was to have special cause to know Julian's generous nature. For in that year came a movement to get Laski dismissed from Harvard for his radicalism, and Julian was of crucial help in scotching that effort. But even without this assistance Laski would have liked Julian because he found his mind always open to new ideas.

Julian's other special friend among *The New Republic* intellectuals was Francis Hackett, the brilliant essayist and biographer. They had known each other casually in Chicago through a mutual interest in Hull House, when Hackett, as editor of the *Chicago Post's* notable literary supplement, had been a major factor in nourishing the then vigorous "Chicago school of literature." When he went to New York to become the first literary editor of *The New Republic*, Hackett maintained a fairly close friendship with Julian.

He vigorously disagreed with Julian on various basic matters. For instance, he tended to scoff at fears about anti-Semitism, viewing them as "over-sensitivity" on the part of Jews or even as something that the Jews themselves provoked. Later, he came to differ sharply with Julian on the desirability of the Jews having a homeland of their own. He vigorously opposed the Zionist idea—a fact which, in view of his own intense Irish nationalism, struck some as odd. But the two men liked each other nonetheless.

Hackett went out of his way to emphasize this in his memoirs, *I Chose Denmark,* where he fondly described an occasion when Julian was host at dinner to Hackett, Laski, and Aaron Aaronsohn, who all happened to be in the Boston area at the same time.

> . . . It was during the period when Ireland was fighting for self-government, and at that time I missed no chance of giving a talk on Ireland. That evening I spoke to the Woman's Club, where I was honored by the presence of Judge Julian Mack, and after the lecture he asked myself and a little black fighting cock called Harold Laski and a large, blond, sleepy, benevolent man called Aaron Aaronsohn, to have supper at the Parker House. I was to take the train to New York when it was over.

> The judge studied the menu with that intensity of concentration with which a jeweler would have studied a diamond. He sought for the flawless. Meanwhile, like a little angry cock, Harold Laski walked round and round Aaron Aaronsohn, who watched him through his light eyelashes with benevolent but apprehensive eyes.

> They were both greatly gifted men, but I felt that unless something was done one or the other would be left dead on the field. Aaronsohn had been up against the Turks in Palestine. He was now up against Laski in Boston. They both had power, but the law of powerful cocks is that only one shall survive in the barnyard. Laski was my black Minorca. I was backing him, but I had yet to learn what the occasion of his ire was. I was

greatly taken with this portly, slow-spoken patriot from Palestine.

Like so many cockfights, it never came off. It was not that the police arrived; the waiter arrived. He arrived with the caviar.

Judge Mack looked at it.

"That," he said in a voice that rose a little, "is Beluga caviar. I did not ask for Beluga caviar. I asked for Astrakhan caviar."

If the Parker House could have blushed, it blushed. The waiter crumbled into a little heap. So did I. It had dawned on me that up till that hour I had not known there could be such a difference. . . .

The Astrakhan caviar must have been in the vault. It came, it was miraculous. Even Laski, who lived on fish and chips by proletarian preference, moved gracefully back to the fish in that incipiency which is known as caviar. Judge Mack, the most hospitable I ever knew, beamed with pleasure. The cockfight was averted forever. . . .

Years later, Hackett wrote to Frankfurter:

. . . I loved Julian Mack's abundance as a host, of course, but along with his rosy benevolence that was apparent to everyone, there was the lovely Jewish warmth, the including-ness, the fraternal comprehension of one's own passionate interest, and then the integrity.

He hadn't any of the stridency of the self-made man. He hadn't been abused and humiliated. That amplitude in his voice and manner, that resonance in him when he greeted you and gave you his good hand, were from a secure world, and it was a helping hand. . . . He was a truly judicious spirit, I believe. He was worth having on one's side.

21. Clouds

Hackett's description of Julian was a perceptive profile of him as he was in 1914, before the outbreak of World War I: the optimist, interested in everyone and everything. The New Art, the New Literature, the New Dances, the New Psychology called Psychoanalysis, the New Politics—none of these held terrors for him. He looked at the world with enthusiasm and found it mostly good.

Much of the time he felt that even the outlook for European Jewry was growing brighter. In Russia there *seemed* to be a decrease in anti-Semitism, partly, perhaps, because the United States had finally denounced the treaty of 1832. There was a lull in the pogroms, and a marked decline in the immigration of Jews to the United States. Moreover, from what Aaron Aaronsohn told him, Julian gathered that the Jewish settlements in Palestine were making good progress. In that promise Julian was becoming more and more interested, intellectually at least.

His spirit of optimism was widely shared. It was expected that the East European Jews already in the United States would become acculturated so quickly to American life, and "melt" so well into the Zangwillian "pot," that they would no longer constitute a social or financial problem. Some even foresaw the early disappearance of the Jewish ghettos on New York's East Side and Chicago's West Side. Indeed, Rabbi Emil G. Hirsch, for one, speculated that were it not for the Zionists who, needlessly in his view, kept agitating that the Jews formed a distinct ethnic group, all American Jewry would be on the path toward an antiseptic brand of Americanized Reform Judaism, only a notch or so different from, say, Unitarianism. And that, Hirsch felt, would be good.

The truth, however, was that there were clouds on the horizon. In particular, there were isolated outbursts of the seemingly perennial "Jewish problem" to remind Julian, among other Jews, that the world was still less than perfect. For example, the scientist Jacques Loeb, whom Julian had known at the University of Chicago, was refused membership in New York's Century Club in

1914 because he had been born a Jew. This incident, though apparently minor, was a disturbing revelation, for it showed how, even in New York, many supposedly cultivated people still felt about the Jews.

Also, there was the Beilis "ritual murder" case in Russia. Even before Mendel Beilis—a Jew—had been placed on trial, the authorities had known, but concealed one fact: Andrei Yustshinski, the boy who allegedly had been killed by Beilis in 1911, had actually been murdered by a prostitute, apparently because he had learned that she was a leader of a group of professional thieves. Yet the Czar himself went along with the demand that a Jew—any Jew—should be punished for the crime.

As with the Mortara affair of the 1850's, and the Kishinev and Bialystok pogroms of the early 1900's, mass protest meetings were held also over the Beilis case. The American Jewish Committee coordinated the American protests with those of European groups and Julian was one of the organizers of these meetings. He viewed the Beilis accusation as another Dreyfus case. Once again, he said, "the whole Jewish people, indeed Judaism itself, was on trial."

Especially dismaying to him, as a proud member of the American judiciary, was the eruption in the United States, even before the end of the Beilis case, of a *cause célèbre* no less hideously overlaid with anti-Semitism. This was the case of Leo Frank in Atlanta.

The Frank case began in April, 1913. Like the Beilis case it started with the discovery of a child's body, that of a girl of fourteen, Mary Phagan. But unlike the affair in Russia, the trial in Atlanta did not end in freedom for the accused, but in his death by lynching. Leo Frank, a young intellectual, graduate of Cornell University and leader in the Atlanta lodge of B'nai B'rith, had moved to the South from Brooklyn, New York, to manage his uncle's pencil factory. His lynching, amidst cries of "Kill the Jew!" came after Governor John Slaton of Georgia had commuted Frank's death sentence for the alleged murder of the girl, because he had become convinced that Frank's guilt had not been proven beyond reasonable doubt, and that, at any rate, Frank had not received a fair trial.

The attacks on Jews in the California legislature in the days of Julian's grandparents, the barring of Joseph Seligman from the

Grand Union Hotel in Saratoga Springs, the discrimination in the employment of Jewish lawyers that had so greatly concerned Julian, the exclusion of Jews from certain clubs, even the attacks upon the immigrant peddlers in Chicago when Julian was with the Juvenile Court—all had been trivial as compared to the orgiastic anti-Semitism engendered by the Frank case.

One of the South's most notorious and effective Negro-hating, Catholic-hating and Jew-hating demagogues was then running amok in Georgia: Tom Watson, former Populist Congressman and later U.S. Senator, at one time a hero of the liberals. By raising "the Jewish issue" in his weekly, *The Jeffersonian,* Watson saw to it that Frank's trial became a travesty. All during the trial, inside and outside the courtroom, crowds spurred by Watson's journalism shouted threats. "Hang the Jew or we will hang you!" they screamed at the jurors.

The mood was such that the presiding judge was afraid to clear the courtroom of the unruly spectators. He did not dare allow Frank to be present in the courtroom when the jury announced its verdict, although the law required the defendant to appear. The judge accepted the jury's verdict of "guilty," though, as he later admitted, he was aware that it was not supported by the evidence.

Years later, Carey McWilliams, an especially perceptive non-Jewish student of "Know-Nothing" outbreaks in American history, studied the Leo Frank case and was struck by the similarity of the Frank trial to the Beilis case. In *A Mask for Privilege,* he wrote:

> . . . that a ritual murder trial, bedecked with fancy nativistic trimmings, could take place in the United States was a possibility that never occurred to the writers of indignant American editorials devoted to the Beilis case. . . .

> Prior to 1913, Tom Watson, the Georgia demagogue, had been violently anti-Catholic; but apparently he had never realized before the Frank case that Jews could be made the target of a vicious demagogic attack. . . .

> But no pogrom organizer in Czarist Russia ever leveled a more savage, ruthless, and unprincipled attack against Jews

than Watson did in this case. "Every student of sociology knows," he wrote, "that the black man's lust after the white woman is not much fiercer than the lust of the licentious Jew for the Gentile. . . ." Following the lynching, Watson continued to repeat the old charge of ritual murder against the Jews and denounced the worldwide campaign to save Mendel Beilis as the same type of "conspiracy" that had won freedom for Dreyfus.

Harold J. Laski, in *The American Democracy,* set down what, of course, was the truth. Even before the Leo Frank case, America had not been free from anti-Semitic incidents. But, he went on, "I think it is true to say that, broadly speaking, there was little organized anti-Semitism in America before 1914."

Of the change that came at this point, Laski wrote:

> American anti-Semitism after 1914 was both wider and more intense than ever before . . . its exponents had less compunction than ever before in shouting their intolerance from the housetops, were more able to secure funds for their activities, and were more successful in securing an audience for their propaganda. . . . The anti-Semitic campaign had a ferocity and a vulgarity about it which might well remind an observer of the methods by which Hitler let loose his atrocities in Europe.

Laski mainly had in mind the vile anti-Semitic campaigns conducted in the 1920's by Henry Ford in his newspaper, *The Dearborn Independent,* and in the 1930's by the "radio priest," Father Charles E. Coughlin. But he also had in mind the Leo Frank case of 1913–15.

Julian was deeply involved in efforts to secure a fair trial for Leo Frank. To a large extent his efforts were made *sub rosa,* for Tom Watson kept drumming on the theme that "organized Jewry" was bent on "subverting Georgia justice, regardless of Frank's guilt, because he was a Jew."

"Frank belongs to the Jewish aristocracy, and it was determined by rich Jews that no aristocrat of their race shall die for the death of a working girl," Watson raged in *The Jeffersonian*. He also kept up a constant barrage about "rich, depraved, Sodomite Jews" working in Frank's behalf.

So as not to give Watson added fuel for such propaganda, the American Jewish Committee as such refrained from taking official action. But individual members of the Committee worked indefatigably on the case. Louis Marshall, the president of the Committee, handled appeals to the Supreme Court on a voluntary basis. Albert D. Lasker, the Chicago advertising man, directed an intensive propaganda campaign in Frank's behalf. Julian worked closely with both Marshall and Lasker and through his influence Julius Rosenwald made a generous contribution to the funds needed for both the propaganda and the legal work.

Up to the last, Julian shared the general feeling that the Supreme Court would intervene. Later decisions by the Court, on the point of what constitutes a fair trial, would have assured such action. Justices Oliver Wendell Holmes, Jr. and Charles Evans Hughes (Brandeis was not yet on the Court) saw the obvious—that a gross miscarriage of justice had been committed in Georgia. But the majority of the Court did not agree. This came as a shock to Julian.

The Leo Frank tragedy, indeed, meant for Julian another link in his acceptance of Zionism. It forced him to reassess old assumptions about the status of Jews in general. But meanwhile, the most decisive link of all in his conversion to Zionism was forged in the war that broke out in Europe in the summer of 1914, a link strengthened by his friendship with Aaron Aaronsohn.

22. A Wartime "Scroll of Fire"

When hostilities had begun in Europe in August, 1914, Aaronsohn, after various visits to the United States, had been in Palestine for some time. Thanks to the financial support Julian had helped arrange for him, Aaronsohn had his experimental station at Athlit well launched. This was the station which now served as a "cover" for the "Nili" in its espionage operations to help the British forces in the Middle East.

"He could see his dreams come true," recalled his sister Rifka, who had lived with the Macks for a time while studying in the United States. "Fields previously barren near Athlit were covered by then with luscious fruit trees. His dry-farming methods proved successful. All the neighboring farmers, Jews as well as Arabs, could learn from the encouraging example." But the outbreak of the war cast a shadow over everything.

The principal economic resource of the modern Jewish settlers in Palestine at the time was their orange groves. But the war had halted all exports of oranges to Europe. Aaronsohn appealed to Julian for American assistance to the orange growers in Palestine, cabling that unless the current orange crop could be sold in the United States, Palestine's Jewish agriculture was faced with ruin.

Julian promptly persuaded Julius Rosenwald and Jacob H. Schiff, among others, to underwrite the import of Palestinian oranges. For several months, along with his other activities, Julian was, in effect, in the orange business, arranging for financing, import licenses, for the packaging, and even for the sale of the oranges. Palestine's orange crop was saved.

In addition, Julian helped arrange for loans to the settlers in Palestine for their future crops. On the basis of other appeals from Aaronsohn, he wrote to Rosenwald: "Unless the orange groves are cared for yearly by proper irrigation, they will go absolutely to ruin and the principal work of the colonists in the past 33 years will be utterly destroyed."

But it soon became apparent that the threat which the Jews in

Palestine were facing was not merely economic destruction. When Turkey entered the war on the side of Germany in October, 1914, most of the Jews living in Palestine were Russian or Polish nationals. They therefore immediately came under suspicion as sympathizers with the Allied powers against Turkey. That was the period, too, when the Turks committed horrible atrocities against the Armenians, and there was fear that a Turkish massacre of the Jews in Palestine would come next.

Though the dreaded massacre did not come to pass, terrible things did happen that tore at Julian's heart, yet inspired him with a new admiration for the idealism, the courage, and the hardihood of the Jewish pioneers in Palestine, pioneers like Ben-Gurion, Jabotinsky, Rutenberg—and, of course, Aaron Aaronsohn.

In the fall of 1916 Julian received from Aaronsohn some moving accounts of the situation in Palestine, particularly in a letter Julian called "Aaron's Scroll of Fire" letter. In strict confidence, and intended for Julian's eyes alone, Aaron spelled out in this letter the background of his "Nili" underground activities, taking up the story from the time of Turkey's entry into the war.

> What we had to bear since that time is undescribable [he wrote]. And every month, every day, every hour, brings some new and more dreadful blow on our frail Jewish enterprises in Palestine. I am still wondering how we managed to keep afloat. . . . For a while, and all too long a while, we thought there can be on Earth nothing worse than the Turks.

> But we were soon to learn, from sad experience, that there might be, for a short while, something worse than the Turks even: the Locusts! . . . The Country looked hopeless after the invasion of the locusts. Food was already scarce, supplies were running short rapidly. . . . famine was staring us in the face. . . .

> The country recovered remarkably quick and well. When one has been given to see how Palestinian products are strongly resisting destruction, one begins to realize where from the *most curious Palestinian product—the Jewish people*—has come its power of resistance, its indestructibility.

You cannot rely on the Turkish sense of moderation. The relentlessness of this class of "rulers" is as much above the human, limited descriptive powers as is the other above-mentioned plague: the Locusts. . . .

At any rate, we went out and worked hard to prepare a new crop, under the most adverse conditions. At the beginning everything was going wrong with the season, and up to February and March last, we had but very little hope of a fair crop. Add to that the pending menace of a second Locust-invasion. Meantime, people were literally starving. We were given to see this dreadful sight: old men, women, and children wandering about with looks of hunger and craze in their dying eyes, dropping dead for lack of food. . . .

I must say, right here, these scenes were less frequent among the Jews than amongst the natives. This for several reasons, the main one being the higher sense of foresight, organization, and solidarity in our Jewish communal life. That helped us through. I leave out of consideration, but do not forget, nor belittle the fact, that we had more money, especially thanks to the helpful hand tendered us by our foreign brethren, our American brethren chiefly. . . .

The natives, and more especially the rural populations, have been decimated. . . . What will become of the country and its ill-fated inhabitants is too horrible to think of, and I wish I knew how one can rid himself of these horrifying thoughts. . . .

And what of your Government, are you going to ask? We have none. We are ruled, ransacked, eaten up by a pack of heartless, predatory, self-conceited and, still worse, German-conceited rulers who do not care a hang of what is becoming of the country, of the people, of themselves even, "*Aprés nous le déluge.*" . . .

What made life and work not only possible but even attractive to us in Palestine, even under the Turkish traditional misrule, was the religious freedom, the autonomous communal life, the possibility of fostering the national culture, the use of our national Hebrew tongue; to feel, if not independent, at least at home in the old cradle of our Nation, to tighten again the old bonds between the Land and the People, to regenerate the people in regenerating the country, to win, if not always the esteem of all, at least the respect of all, and to get a high prestige.

That was what we were striving for, and thanks to our honest endeavors, we got it. And how brutally, and at the same time how methodically we have been robbed of it all, in no time! . . .

Indeed, Aaron suggested, because of the Turks and in view of the general war situation, there was basis for real fear that the dream of a Jewish Palestine would come to an end. For, aside from the physical and economic situation of Palestine's Jewish community, there were political dangers—behind-the-scenes agreements, or supposed agreements, by British and French agents with Arab chieftains that spelled future trouble for the Jews.

But Julian and others began to see even in this perilous situation a bright prospect—that the war might bring about the rise of a Jewish state in Palestine. If that happened, the new political situation in Palestine could mean the fulfillment of Herzl's vision.

And what of the Arabs? They were then in the same position as the Jews; both the Jews and the Arabs in Palestine were subjects of the Ottoman rulers. If the Arab natives then had an "enemy," it was not the Jews but their fellow Moslems, the Turks.

In his "Scroll of Fire" letter, Aaron Aaronsohn brought all this home to Julian. He cited one particular example of how the Turks treated the Arabs. During the wartime famine period, when Turkey forbade import of food, the Turkish authorities, in distributing what food there was, took good care of the Turks. But Arabs were deliberately allowed to starve. Aaron wrote:

In the region of Beyrouth and the Lebanon only, more than fifty thousand people were actually dead of starvation . . . the highways were lined by unburied bodies. . . . In going in my carriage from Beyrouth to Damascus, I quite went out of my mind, seeing on the roads hundreds and hundreds of aimlessly wandering, starving people and dozens of dead bodies bordering the main arteries.

This Turkish policy caused Aaron, at the risk of his own security as a Jew, to protest to the Turkish military authorities, urging them to help the Arab natives, including "hundreds of babes in the streets crying for food and dying off in the arms of their starving mothers."

Lt. Colonel Ali Fuad Bey, Chief of Staff of the Fourth Army, a gentleman, nay, a Turkish officer with a catching, superficially European varnish, got wild when I mentioned the distress of the people. "Now, look here, Aaronsohn," he went on. "You are a healthy, strong fellow; you are not going to be mollified [taken in] by the *'larmes de crocodile'* of a half a dozen hysterical, mendicating women."

At that time we had . . . fifty thousand dead of starvation. *Excusez du peu!* . . . Who is starving in fact? No Turks! mind you. Only Christian dogs, Jewish dogs, and unfaithful Arabs, *le bon debarras!* And to get rid of those "Undesirables," in such a natural way, by the will of Allah, without the shedding of blood, without giving any outside Nations any possibility to interfere! . . .

Aaronsohn was not the only Jewish settler in Palestine who tried to help the Arabs. Jewish policy generally, then as later, was to seek friendship with the Arabs. Jews in Palestine shared with the Arabs their skills for improving the yield of the land. They also shared with those Arabs who cared a common goal—that both groups, Arabs and Jews, should again be free in their own lands. Few then foresaw that Arab "nationalists," once they had been helped toward independence, would turn on the Jews for seeking the same goal—in a land to which the Jews had legal, historical, and spiritual connections as valid as those of the Arabs. Obviously, there was land enough for both the Arabs and the Jews.

As early as 1913, Aaron Aaronsohn saw the possibility of British control of the region. England, he sensed, might sponsor a future Jewish homeland in Palestine on the basis of steps that would also assure the creation of independent Arab states in the region. Aaron's prescience in this regard impressed all who met him—including Julian, and eventually, through Julian, Louis D. Brandeis.

In April, 1913, Aaronsohn had a significant meeting, arranged by Julian, with Brandeis. As of 1913, the "official" Zionist doctrine had been that if a Jewish homeland in Palestine came into being, it would be under a Turkish protectorate, perhaps by purchase, in accordance with the early ideas developed by Theodor Herzl. But Aaronsohn, with his usual eloquence, presented to Brandeis the view that Great Britain would be the more logical protector. Neither of the two men foresaw then that, in the end, Britain would prove untrustworthy.

Through Julian, as well as Felix Frankfurter, other doors were opened to Aaron for the propagation of his views on the future of Palestine. "I remember in Washington," William C. Bullitt recalled, "how the diplomats sat openmouthed, astonished by his knowledge and his insight, and were warmed by his picture of the Zion that was to be."

To be sure, Aaronsohn was not alone among those Jews and non-Jews who at that early stage of World War I saw the possibility, the desirability, both for Jews and for British interests, of the restoration of a Jewish Palestine under the protection of England. In England, Chaim Weizmann was already working through influential friends, notably the editor of the Manchester *Guardian*, C. P. Scott, to translate that possibility into fact.

There was also another British Jew, even more prestigious in top British circles than Weizmann, who, though not himself a Zionist, had the same vision. He was Herbert Samuel, later Viscount Samuel and first British High Commissioner for Palestine. Samuel, in some interesting aspects, was a British counterpart of both Julian Mack and Louis D. Brandeis—a wholly "emancipated," not very religious Jew, who nevertheless had a strong feeling of sympathy for his fellow Jews. Like the two Americans, he was a brilliant and highly successful lawyer, concerned at the same time with social welfare causes. Like Julian in America, Samuel in England was the leading exponent of a Juvenile Court movement patterned on the Chicago system.

Almost precisely at the time that Brandeis assumed leadership of the Zionist movement in America, Samuel, as a member of the British cabinet, had a most interesting talk with Sir Edward Grey, the British Foreign Secretary, about Palestine.

"I spoke to Sir Edward Grey today about the future of Palestine," he wrote in his record of that talk in November, 1914. "In the course of our talk I said that now that Turkey had thrown herself into the European War and that it was probable that her empire would be broken up, the question of the future control of Palestine was likely to arise. . . . Perhaps the opportunity might arise for the fulfillment of the ancient aspiration of the Jewish people and the restoration there of a Jewish State. . . .

"I said," his note, as published in his autobiography, *Grooves of Change,* continued, "that I myself had never been a Zionist, because the prospects of any practical outcome had seemed so remote. . . . But now the conditions are profoundly altered. If a Jewish State were established in Palestine it might become the centre of a new culture."

To this, Samuel added a practical comment:

"I thought that British influence ought to play a considerable part in the formation of such a state, because the geographical situation of Palestine, and especially its proximity to Egypt, would render its goodwill to England a matter of importance to the British Empire."

In the event, after talking also with David Lloyd George, who was soon to become Prime Minister, and whom he found "very keen to see a Jewish state," Samuel was invited to submit a memorandum on the subject to the Asquith cabinet; he did so on January 28, 1915.

Thus, not just Aaron Aaronsohn was discussing British sponsorship of the Zionist goal. Englishmen of the highest status were also beginning to press the concept—to be sure, also from military, political and imperial considerations not necessarily relevant to "the Jewish Problem." But Aaronsohn was certainly among those who played an important role in stirring up the issue—a role much more important than is recorded in many accounts of the Balfour Declaration and the subsequent establishment of the Jewish State.

At the outbreak of war in 1914, however, the important thing was to help prevent the pioneer Jewish settlements in Palestine from becoming casualties of the fighting. Saving the *Yishuv* (Palestine's Jewish communities and settlements) became a paramount consideration, not only for Zionists, but also for non-Zionists, and even some anti-Zionists as well.

Step by step, Julian became more and more involved in helping further Zionist goals. Even before the outbreak of the war he had played a role in wresting control of Haifa's "Technikum" from the German Jews who then dominated it and who had insisted that no other language but German should be spoken at the institution. Because Hebrew was favored by most of the Jewish settlers in Palestine as the official language of the Jewish homeland, Aaronsohn urged that the institution be brought under American sponsorship, thus thwarting the "Germans." Jacob Schiff, Julian, and others did this by assuming financial control over the school.

The "language war," as this conflict came to be known, turned out to be a milestone—not a big one, to be sure, but a milestone nonetheless—on the road to Jewish statehood. The victory of the Hebrew language over German at the "Technikum" helped turn the Jews of Palestine away from Germany and her Turkish allies and toward England. More important, the "language war" helped establish Hebrew as the common language of the future State of Israel.

Julian was occupied also with an even graver Jewish problem arising from the war. It was more serious than the Palestine situation, for though it eventually became linked to Palestine, it covered a vaster area: the plight of the Jews in Eastern Europe. Fighting and destruction were widespread on the Eastern front and as a result East European Jewry in World War I met with a disaster that would be exceeded in modern times only by World War II a generation later. In *Zionism and World Politics,* a brilliant book that Julian had encouraged him to write, Horace M. Kallen described the disaster.

> The Jews had become the supreme victims of the war. No people on the battlelines, except possibly the Armenians,

suffered as the Jews had suffered. The war on the Eastern front was being fought within the Jewish pale of settlement. The treachery and incompetency of the Russian bureaucracy; the malice, intrigue, and disloyalty of the Poles; the brutality of the Germans were alike cloaked by means of charges and assaults against the Jews. More than 10 per cent of the entire Jewish population of Europe was on the battlefield and more than 90 per cent of these were engaged in the armies of the Allies. But in Eastern Europe it was their ironic fate that the battlefield should be nothing else than the Pale and that Jewish soldiers should battle for the Allies amid the familiar scenes of their own homes, should be required to burn and raze their own communities, should be compelled to stand by while fathers, sons or brothers were executed on trumped-up charges and wives and sisters and mothers were raped and maimed and killed. . . .

The East European Jews indeed were in desperate need of help, which could come only from the American Jewish community. In the fall of 1914 there was formed the American Jewish Relief Committee, forerunner of the larger American Joint Relief Distribution Committee. Julian was a key factor. He threw himself energetically into this work. From Denver, in January, 1915, he wrote to Ruth, who was then at Radcliffe:

> I was called on to talk about philanthropy at the annual meeting of the Denver hospital yesterday, but I can't talk to a Jewish audience today and stick to that theme. The only subject I can really talk about is the Jewish war relief situation, which I did.

He was not, of course, alone. The Schiffs, the Warburgs, the Marshalls, the Lehmans, the Rosenwalds, indeed, practically all influential American Jews rose magnificently to the cause. But Julian, as in the days of the Russian immigrants, was in the vanguard.

23. The "American Herzl"

Soon he was also talking quite as much about a subject which, though related to philanthropy, was different from ordinary charity. In March, 1915, he received from Louis D. Brandeis a message that tipped the scales in his decision to identify himself at last officially with the Zionist cause.

Julian was then holding court in Chicago. Frankfurter, who, since his appointment to the Harvard law faculty, had enjoyed a close association with Brandeis, personally brought to Mack a note from Brandeis, dated Boston, March 16, 1915:

> Frankfurter goes to you as Envoy Extraordinary from me on an important mission, and I bespeak a favorable reception.

The tongue-in-cheek tone of this note was a Disraelian touch of which Brandeis was peculiarly capable. But it was a prelude to the wholly serious nature of Frankfurter's request to Julian.

The year before—in August, 1914—Brandeis had assumed the leadership of the Zionist movement in the United States. Indeed, he was, or seemed to be, the leader—*pro tempore* at least—of organized Zionism the world over, an unexpected organizational situation brought about by the war.

Until the war, the headquarters of the World Zionist Organization had been in Berlin. The Zionist Executive there represented Zionist groups, or federations of groups, in various parts of the world. The largest Zionist organizations were in Russia, Germany, and Austria. In England there was also a Zionist organization, but it was a smaller one—the English Zionist Federation, led by a professor of chemistry at the University of Manchester, Dr. Chaim Weizmann.

In the United States, the Zionist movement on the eve of World War I was also relatively small. It consisted of various separate groups allied in a Federation of American Zionists, then led by the chairman of its executive committee, Louis Lipsky. A brilliant

172

journalist, Lipsky was responsible in Zionist affairs to an executive committee that included Henrietta Szold, Rabbi Judah L. Magnes, Nathan Straus, Stephen S. Wise, and Dr. Harry Friedenwald.

The war necessitated a substitute for central Zionist direction from Berlin. No other European center seemed capable at the time of filling the breach so long as the war went on. Thus leadership of world Zionism fell to the Zionist movement in the United States. While no one knew how long the situation would continue, nor to what extent the world Zionist movement would, in fact, accept American leadership, the American Zionists set about to form a new committee with self-assumed caretaker responsibilities: the Provisional Executive Committee for General Zionist Affairs. It represented not only the General Zionists but also the Orthodox (religious) Zionists and, most important in view of their later role in Israel, the Labor Zionist movement. Among the members of the committee were two men close to Julian—Stephen S. Wise and the young philosopher Horace M. Kallen. Its chairman, active as well as titular, was Louis D. Brandeis.

The new committee was not exclusively American. Shmarya Levin, a member of the World Zionist Executive, had participated in its formation. He had just set sail from New York to return to Europe at the close of his visit on behalf of the Haifa "Technikum" when his boat was turned back because of the war. He thus spent the war years in America and, as a member of the world Zionist leadership, gave the Provisional Executive Committee a color of Zionist legitimacy as an interim substitute for the World Zionist Executive.

Thus, the American Zionists suddenly attained a place of major importance. Meeting at the Hotel Versailles in New York City on August 30, 1914, to establish the Provisional Executive Committee for General Zionist Affairs, they considered it vital to obtain leadership of outstanding stature. The obvious candidate was Louis D. Brandeis.

Years later, at the dedication of Ein HaShofet, a kibbutz named for Brandeis, Henrietta Szold would recall the moral inspiration she had received from the 1914 meeting at which Brandeis accepted the chairmanship of the Provisional Committee. "The spirit of a quiet,

grave, yet dominating personality was infused into it," she related.
"To be of it, was like standing on a mountain top. . . ."

In a milestone article in the *American Jewish Year Book* for 1915,
"Recent Jewish Progress in Palestine," Miss Szold observed that
under Brandeis, the Provisional Committee had saved Jewish
Palestine by raising funds, shipping food and medical supplies to
Palestine, and enlisting the cooperation of such organizations as the
American Jewish Committee.

Writing to Israel Zangwill in London in 1917, Stephen S. Wise
summarized a generally-felt view:

> Brandeis is our leader and in some ways he is the first Jew in
> the world . . . I do not know that you have any Jew in
> England to match him.

Hyperbole? Not necessarily.

Probably, by the force of events, the American Zionist movement
would eventually have attained great prestige in any case. But as its
chairman, Brandeis expedited and assured the transformation. It
was in pursuit of this end that he sent his message to Julian with
Felix Frankfurter. It was a request that Julian actively join Brandeis
in the Zionist enterprise.

Events at home, as well as in Europe and in Palestine; the
influence of close association with Aaron Aaronsohn; the Zionist
sympathies of others among his associates whom he respected, and,
finally, Brandeis' pressing invitation to join him in this crucial
step—all now closed in to convert Julian's drift toward Zionism into
full-scale participation in the Zionist effort. The complete American
Jew was being forged—at last.

Brandeis was a nonreligious Jew who, like Herbert Samuel in
England, had for years seemed wholly isolated from Jewish
interests. Hence, that he should have emerged as a Zionist leader
was considered freakish, even presumptuous, by some other
important Jews at the time.

Jacob H. Schiff, for example, did not regard Brandeis as a
"representative Jew" at all. In 1913, President Wilson asked Schiff to
give him his opinion of Brandeis. Schiff replied that he only knew

Brandeis "passingly." He believed his achievements were "of a high and unselfish order." "If President-elect Wilson thinks . . . favorably of Mr. Brandeis for a Cabinet position, he will find him a most efficient adviser and co-worker." But: "I have been asked from time to time recently whether Mr. Brandeis may be considered a representative Jew, and to this I was able to give a qualified reply only, but he is, without doubt, a representative American."

Such comment, coming from Schiff, could have been interpreted as an attempt to "excommunicate" Brandeis, as it were—a rebuke for his previous aloofness from the Jewish world. Apparently Schiff from the start feared Brandeis' influence on other Jews, even on the "representative" Jews. Thus, while vacationing at the Greenbrier at White Sulphur Springs in November, 1914, Schiff was disturbed to read a Chicago newspaper story to the effect that Brandeis had converted Julius Rosenwald to Zionism. He wrote to Rosenwald about this and was much relieved when Rosenwald told him that the newspaper report had given a wrong impression.

What had actually happened in Chicago was that Mack had arranged with Rabbi Hirsch to let Brandeis give a talk before the Sinai Congregation to raise funds in aid of the Jewish settlements in Palestine, and Rosenwald had been in the audience.

Accompanying Brandeis in Chicago was the master Zionist orator, Shmarya Levin—doubtless by Brandeis' express desire, for Brandeis not only valued Levin's persuasiveness, but also enjoyed his company. "I recall," Louis Lipsky wrote in *Thirty Years of American Zionism*, "[Brandeis'] eagerness to hear Jewish wisdom from Shmarya Levin; how moved he was by tales of Jewish life exemplifying courage, or piety, or primitive humor."

They made a striking pair; the one calm and cool, the other emotional and warm. How effective they were in their proselytizing for Zionism is probably attested by the recollections of Ben Hecht, then a young newspaper reporter, who interviewed them for the *Chicago Daily News* and, years later, in his book, *A Guide for the Bedevilled*, recalled:

> I was used to wit and men of learning . . . but I had never heard the likes of these two. . . When Brandeis and Levin left Chicago, I was a slightly muddled convert to Zionism.

Brandeis' theme at Sinai Congregation was that American Jews, even those opposed to Zionism, should help the Jews of Palestine simply because they were Jews. Rosenwald, as well as Dr. Hirsch, agreed. With Aaron Aaronsohn in mind, Rosenwald that evening made a speech of his own, seconding Brandeis' appeal. He pledged $1,000 a month to the Zionists' fund for Palestine relief for the duration of the war. But Rosenwald's generosity did not mean that he accepted Zionism.

"I am not one bit more of a Zionist than I believe you to be, nor am I Anti-Zionist," he wrote to Schiff. "I consider their Nationalistic idea a wild scheme. . . . I doubt very much, even if they could accomplish what they are after along that line, that it would be to the best interest of the Jews." Not even Julian, incidentally, could ever get Rosenwald to change his mind. Ironically, Julian was to be more successful with Schiff—in due time.

In his reply to Rosenwald about the Sinai meeting, Schiff said of Brandeis: "Like all new converts, he goes to extremes in things of which he understands little. It appears to me he should have become a follower for a while, instead of an immediate leader."

Contrary, however, to Schiff's judgment, Brandeis had come to understand Zionism very well. He had already studied it with the intensity that had made him so outstanding an advocate of other causes. Besides, Brandeis had not been so isolated from Jews and Judaism as Schiff and others, including even Julian Mack, had assumed.

His maternal uncle, Lewis Naphtali Dembitz, a Louisville lawyer and an Orthodox Jew, had written articles for the *Jewish Encyclopedia*—and had been an early Zionist. Brandeis so greatly admired this uncle that, during his teens, he changed his own middle name from David to Dembitz.

Brandeis also had worked on a number of law cases for Jewish clients, including a case involving the United Hebrew Benevolent Association; also a minor litigation on behalf of a group of Jewish students at Harvard, among them Horace Kallen, and, in 1911, on the great garment workers' strike in New York, where he was called in as an arbitrator and helped devise the famous "protocol" by which the garment strike was ended. This latter experience gave him much insight into the character of Jewish workers, for most of the workers involved were Jews. It awakened him to traits in East European Jews that evoked his deep admiration. He began to feel an identification with Jews that he had not felt before. There was more, he began to sense, to being a Jew than practicing the religion which his own parents had discarded before he was born. This feeling grew stronger with him through the years.

As for Zionism, when he read about the first Zionist Congress which Herzl had called at Basle in 1897, Brandeis said to his wife, "There is something to which I could give myself!"

The following year, the Jewish Publication Society of America published his uncle's book, *Jewish Services in Synagogue and Home,* which contained much Jewish lore that Brandeis, then 42, must have found fascinating. It also contained a term referring to a Jewish state, which Brandeis had occasion to remember, and which he himself was to use often: "Commonwealth."

From that time on, Brandeis read a great deal about Zionism. Then, about 1908, he met the journalist Jacob De Haas, who had been Herzl's honorary secretary in England—"my faithful De Haas," as Herzl called him in his diary. Settling in the United States in 1902, De Haas had become secretary of the Federation of American Zionists and editor of the *Jewish Advocate* in Boston. Following a meeting on a labor matter, De Haas and Brandeis became friends.

De Haas fascinated Brandeis with his stories about Herzl. "You know, fate destined me to be a potent factor in bringing Dr. Herzl before the Jews of the world; and now I believe that I am destined to bring a new American Herzl to the Jewish people—Louis D. Brandeis," De Haas was to tell Julian's Chicago friend, Bregstone.

Brandeis himself referred to De Haas as "my teacher" in Zionism. In the 1920's he authorized him to write an official biography of himself, from the standpoint of his Zionism. The book was dedicated to Julian Mack, the only other person De Haas then considered to be as close to Brandeis as he, De Haas, himself.

Also of influence on Brandeis was another able Zionist journalist, Bernard G. Richards, who, in 1909, had blasted Julian for his testimony before the Immigration Commission. At that time Brandeis had sent Richards a telegram regretting his inability to attend the celebration of the anniversary of a Zionist publication. "My sympathy with the Zionist movement rests primarily upon the noble idealism which underlies it, and the conviction that a great people, stirred by enthusiasm for such an ideal, must bear an important part in the betterment of the world." The telegram was accompanied by Brandeis' check for $25.00—in a sense Brandeis' personal *"shekel,"* by which one formally became a Zionist.

Thus, it was as an official, dedicated, zealous Zionist that Brandeis, the Bostonian as "proper" as any Bostonian, the ultra-assimilated Jew of impeccable social status, sent his message, that March 15, via Felix Frankfurter to Julian Mack.

24. Hirsch versus Kallen

Would Julian Mack embrace Zionism? Julian's concern with Palestine gave Brandeis ample reason to assume that his response to his message would be in the affirmative.

Yet, Brandeis could not have been wholly sure. For Julian's public image, as of 1915, still was that of the "emancipated" Jew who kept aloof from Zionism, although he was not actively hostile to it, and had, in fact, proven to be genuinely sympathetic to the Jews in Palestine. But such firm non-Zionists as Schiff, Louis Marshall, Julius Rosenwald, and even Rabbi Emil G. Hirsch, had also shown their sympathy for those courageous pioneers. Thus, Brandeis as yet had no definitively clear private image of Julian Mack in this regard.

Over the years, since their first meeting during Julian's *Harvard Law Review* days, Julian and Brandeis had had some contact, mainly in connection with Harvard Law School alumni matters, or various social welfare causes. In 1911, for example, they had been fellow delegates to a meeting in Boston of the National Conference of Jewish Charities, where Julian presided over a section on juvenile problems in which Brandeis also participated. Likewise, they had had some association when Julian was active in the National Conference of Social Work, meetings which Brandeis attended from time to time, frequently as a featured speaker who would be introduced by Julian.

They had been associated also as fellow supporters of the *Survey*, a pet interest of both. They had had some social contact, too. For Brandeis' daughter, Elizabeth, had been at Radcliffe at the same time as Julian's daughter, Ruth, and their friendship brought the two families together. Incidentally, both girls had helped found Radcliffe's first Jewish students' group, the Menorah Society.

But Julian's association with Brandeis was then not yet a close one—certainly not close enough for Brandeis to assess clearly how near Julian might be to committing himself to Zionism.

Paradoxically, Julian's active connection with Jewish affairs was no help as an indicator of his position with regard to Zionism. If anything, a decision to opt for Zionism could have been more difficult for Julian than for Brandeis precisely because Julian was so active in such organizations as the American Jewish Committee—in short, because Julian was so clearly a "representative Jew." Brandeis knew that Julian leaned toward Zionism. But whether or not he would lean all the way was still a question in March, 1915.

Indeed, before Julian could finally decide in favor of Zionism, he first had to make an intellectual judgment between differing views of Judaism symbolized by two friends whose intellects he admired equally: Emil G. Hirsch, his rabbi at Sinai Congregation, and Horace M. Kallen.

Dr. Hirsch, as already noted, had been railing persuasively against Zionism ever since he and Julian had first become friends back in the 1890's. In later years, especially after the concept of a Jewish homeland in Palestine had been approved by the League of Nations, Hirsch was to undergo a change. An associate quoted him as having said in 1923, the last year of his life: "If I were a young man, I believe I would embrace Zionism after all. . . ." But in 1915, Hirsch was still uncompromisingly opposed to Zionism.

The other friend, Horace M. Kallen, Julian had first met at Harvard around 1911. In 1915, when Kallen was teaching philosophy and psychology at the University of Wisconsin, he often came down to Chicago, as when he lectured before the Book and Play Club, and always was made especially welcome at the Mack home.

Even at that early date, Kallen already had chalked up a career that interested Julian greatly. Born in Germany, the son of an Orthodox rabbi, he had grown up in Boston. At Harvard, where he had obtained his Ph.D., he had been a favorite of both George Santayana and William James, emerging with the belief that for him, Judaism was just another "ism," like Hellenism or the "systems" of Joyce and Santayana.

His re-education began in 1904 at Princeton University, where he received an appointment as an instructor in English. Everyone at Princeton conceded that he was a splendid teacher. But in 1905, after only one year, he was advised that he should leave. He could not expect to be promoted, he was told. Indeed, he would never have been appointed in the first place had it been known that he was a Jew. As he wrote in *The Menorah Journal* in 1962:

> In short, as the Princeton authorities saw me, I was one who had come to live and work among them under false pretenses: a Jew who "passed." No sooner did they discover I was a Jew than they decided that I must be cut off and shut out. In those days, such a frame of mind was anything but unusual. It prevailed in all the institutions of higher learning, and the "self-hatred" of the generality of Jews in them was their adjustment to it.

This experience did not destroy Kallen. It made him. He became one of the most creative thinkers in American life, not only on Jewish matters, but on the full spectrum of philosophy, sociology, politics, and economics. He also became, quite early, an ardent Zionist, working energetically with, and for, Brandeis in that cause.

"Your enlistment in the Zionist movement," Kallen wrote to Brandeis from Madison in December, 1913, "has renewed the courage of many of us who are deeply concerned in it. It has given us the hope that its program and policy might be changed from the piddling charity and ghetto-building, into which it had fallen, back to the high level of statesmanship in which it had been begun. We feel that there is with us at last a statesman & a leader."

"I have known in my life two great men," Kallen told Chaim Weizmann in 1915. "One was William James; the other was Louis D. Brandeis." To Brandeis himself that year Kallen gave assurance that "we who have been concerned about the destiny of the spirit of our people are ready to follow wherever you will lead."

Though the public did not know it, Kallen later drafted major documents on Zionist matters that became official statements bearing the signatures of both Louis D. Brandeis and Julian Mack.

Kallen did not, however, return to religious Judaism. On the contrary, he remained definitely nonreligious. But he did become a leading exponent of "Hebraism" which held great regard for the cultural elements, past and present, of Jewish life. It was he who first gave currency to the concept of "cultural pluralism," an outgrowth, he would generously say, of William James' philosophy and the writings of the Negro thinker, Alain Locke. A few decades later, Kallen's "cultural pluralism" was to supplant Zangwill's idea of the "melting pot."

Though Kallen by 1915 was already recognized as an exceptionally creative thinker, having published a number of important works that revealed a subtle and deep understanding of both Jewish culture and Hellenism, Dr. Hirsch publicly referred to Kallen as an "ignoramus." He belittled him as "this anti-Rabbinic expounder of Judaism à la James and Bergson, and Nordau."

Much of Dr. Hirsch's antagonism undoubtedly came from his fear of the effect of Kallen's "Hebraism" upon Jewish religious life in general. But the rabbi assailed Kallen also because he knew that Kallen was influencing Julian in the direction of Zionism. It did not sit well with Dr. Hirsch that his star "parishioner" was turning increasingly to Professor Kallen for explanations of Jewish problems that puzzled him, including some involving Dr. Hirsch's own special field, theology.

Julian had taken to doing this not only because he admired Kallen's mind so greatly, but also because his daughter had developed an admiration for Kallen and, as a student, took her own problems about Judaism to him also. In fact, Julian felt that Dr. Hirsch was wrong in believing that Kallen's "Hebraism" led to irreligiosity. To Ruth, who had raised the point in January, 1919, Julian wrote:

> If people really study Jewish tradition or, as Kallen prefers to put it, Hebraic tradition, they will become more and more religious and, inevitably, the particular form of religion that will be most sympathetic to them will be some form of Judaism, whether it be orthodox, conservative, reform, or as radical as we are at the Sinai Temple. In any event, no student of the Hebraic tradition can in my judgment ever be a scoffer at religion, particularly at Judaism.

Obviously, then, Julian was not to be influenced adversely by Rabbi Hirsch's opinion of Horace Kallen.

Ruth, incidentally, became a convert to Zionism through Kallen before her father did. Probably this was one more influence toward Julian's own conversion. In this connection, Rifka Aaronsohn recalled Julian's tendency to adopt, or to seem to adopt, Ruth's views on various subjects. "Close friends," she remembered, "used to tease him by quoting him as often saying, 'Ruth and I think.'" So when Ruth became a Zionist (though, as it turned out, only temporarily), Julian's leaning toward Zionism also became apparent.

However, in the tug-of-war over Julian, it was for Brandeis rather than Kallen that Rabbi Hirsch reserved his most thunderous blasts, calling Brandeis' speeches on Zionism "pernicious exaggerations." In particular, Dr. Hirsch reacted adversely to views which Brandeis had expressed in an address entitled, "The Jewish Problem and How to Solve It," before the Eastern Council of Reform Rabbis in 1915.

> The rebirth of the Jewish nation [Brandeis then said] is no longer a mere dream. It is in process of accomplishment in a most practical way, and the story is a wonderful one. . . .
>
> To the wordly-wise, these efforts at colonization appeared very foolish. Nature and man presented obstacles in Palestine which appeared almost insuperable; and the colonists were in fact ill-equipped for their task, save in their spirit of devotion and self-sacrifice. . . . but at last success came. Within a generation these Jewish Pilgrim Fathers, and those who followed them, have succeeded in establishing these two fundamental propositions:
>
> First: That Palestine is fit for the modern Jew.
>
> Second: That the modern Jew is fit for Palestine.

By indirection, Brandeis thus answered the viewpoint represented especially by Julius Rosenwald. In 1914, mainly at the urging of Aaron Aaronsohn and Henrietta Szold, Rosenwald and his family had visited Palestine. Aaronsohn in particular was confident that the Rosenwalds would be favorably impressed, as other American Jews had been, when they saw what the pioneers there were

accomplishing, especially since Rosenwald was supporting Aaronsohn's work. "Will your Palestinian trip make you a Zionist, you ask?
Not necessarily," Aaronsohn wrote to Mrs. Rosenwald—intending
the question for her husband's eyes also. "But I have no doubt
whatsoever that your Jewish selfconsciousness will find . . . tonici-
ty in such a trip. What action will result? Let the future take care of
itself." Indeed, "Gussie" Rosenwald was really a Zionist.

Mrs. Rosenwald was favorably impressed. But her husband held
to his preconceived notions. Palestine was still "impracticable," he
said on his return. He even tried to persuade Aaronsohn to leave
Palestine, offering him $500,000 (which Aaronsohn refused) for his
work if he would settle in the United States. "All he [Rosenwald]
could see," as Julian lamented some time later," [was] the flies."

Brandeis also developed again in his speech the theme that had so
appealed to Julian—that a Jewish state in Palestine would mean an
uplifting of the character of Jews everywhere. He commented on
the argument that Zionism would cast a shadow of "dual loyalty"
over Jews in America.

Let no American imagine [Brandeis said] that Zionism is
inconsistent with Patriotism. Multiple loyalties are objection-
able only if they are inconsistent.

A man is a better citizen of the United States for being also a
loyal citizen of his state, and of his city; for being loyal to his
family, and to his profession or trade; for being loyal to his
college or his lodge. Every Irish American who contributed
towards advancing home rule was a better American for the
sacrifice he made.

Every American Jew who aids in advancing the Jewish
settlement in Palestine, though he feels that neither he nor his
descendants will ever live there, will likewise be a better man
and a better American for doing so.

We must [he continued] protect America and ourselves from
demoralization which has to some extent already set in among

American Jews. . . . The sole bulwark against such demoralization is to develop in each new generation of Jews in America the sense of *noblesse oblige*. . . . That spirit can best be developed by actively participating in some way in furthering the ideals of the Jewish renaissance; and this can be done effectively only through furthering the Zionist movement.

Julian, listening carefully now to both Kallen and Brandeis, and tending to disagree more and more with Hirsch, had arrived at the point of decision.

25. Decision

To reach his decision on Zionism, Julian proceeded in the same studious way in which he made his decisions on the bench. He weighed the arguments carefully. Horace Kallen once said, comparing Julian's attitude toward Zionism with that of Brandeis, that Brandeis was "the prophet" and Julian "the judge." Kallen, incidentally, saw to it that Julian had all the Zionist arguments. His success was such that by December, 1914, Dr. Hirsch in his *Reform Advocate* was sadly referring to Julian as being "Zionistic." And by 1915, Kallen was able to tell Brandeis:

"Mack is now likely to go all the way."

Some years later, Kallen stressed the democratic ideology that was involved in Julian's moving "all the way." For the *American Jewish Year Book*, Kallen wrote:

> . . . . his studies of the situation of Jews tended to shift the direction of his thought, and gradually to bring his sense of the meaning of democracy away from the prevailing assimilationist conception of Reform Judaism to that of the older, somewhat overlaid one of which Thomas Jefferson was the avatar. This led him to Zionism. The symbolic expression for the Judaist conception was "the melting pot"; the symbolic expression for the Jeffersonian one became "cultural pluralism." As was the case with Louis Brandeis, it was no more Julian Mack's sympathy for the Jews as pitiful victims of injustice than his revision of his idea of democracy that made a Zionist of him as well. "We ask no more," he told the peacemakers at Versailles, "for the Jew than we do for any one else." Nor, as a loyal servant of freedom and justice, would he stop with less. . . .

Remarks made by Julian himself, at a dinner in New York at the Astor Hotel in November, 1922, confirmed this aspect of his conversion. "We hear much about Palestine as a refuge of the oppressed," he said. "Of course there are many people who need Palestine because they must get away from the hell in which they are living. But that is not what inspired the Zionist movement. What led us is pride in the people from whom we have sprung, pride in our cultural inheritance and a desire to see that develop."

It was one more step in Julian's thinking that he wholeheartedly accepted Kallen's Jeffersonian concept of "cultural pluralism." For *The Nation* Kallen had written a two-part essay entitled "Democracy Versus the Melting Pot—A Study of American Nationality." This essay, published in February, 1915, was of seminal significance and persuaded Julian that Jewish distinctiveness, as implicit in Zionist nationalism, was beneficial to American life.

Gradually, Julian found himself increasingly active in Zionist projects. But the friends and acquaintances who continued to try to get a definitive commitment from him were not yet successful. Then, in September, 1914, during a discussion of the importance, and the difficulty, of winning wealthy Reform Jews over to Zionism, Kallen made an important suggestion to Brandeis. The Provisional Executive Committee for General Zionist Affairs, he urged, should enlist the cooperation on a formal basis, if not the formal membership, of certain outstanding Reform Jews who would act as liaison between the Committee and the Reform community. Julian was one of those he prominently mentioned. Out of this idea came an "advisory council."

With the hope that he would accept a place on such a council, Julian was sounded out at the time, at Brandeis' request, by Eliyahu Zev Lewin-Epstein, treasurer of the Provisional Executive Committee.

Julian indicated then that he might be willing to serve. Frankfurter, too, was sounded out about accepting membership on an advisory council.

On March 11, 1915, the Provisional Executive Committee, meeting in the offices of Nathan Straus in the Aeolian Building in New York, officially took up the matter of the advisory council, as recorded in the minutes of that meeting:

BRANDEIS: We have been having to an extraordinary degree, the sympathetic cooperation of Judge Mack who, I think, is becoming more and more Zionistic in all his endeavors. I think nothing could be better than to have Judge Mack associated with us, publicly and actively, and I have been considering Prof. Felix Frankfurter in the same position. If we could get them, and possibly some others definitely associated with us, we would get a good deal. We have been considering in what form it could be done. A suggestion has been made that they be members of an Advisory Council. If they were willing, I feel we should gain very much by their public declaration that they are acting with us, as they are, in fact. I think before we elect them, that I would sound them, and we would invite them with the assurance that it would be accepted.

GOTTHEIL*: I would also suggest Judge [Irving] Lehman, and Mr. [Maurice] Wertheim [son-in-law of Henry Morgenthau, Sr.].

BRANDEIS: Yesterday we organized our Loan Committee, raising $120,000, and Judge Mack was President, and Dr. Julius Goldman, Treasurer, and Mr. Wertheim, Secretary. At all events, we are making definite progress with these men, especially Judge Mack. I should like to have an informal expression, whether, if Judge Mack and Prof. Frankfurter are willing to come, we are willing to have them.

It is moved and seconded that an Advisory Council be created.

MOTION PASSED.

Such, then, was the background of the message from Brandeis to Julian Mack.

Julian's answer, in a letter on March 18, 1915, conveyed to Frankfurter and later to Brandeis himself, was that he "would be glad to act on such a committee with Felix and a few others."

---

*Richard J. H. Gottheil (1862–1936), president of the Federation of American Zionists from 1898 to 1904.

As it turned out, there were no other acceptances, and there was to be no "committee"; there were only Julian and Felix Frankfurter. In April, 1915, the Provisional Executive Committee for General Zionist Affairs announced that it had an "advisory council" consisting of Judge Julian W. Mack and Professor Felix Frankfurter, who were referred to as "councilors." Thus, Julian's career in Zionism was launched.

Kallen, as might have been expected, was especially exultant. That May, he ecstatically reported to Brandeis on Julian's "first public Zionist address," given at a Menorah Society dinner at the University of Wisconsin. True, an anti-Zionist Reform rabbi from Milwaukee had taken umbrage publicly to Julian's theme, but Kallen was certain that Julian's presentation, "very forceful and eloquent, true doctrine," had been more than a match for the rabbi's angry criticism. At about the same time, Judge Bernard Rosenblatt of New York, who was to become a leader in American Zionism, commented on a talk Julian had given in Boston that, he said, "was one of the greatest speeches I ever listened to . . . a most eloquent plea for Jewish nationalism, a very fine repudiation of his own testimony before the Immigration Commission."

Indeed, Julian soon became one of Zionism's most influential spokesmen. His formal affiliation was with a group called "the Intercollegiate Zionist Association of America," a federation of college Zionist societies, a catch-all group, so to speak, for confirmed Zionists of all shades. Later, he accepted the honorary presidency of the "Knights of Zion," the Chicago Zionist organization, whose leaders back in 1903 had decided, with some diffidence, to take a chance on supporting him as a candidate for judge of the Circuit Court of Cook County.

The decision that he made represented a long intellectual and emotional journey. Deep concern over the plight of the Jews of Eastern Europe; recognition that the United States was closing its portals to such Jews; and above all, a matured awakening to the cultural importance of the Jews as a people—his people—in the context of Kallen's "cultural pluralism": these were the basic milestones in his journey, one much like that of Louis D. Brandeis. In effect, he had crossed an intellectual continent as wide as that from his native San Francisco to his new base, New York. And the result, clearly, was a sense of ease with himself concerning his Jewishness that he had not felt before.

Certainly he had come a long way from the Judge Mack who in 1909 had so vigorously argued before the U.S. Immigration Commission against the idea that Jews were a "race"—and had been attacked by Zionists for his testimony. In contrast, he was soon saying from a speaker's platform:

"Zionism rests, as I view it, on this fundamental assumption, that the Jews are a people. I mean that all the Jews, no matter of what country they may be citizens, are one people."

If it was inferred that he had come close to calling Jews a "race," whatever the word meant, that issue no longer really bothered him. Nor did it really disturb him that some Jews, including relatives and close friends, subjected him to sneers and even slurs because he had become a Zionist. Truly, he had experienced in a sense what in theology is called a "conversion."

In 1943, Solomon Goldman, the Chicago rabbi who later became a leader in American Zionism, wrote of the nature of Julian's "conversion":

> Judge Mack lived and moved for a long time amidst perhaps the extremest *anti*-Zionists to be found anywhere in the country. . . . Why, asked many of those who knew him in his early years, did he go over to Zionism? He came, as do all men whose eyes are opened to the circumstances of Jewish existence and the logic of Jewish history. He was frightened of the smugness and obtuseness of Jewish isolationists who assumed that all was right with Israel because all was well with them, and that what was wrong, their charity could right. . . . He was pained because much of American Jewish talent was untouched by the pathos of Jewish destiny and the sublimity of the Zionist dream. He had come to see clearly the superficiality, the lie, and the cowardice of assimilation. . . .

From then on, too, his life was closely interwoven with that of Brandeis. "Zionist affairs are really the important thing in life now," Brandeis wrote to his brother that April—and this was nearly the case with him even after he went to the Supreme Court. So it was also with Julian.

In that common interest, the two functioned almost as one during most of the time when, as Judd L. Teller was to note, American Zionism entered its "golden age." To be sure, Brandeis was the leader. But this was quite in accord with Julian's personality—especially when the leader was Brandeis.

When they first began their active association, Brandeis was approaching sixty. In physical appearance he was then, as always, impressive. In his last years on the bench, when the popular impression of Brandeis was shaped by Franklin Roosevelt's description of him as "Isaiah," he evoked an image of asceticism, a patriarchal image reinforced by numerous accounts of his simple living arrangements, the frugal furnishings of his home, and his Spartan meals. Julian good-humoredly contributed to this Brandeisian lore. Once, when asked to bring an associate to Brandeis' apartment for dinner, Julian, the gourmet, warned: "Let's stop and get a sandwich first!"

But in this earlier period, Brandeis cut the handsome figure of a man of the world, strong, self-assured, rugged and erect, appearing to be taller than he really was. Brandeis' style, reflected in a wide-open, penetrating look from piercing blue eyes, was then more that of the vigorous leader and man of affairs than of the philosopher, though philosopher he was. For all his "Isaiah" role in America's conscience, there was in him a strong practical streak, Emersonian, with a bit of Thoreau, also a trace of the inventor-engineer. Some called him "Lincolnian."

Temperamentally, two more unlikely close associates could hardly have been imagined than the seemingly steel-like Brandeis and the usually amiable Julian Mack. Indeed, Julian might have been expected to shy away from one so different from himself, from the Brandeis variously described as ". . . dominating, intransigent . . . prone to read evil motives into obvious actions," and so forth. But Julian did not see him so. "This profound jurist, uncompromising idealist . . . dauntless Jew"—so he once described Brandeis. His high regard for Brandeis was always apparent, specifically or between the lines, in the correspondence between himself and Brandeis that extended over many years.

In view of Brandeis' temperament, it was not surprising, however, that their friendship developed gradually, not instantaneously as it had between Julian and Aaronsohn. They addressed each other for some time with an almost curious formality: "Mr. Brandeis" and "Judge Mack," or, at the most, after a while, "Dear Brandeis" and "Dear Mack." It was a long time before they relaxed into the comradely "L.D.B." and "J.W.M." It took still longer before their correspondence included personal references and, finally, messages of affection that reflected the tenderest concern for each other's welfare. This, when it came, was not unexpected in Julian. But for Brandeis it was unusual, showing his special high regard for Julian. It also revealed, despite commonly-held views of him, that Brandeis, too, could be "human."

In the Brandeis circle devoted to Zionism that took shape as a kind of Arthurian Round Table, Julian's status became unique. In this group—Robert Szold was notably included later—there were some especially "able knights," men like Stephen S. Wise and Felix Frankfurter, who paid reverent homage to Brandeis, referring to him as "The Chief" and following his leadership with noteworthy loyalty. But after 1915, the first of the "knights" was Julian. Not the least of his functions, it may be noted, was to keep peace within the circle, often smoothing feathers that Brandeis' manner at times ruffled. But for the most part, in Zionism, Mack was *the* co-worker of Brandeis, the one who could always be depended upon to see to it that policies agreed upon were carried out or championed. He was part of every Zionist move that Brandeis made from then on until the end of their lives.

Again Julián's own intimate circle widened. This time it included, along with Brandeis, a number of other Zionists such as Shmarya Levin and that valiant head of Hadassah, Henrietta Szold. To these leaders, Mack had become a "brother in Zionism," signing his letters to them as "Yours in Zionism."

Had some of his older friends—Emil G. Hirsch, for example—seen such letters, they would have been shocked indeed. Julian Mack—pride of Chicago's Sinai Congregation, the citadel of "radical" Reform Judaism; Julian Mack, personification of the assimilated American Jew of German-Jewish stock, of the Harvard Law School, a founder of the American Jewish Committee, a Federal judge only one rung below the Supreme Court, all this and more—he a Zionist! If at times he himself was ever shocked or even ambivalent about his Zionism, there was his friendship with Aaron Aaronsohn to give his Zionist activities a personal content and to help sustain his enthusiasm for Zionism when otherwise it might have flagged. From Aaron's "Scroll of Fire" letter, Julian had learned that his friend's zeal for a Jewish Palestine had led him to carry on espionage activities there for British military forces as leader of the "Nili," which was probably the main source of British intelligence about Palestine, its terrain, water sources, and about the deployment there of Turkish forces. The information supplied by Aaronsohn played a crucial role in the British victory in Palestine. By the time General Allenby's forces marched into Jerusalem in December, 1917—during the Jewish festival of Hanukkah—Aaron was actively, though secretly, on Allenby's staff, working closely with the noted Col. Richard Meinertzhagen and the even more noted Lawrence of Arabia.

The headquarters for the "Nili" was at Aaron's agricultural station at Athlit, the project supported by the American group Julian had helped to organize. Hence Aaron's activity was not only worrisome but also potentially embarrassing to Julian. In 1916 the United States had not yet entered the war. Thus Aaron's activity might have been interpreted as involving Julian and his other American backers in a technical violation of American neutrality.

Aaron was aware of this. He apologized, hoping that at least Julian, if not Schiff, Rosenwald, and some of the others, would "understand."

"I felt from the beginning," Aaron wrote, "the necessity that you, of all men, should know as early as possible. I cannot keep you in ignorance. It is up to you to make your own opinion and to give your verdict: Can you or can you no more reach me your hand? Is it adieu or au revoir? . . ."

It was not "adieu." Naturally, as a United States judge, Julian could not allow himself to be associated with Aaron's activities against a foreign power, even for Zionism. Therefore, he had to approve the stoppage of American funds for Aaron's station "for the duration." But he could not, and did not, cut off Aaron Aaronsohn.

If, by usual standards, Aaron's wartime activities seemed quixotic, the same might have been said—and indeed, was said—of Mack's and Brandeis' activities on behalf of Zionism. For these two men were involved in bringing about an "impossible" thing: the ultimate re-creation of a nation, in its original land, by a people dispersed from it many centuries before, a return which pious Jews, incidentally, felt could be achieved only by miraculous, direct intervention from God in some future messianic era.

At the time, the major established Jewish organizations, religious and otherwise, in Europe and America, were for the most part either indifferent to Zionism or actively hostile to it. If they supported the Zionist settlements in Palestine, that support was philanthropic, not political.

Only the most highly "political" Zionists envisioned the development of the settlements in Palestine into a Jewish state—and even among them many saw it as a utopian concept more than as a program capable of realization. Most of the Zionist sympathizers were like the socialists who discussed and propagandized, but never expected to see a socialist state.

The outbreak of World War I, however, changed matters. It gave promise that the Zionist dream, as Aaron Aaronsohn perceived it, might, in some form, become reality. Regardless of which side won, it seemed certain that a political reshaping of the world would take place when the war was over. The Poles, the Czechs, the Irish, and the Arabs, among other peoples, felt their national aspirations quickened by the war. It could hardly have been otherwise for Zionist Jews, even though their leaders remained most cautious for some time in expressing themselves.

This caution is shown by the fact that they did not use the word "state" when they discussed their aims. With some of the Zionists, this was due to their own uncertainty as to whether a "state" could, in fact, be achieved or whether it would even be immediately desirable. With others, caution was dictated by the knowledge that many Jews, while rejecting the idea of a reborn Jewish "state," were nevertheless sympathetic to the concept of a Jewish "homeland" in

Palestine, or to the concept later defined as a Jewish "common-wealth," concepts which seemed less emotionally charged than that of a "state," and which they were willing to help support.

But whatever the concept, so long as new boundaries were to be drawn, possessions transferred, old states re-formed or abolished and new states created, why should not a small area, specifically Palestine, be set aside for the Jews?

Ironically, it was not American Jews but certain American non-Jews who began talking most openly of the establishment of a Jewish state after the war. In 1916 the Rev. Dr. Blackstone resurrected the memorial he had sent to President Harrison in 1891 and persuaded the Presbyterian General Assembly to endorse a Jewish homeland in Palestine. Also in 1916 former President William Howard Taft came close to advocating the same idea in a talk before the National Geographic Society. And the American Federation of Labor, led by Samuel Gompers, a non-Zionist, non-practicing Jew, chimed in with an official resolution for a Jewish Palestine.

Then, during the war, the idea took hold that the Great Powers—whichever set of them would emerge victorious—could in fact be persuaded by political action to secure Palestine for the Jews.

In September, 1915, speaking to a group of fellow Labor Zionists in New York, young David Ben-Gurion examined the idea that the Jewish homeland could come into being by fiat of a peace conference after the war. Not so, he warned.

> We will receive it, not from the Peace Conference, or the nation that rules it, but from the hands of the Jewish worker who will come to take root in it, to bring it life and to dwell in it. The Land of Israel will be ours when, in best part, its workers and watchmen are from our own ranks. The real conquest of the Land through labor—that is the transcendent duty which faces the nation's pioneers. . . .

Brandeis, too, emphasized the need for the development of viable settlements in Palestine by the Jewish pioneers as a prerequisite to the establishment of a permanent base for the eventual homeland.

But neither he nor Ben-Gurion lost sight of the fact that international politics after the war would certainly play a role. There would have to be politics *and* settlement of the land, as well as a defense of it once it was settled.

As a political realist, Brandeis knew the sources of political action. He therefore understood that it would be necessary to exert political pressures upon statesmen in behalf of the Zionist goals, and that Jewish mass opinion, in particular, would have to be mobilized. Otherwise, the Zionist aspirations would have no more vitality than the Reverend Mr. Blackstone's "memorial" of 1891.

Brandeis was not alone in that understanding. There was a new stirring among Zionist leaders everywhere, particularly in Russia in the person of the rugged leader Menachem Mendel Ussishkin, and in England in the person of the politically knowledgeable scientist, Chaim Weizmann.

Zionist recruiting was stepped up. The goal was to have a movement so strong that Zionism would be accepted as an acknowledged aspiration, like the movements for Irish freedom and Czechoslovak independence. Then, perhaps, the peacemakers and map-drawers would act favorably.

But it was *Jewish* opinion, more than non-Jewish opinion, that had to be won over to the dream which Julian now shared.

Ironically, Julian's efforts to win Jews of his own class to Zionism were least effective in the cities where he had the deepest personal roots—Cincinnati and Chicago. In Cincinnati, of course, he met with resistance from the partisans of the Isaac Mayer Wise tradition, specifically, from the Hebrew Union College, which was then still the center of "German-Jewish" classic Reform Judaism. When Julian spoke there, he was openly rebuked by David Philipson, who had been one of the officiating rabbis at his marriage ceremony. Nor was he able to convert his own brothers, especially not Ralph Mack, whose anti-Zionism later, in fact, led him into the anti-Israel American Council for Judaism.

In Chicago, the anti-Zionist position of Julius Rosenwald and Rabbi Emil G. Hirsch was like an impenetrable wall against Julian's attempt to bring Chicago's Jewish establishment into the Zionist

fold. Of one gathering at Chicago's Sinai Congregation, Julian had
to report to Stephen Wise that

> While I had a fairly good audience . . . I did not convince
> J.R. [Rosenwald], who was there, or A.G. Becker, or Max
> Epstein. . . .

Rosenwald's unbending resistance was particularly distressing to
Julian, especially as he knew that Mrs. Rosenwald tended to favor
the Zionist idea.

"I perhaps ought to have been more aggressive with Rosenwald,"
Julian later said. "But it was just not my character to be so. I gave
him the facts as I knew and saw them, but could not go further with
him."

Nor would he denounce Rosenwald, as some Zionists did.

Yet, in other localities, Julian, like Brandeis, was highly
successful in making recruits for Zionism, or at least in developing
cooperation with Zionism from some influential figures—some of
whom, admittedly, drifted away later. One such person was Eugene
Meyer, later a well-known banker and newspaper publisher.
Another was J.M. Kaplan, whom Julian as judge had permitted to
take over equipment from a sugar company in Cuba, thus boosting
him on his road to wealth. Until the 1930's Kaplan had been totally
indifferent to Zionism and Palestine. "Frankly," he said, "I had my
doubts about the Zionist dream of settling Jews on land that I
thought was merely a strip of desert . . . dry sand fit for camels
rather than for human beings." But along with Brandeis and Robert
Szold, Julian persuaded Kaplan to visit Palestine, with the result
that Kaplan contributed to the Jewish settlements "considerably
more than the $50,000 that Judge Mack had originally suggested."
Julian, Kaplan later recalled, "smiled, as if to suggest that his
confidence in a nervy young businessman many years earlier had in
this way been rewarded."

It was Julian, too, who cinched the conversion to Zionism of
Benjamin Nathan Cardozo. The future Supreme Court Justice, of a
temperament much different from that of Brandeis, had been

diffident about following Brandeis' lead into Zionism. But in January, 1920, Julian was able to advise Jacob Schiff, with much enthusiasm, that Cardozo "is most heartily with us and will permit his name to be used for any proper purpose."

Mack was to win large numbers of such converts. As *The New Palestine*, the official publication of the Zionist Organization of America, was to say of Mack in September, 1943:

> He was a complete, an integrated personality, kin to Justice Brandeis in his ability to capture and harmonize the essence of both Americanism and Zionism. Unnumbered are there in Zionism today who owe their inspiration, their early guidance, to him. . . . Judge Mack was one of the giants in American Zionism.

However, Julian suffered some disappointments in his efforts to make formal converts to Zionism, particularly with Jacob Schiff. Before his death in 1920, Schiff had agreed to let Julian announce that he had "officially" become a Zionist, but with one explicit proviso: the announcement should also say that Schiff was joining on the understanding that one Zionist objective in Palestine should be the furtherance of religious Judaism. Julian accepted the condition. But other Zionist leaders, including Brandeis and even Rabbi Wise, did not want to let Schiff impose this condition. They felt, probably with justification, that, since many Zionists were not religious, another harmful controversy would result. Besides, they did not believe that any prospective member of the Zionist Organization of America, not even Schiff, should be permitted to set his own conditions for joining. Thus, to Julian's keen chagrin, Schiff was lost to the movement—and so, most likely, were many others who might have followed Schiff's lead, including, perhaps, even Julius Rosenwald.

26. Continuing Commitment

To win over American Jewish opinion was the major task in which Julian Mack became engaged as a collaborator with Brandeis and other Zionists. A remarkable degree of success was achieved. Of course, that success was owed also to the work of many other leaders, and to the influence of "history," including new tragedies of unforeseen magnitude in Europe. But Julian's importance in the effort was considerable.

One particularly fruitful phase of his activity resulted from his friendly contacts with newspaper and magazine editors. Not a few articles favorable to Zionism were due to his influence—even in the then anti-Zionist *New York Times*. His prestige as a judge, as well as his personal acquaintance with journalists such as Walter Lippmann, Hackett and Franklin P. Adams, opened editorial doors that were closed to the regular Zionist publicists.

Indeed, his impeccable status as a Reform Jew, along with his position in American public life, made the fact of his own conversion a strong argument for Zionism. The essence of his contribution lay there, and in his exceptional ability to be a conciliator among disputing factions and personalities.

There was great need at that time for his talent as a mediator. For Zionism involved not only much controversy with anti-Zionists, but also, as already noted, much division within Zionism itself.

Perhaps more than anyone else on the scene, Julian was a figure in whom nearly all parties in the Jewish community, both within and outside the Zionist movement, had confidence. There were numerous instances of leaders who had refused to sit down together but were able to negotiate with Julian. He thus exercised an important function and at times a crucial one. And in the end he, too, was to be caught up in a dramatic collision between Brandeis and Weizmann.

In fact, Julian was immediately drawn into a stormy situation that developed from a movement to establish a central agency which would speak for the entire American Jewish community with respect to Jewish problems arising from the war. It seemed clear that, aside from the Palestine question, some stand would have to be taken on the political and other rights of Jews in the war-torn countries, once there was peace. But who, or what group, would be able to speak with authority for all the Jews in America?

That question exposed a tender nerve in American Jewish life. There were too many different kinds of Jews—in religious affiliation or nonaffiliation, in economic status, in national origins, in political views—for any existing organization to be considered fully representative. Then, too, there had existed historically a kind of tacit understanding in the American Jewish community that there ought not to be any single representative Jewish organization. One of the closest approaches to such an agency up to that time had been the American Jewish Committee. But this committee had sidestepped the issue by establishing itself as a self-constituted committee of prestigious upper-class individuals. Moreover, working-class Jews, for example, who had formed strong labor unions and socialist societies, did not recognize the American Jewish Committee as representing them. In his *Thirty Years of American Zionism*, Louis Lipsky expressed the dominant Zionist position with regard to the American Jewish Committee at that time when he wrote:

> We just could not abide its undemocratic constitution. . . . We, organizers of a free Jewish opinion, upon which Zionist success depended, felt that we had to fight the American Jewish Committee or be faithless as Zionists and Americans.

In later years, the American Jewish Committee underwent substantial change, becoming more democratic and to some extent developing a mass membership. But Lipsky's view at the time was valid and Julian, a founder of the Committee, was not far from agreement with it.

In point of fact, other important leaders of the American Jewish Committee themselves recognized the Committee's shortcomings and realized the need for a more representative voice on the issues that would arise from the war. Thus, when various Jewish groups began to advocate the idea—articulated early by the Zionist journalist Bernard G. Richards—of a widely representative American Jewish Congress, the dominant leadership in the American Jewish Committee seemed to favor it, with certain reservations. It even sponsored a call for a conference in which already established leaders of all major Jewish organizations would participate. In the meantime, the Zionist movement vigorously took up the idea of such a congress.

Conflicts, however, developed on such issues as how the delegates would be chosen. Then, too, there were those in the American Jewish Committee who began to ask whether there should be a congress at all. Louis Marshall, the president of the Committee, for one, labeled the Congress idea as "juvenility" and as a project that would permit "blatant and flamboyant orators . . . to make themselves conspicuous." Other leaders of the Committee feared that the Congress movement represented an effort on the part of the Zionists to have their particular aims presented in the name of American Jewry.

Also involved was the question of sympathy for one or the other of the belligerents in Europe. Related to this issue was the equally heated debate about "neutrality" versus "preparedness," with pacifism, notably represented by Jane Addams, thrown in. The idea of a Jewish gathering debating such matters in public alarmed many Jewish leaders, who felt, not without historical basis, that no matter what position Jews took on such questions, they would stand to be damned, and that aspersions would be cast upon their patriotism.

The basic issue, however, was stated by Horace Kallen:

> All sorts of things were argued. But the one thing which was really fundamental in the quarrel over the Congress was the fact that it was a struggle between . . . a democratized Jewry and a traditional Jewish oligarchy.

Naturally, deep emotions were stirred. Indeed, at one point, Jacob Schiff became so agitated by criticism of his stand against the Congress idea, especially in the Yiddish press, that in an almost tearful address, in June, 1916, he announced: "I have been hurt to the core, and hereafter Zionism, Nationalism, the Congress movement, and Jewish politics, in whatever form they may come up, will be a sealed book to me." He did not keep the vow. But the fact that he made it was indicative of the passions that flared.

Nor did it help, at least not with the leadership of the American Jewish Committee, that the exponents of the Congress idea selected Brandeis as their official spokesman.

Both as a Zionist and as a member of the American Jewish Committee, Julian took the middle ground. Felix Frankfurter and Dr. Harry Friedenwald resigned from the Committee. But Julian (though he later resigned over another issue) remained on the Committee.

> I do not as yet find it difficult [he wrote to Brandeis] to be actively engaged both in the work of the American Jewish Committee and in that of the Zionist organization. Whenever the time comes when I shall feel . . . that there is injury to one or the other because of my service to both, I shall have to choose . . . but until that time, I hope that my usefulness to both may be increased rather than diminished. . . .

Actually, Julian at the time tended to favor the American Jewish Committee's position, as he candidly informed Brandeis in August, 1915. But he also informed Brandeis that, if the Zionist group stood firm, "I will yield my personal judgment."

As it happened, his ambivalent stance was a fortunate one. To achieve a united Jewish program on the war issues, negotiations between the American Jewish Committee and the Brandeis-led forces had to be continued.

Julian, the mediator, was the perfect bridge.

In the tug-of-war that went on, there was one important interruption, which seemed unrelated to the question of whether or not there would be a congress, but which, in fact, had a decisive impact on the outcome of that debate: The political battle that began in January, 1916 and centered in the United States Senate, when President Wilson named Brandeis to the Supreme Court.

No other nomination to the Supreme Court, not even nominations that three later Presidents, Hoover, Johnson and Nixon, were forced to withdraw, was fought so bitterly as was that of

Louis D. Brandeis. During the long battle, Brandeis was unconscionably and falsely vilified in and out of the Senate. Even Elbert Hubbard, the "Sage of Aurora," ostensibly a liberal philosopher, took part—as a mercenary publicist—in the disgraceful attempt to smear Brandeis' reputation as a lawyer.

The legal profession was torn apart. It was a shocking spectacle not only for Brandeis, but also for Julian, who wanted to view the legal profession as one dedicated to the highest ethics. The division over Brandeis made it hard for him to retain that image of the bar, so low did many fellow members of both bar and bench stoop in their attacks upon Brandeis.

Also to Julian's dismay, even the usually sedate Harvard Law School was split. For though most of the Harvard law professors, including Dean Pound, supported the nomination, President A. Lawrence Lowell led a scathing attack on Brandeis. William Howard Taft, who had sponsored Mack's own nomination as a Federal judge, joined the pack against Brandeis along with other "respectables." Their conduct caused Senator Robert M. LaFollette, Sr., to exclaim to Brandeis: "These hell-hounds must get what is coming to them—I mean these Bar Association presidents —University presidents—these sleek respectable crooks whose opinions have always been for sale!"

The basic issues, of course, were Brandeis' alleged "radicalism" and the "New Freedom" policies of President Wilson, who, in the assessment of John Chamberlain, had made his "most logical move" in sending Brandeis' name to the Senate. But anti-Semitism was also involved. Deep emotions were stirred among conservatives and liberals—and especially in the Jewish world.

And Julian? As a judge, he was expected to keep aloof from the Brandeis struggle—a painful stance for him. So far as the public knew, he played no part in the battle. But in fact, mainly in association with Frankfurter, he was quite active behind the scenes rounding up support for Brandeis, supplying answers to the slanders against Brandeis, and getting influential citizens to exert pressure on senators in Brandeis' behalf.

Jewish organizations, notably the B'nai B'rith, went into action with telegrams and letters to the senators; so, too, did the Zionist groups—all with Julian's aid in association with other Jewish leaders. He helped also to galvanize various liberal groups, such as the *Survey, New Republic,* and *Nation* people, into action.

In addition, he made a highly personal contribution to the fight on behalf of Brandeis—by his reaction to a movement of his friends to get Julian himself "considered" by the President for the court in case the Senate became deadlocked over Brandeis. There was considerable power behind this movement. Its leaders included Julius Rosenwald, Lessing Rosenthal, and Levy Mayer of Chicago, who worked with certain leaders of the Foreign Policy Association in New York. In fact, Lessing Rosenthal had begun a movement for getting President Wilson to name Julian to the Supreme Court even before Brandeis' nomination had been announced, and now, even after the nomination of Brandeis, was using his many contacts to follow through on his effort.

Still earlier, various liberal groups had loosed trial balloons in the press for several potential appointees, including Learned Hand, Samuel S. Seabury—and Julian Mack.

When Julian discovered this activity on his behalf, he saw at once that it was playing into the hands of Brandeis' opponents. There was no hesitation in his response. "It was the first time I ever observed Judge Mack stern, even harsh, with life-long friends," Lawrence Berenson, then his secretary, recalled. "He warned all in no uncertain terms that he would terminate his association with them—forever—if they persisted." And so the movement was called off.

When Brandeis was finally confirmed, Julian, of course, was "extremely delighted," as he wrote to Brandeis from Chicago. As might have been expected, it was his undeviating view that "Brandeis deserved the appointment beyond any other man," himself included.

After confirmation, Brandeis took on a new image on the American scene, that of a national figure of towering stature, particularly that of an authentic American Jewish "hero." No longer did Jews such as Schiff or Rosenwald scoff at him, his Zionism notwithstanding. Indeed, both Schiff and Rosenwald in the end worked energetically for Brandeis' confirmation.

Pride in the honor that had come to a fellow Jew, the first to sit on the Supreme Court, had taken precedence over their objections to his Zionism and even to his economic views. Such, indeed, was the general Jewish view, regardless of class or politics.

Alpheus T. Mason's biography of William Howard Taft quotes an odd comment by Taft that is obliquely pertinent. "The intelligent Jews of this country," said Taft, "are as much opposed to Brandeis' nomination as I am." But Taft could not have been more in error. The truer view was that of Nathan Straus, Jr., who, on hearing of Brandeis' confirmation, wrote to him:

"As a Jew, it means more than I can tell you to know that so conspicuous a public office will be filled by so wise and good a man of our race."

So Julian, as a Jew, also felt.

The effect of Brandeis' appointment on the proposal for a Jewish congress was immensely potent. So striking was the enhancement of Brandeis' personal authority—it was already apparent that he was destined to become America's Number One Jew—that there was a marked abatement of opposition to his views on the Congress idea. From then on, even the most respected Establishment Jews considered head-on opposition to Brandeis as dangerous to their standing. At any rate, a compromise agreeable to him was worked out with the American Jewish Committee.

Brandeis' new status was not the only factor here. The leaders of the American Jewish Committee were forced to recognize the fact that mass Jewish opinion behind the Congress idea was too strong for them to ignore. But the Brandeis image was undoubtedly also a strong factor, as Julian learned when he acted as a go-between in the Congress negotiations.

"The Committee yielded much," Julian wrote to Brandeis at a crucial point while the compromise was being worked out. He urged that Brandeis, in turn, yield on two matters presented by the American Jewish Committee: that the Congress should be postponed until after the end of the war; and that such a gathering should be merely an *ad hoc* organization which would cease to exist after a peace settlement had been made among the belligerent nations.

Julian admitted that the first concession was asking a great deal of Brandeis, who had told him:

"A congress *after* the termination of hostilities may mean a

congress after the time has passed when Jews could accomplish
something by participating in a [peace] conference. It is perfectly
clear that there might be a peace conference while hostilities were
still under way."

This, it should be noted, was in 1916—before the United States
had entered the war, and before the issuance of the Balfour
Declaration in 1917. What Brandeis particularly had in mind was
the hope that from a peace conference there would emerge a Jewish
homeland in Palestine.

Finally, Brandeis did agree to the compromise. A contributing
factor—part of the behind-the-scenes history of Jewish Palestine—was a discreet word from the White House to the effect that
the predictable action by an American Jewish Congress, before the
war was over, in favor of a Jewish homeland in Palestine would be
embarrassing to the United States in its relations with Turkey—in
effect, that American "neutrality" would be compromised.

Brandeis found it hard to ignore this plea from the White House,
regardless of whether it was sincere with respect to Jewish hopes for
Palestine, and of whether it had really come from Wilson or had
been, in fact, a ploy of the State Department. Then, too, there is
evidence that some strong representations were made to Brandeis,
especially from British sources, that a congress held while the war
was still going on, and before the United States had entered it,
would provide a "disturbing" forum for Jewish pacifists. Judah L.
Magnes, then prominent in "The People's Council for Peace and
Democracy," was especially singled out in that connection.

That Magnes would seek to commit the Congress to a pacifist
position was viewed as more than a possibility. In Brandeis' view,
the chance that America's participation in the war might become a
topic of heated debate at an American Jewish Congress was
definitely to be avoided as a disservice to Jewish interests, regardless
of anyone's stand on the war issue itself. In any case, for this and
other reasons, Brandeis agreed with Julian's endorsement of the
compromise with the American Jewish Committee.

The path was then cleared for the epochal American Jewish
Congress that convened in December, 1918—a month after the
armistice that ended World War I. When the Congress met in
Philadelphia, Julian was its president.

27. Wartime Interlude

"He refused to imprison the citizen in the judge, or let the bench contain him," Horace Kallen was to comment about Julian. This was true throughout his judgeship, but especially so during the period when America became involved in the European war.

His leadership in the *ad hoc* American Jewish Congress of 1918 was just one example of his non-judicial activity. Earlier in 1918, he also became president of the newly-formed Zionist Organization of America, successor to the Federation of American Zionists. As for the war itself, it was one of the busiest interludes in his life, for he took on several major activities related to it and did so though there was little, if any, of the martial spirit in him.

His instincts were clearly with those other Americans—perhaps the majority—who preferred that the United States stay out of the war. In the debate that went on, his position was adherence to the strict neutrality that President Wilson had proclaimed—until Wilson himself called for war in April, 1917. This is not to say that Julian Mack was a pacifist. Peace-minded, he supported organizations dedicated to settling international disputes by rule of law instead of by war. He was much troubled by the attacks made upon Jane Addams because of *her* pacifism. But he did not join her in her denunciation of the war spirit or, later, of the war itself. Publicly, he was silent, and basically ambivalent, until Wilson decided the issue.

Yet he entered upon war service wholeheartedly. Indeed, as in the days of Taft, he served as a kind of "trouble-shooter" for the Wilson administration on various problems relating to the war, including the wartime takeover of the railroads by the government. At times, his war work in several fields was so heavy that he had a special office at the Treasury, or in the Interstate Commerce Commission Building, in Washington—a judge who, like the nation, had "gone to war."

In assuming his special wartime tasks, Julian's desire to be patriotically useful was, of course, obvious. But there was more to it than that; more, even, than the motive of personal patriotism. Involved, too, was the matter of the common Jewish "image" with respect to the war, about which he, along with other leaders in the Jewish community, was especially sensitive. For, historically, in practically every nation, war has been a breeder of anti-Semitism. Suspicions as to loyalty, especially concerning people who are in any way "different," or considered to be "different," are easily aroused in wartime. Julian was apprehensive—instinctively, it might be said—that such suspicions would arise also with regard to the American Jewish community after the United States entered the war in 1917. The fact is that these suspicions were rife before and also after America's entry into the war. Both "German" and "Russian" Jews were subjected to vicious, or merely uninformed, attacks on their patriotism, the "German" Jews simply because they were of German origin, and the "Russian" Jews because, as a group, they could hardly have been expected to be enthusiastic supporters of Czarist Russia. *Harper's Weekly* in April, 1916, for example, falsely accused even the American Jewish Committee of being "pro-German." When the Czar was forced to abdicate, in the first phase of the 1917 revolution, just before the United States entered the war, concern over the attitude of the "Russian" Jews diminished. But it did not wholly disappear. Certain public statements made by Jews *before* the United States had entered the war were twisted out of context and used against the Jewish community. Cases in point were a comment by Horace Kallen in the *Menorah Journal* of April, 1915, to the effect that the Yiddish newspapers in America "do not celebrate German victories—they celebrate Russian defeats," and a public statement, that same year, by Jacob Schiff: "It is well known that I am a German sympathizer." Such statements later became grist for the mills of anti-Semitism.

The American Jewish Committee in particular recognized this potentially dangerous situation. At a meeting of its executive committee on November 11, 1917, which Julian attended, the Committee felt obliged to adopt a report that stressed an obvious point: "The Jews of America are just as loyal to the ideals of the United States and just as eager to live and, if need be, to die for them as is any other of the component parts of our citizenship."

Certainly, Julian conducted himself accordingly and thus, in addition to all his other duties, he welcomed every opportunity to serve the government during the war.

In July, 1917, he accepted an appointment to the Advisory Commission of the Council of National Defense. His .main assignment here was to help work out a new program for compensation and aid to dependents of soldiers and sailors killed or wounded in the war, a program that would be an improvement upon the traditional "pension" system. As chairman of the Section on Compensation of the Committee of Labor within the Council of National Defense, under Samuel Gompers, president of the American Federation of Labor, it was he who directed the drafting of the War Risk Insurance Act of 1917. This law provided for the first time in American history—indeed, in the history of any belligerent nation—that servicemen would be able to obtain, at low rates, life insurance up to $10,000, with the government meeting most of the cost. Previously, soldiers and sailors had been considered "uninsurable." Under the new law, veterans of World War I and of subsequent American military actions, including service in Vietnam, ultimately received billions of dollars in "compensation." Likewise, Julian helped draft legislation for the care of wounded servicemen, thus laying the groundwork for the later Veterans Administration.

The War Risk Insurance program, although simple in basic principle, involved many complicated factors and also encountered opposition that had not been fully anticipated. Certain segments of the private insurance industry organized a powerful bloc against it.

In hearings before Congressional committees, it fell to Julian to be a major defender of the program. To the charges that the plan was "socialistic," he retorted that the government insured ships and their cargoes; why, then, should it not insure the lives of its defenders in times of war? "We believe that the government should also do justice to its soldiers and sailors," he added. "If that be socialism, I am willing to stand for socialism."

As it turned out, a majority in both houses of Congress agreed with him and the War Risk Insurance Act was passed.

In May, 1918, he accepted another assignment, this time from Secretary of War Newton D. Baker. "I am touring the country on conscientious objectors," he wrote to Jacob Schiff. In the course of this work, Julian had to visit military establishments in all parts of the country as a member of a board of inquiry to investigate, for

Baker, how the Army was administering the nation's first code for dealing with conscientious objectors. It was an onerous and often heart-wrenching task.

The code provided that if a person was "a member in good faith and in good standing of a well-recognized religious sect or organization . . . whose existing creed or principles forbid its members to participate in war in any form," that person, if he adhered to such a creed, could be excused from combat service. However, he was not exempt from Army control. The alternative to combat duty was assignment to hospital service, and the like, in the Army or, if a man had legitimate scruples against even such duties, to agricultural or similar work at Army pay. Then, too, men who had conscientious objector status but refused to do noncombatant service were court-martialed by the Army in the same manner as men who refused to serve as combatants after having been denied the legal status of conscientious objectors. This provision often led to harsh punishments, for there was little sympathy for "C.O.'s."

Various organizations, including the Civil Liberties Bureau organized by Roger N. Baldwin, gave publicity to charges that in some cases the Army was ignoring the law, that it was acting too harshly in disciplining "recalcitrant" C.O.'s, and that the C.O.'s were being subjected to ugly abuse in various Army camps. It was these cases that Julian and fellow inquiry board members had to investigate.

Secretary Baker, who once had been a pacifist, was especially sensitive to such charges. In appointing Julian to the board of inquiry, along with Harlan F. Stone, the later Chief Justice, Baker obviously sought to give assurance to the protesters that there would be a fair inquiry, which Julian, Dean Stone, and a third member, an open-minded Army officer, did in fact achieve.

The C.O. board held hearings at ten military camps across the country, giving men who had been denied assignment to noncombatant work an opportunity to appeal. Sadly for Julian, in most cases, the appeals had to be denied, for generally they were made by men who, though they were sincere, could not prove membership in religions that forbade military service. The law, which has since been changed, permitted no leeway on that point.

But the board was at least able in various instances to impress upon certain Army officers, who needed the lesson, that there *was* such a thing as legitimate conscientious objection to war.

Except for his association with Stone, a good-humored fellow gourmet, this assignment, as already noted, was not a pleasant one for Julian. The question of conscientious objection raised problems that seemed to pit idealism against patriotism—a tough choice. But it was not in Julian's power to change to any marked extent the hostile military attitudes that prevailed. Besides, the Judge Advocate General's office bitterly challenged the right of the board to review court-martial decisions, though the board had been specifically requested to do so by the War Department. This attitude only served to increase Julian's unhappiness.

Even so, the board obtained leniency in some cases and amnesty for about 100 C.O.'s at Fort Leavenworth at the end of the war. It won praise from such critics of militarism as Miss Addams, Norman Thomas, and Roger Baldwin and prompted the *Survey Graphic* in 1943 to recall of Julian that "champions of civil liberty hailed his humanization of the Army approach to conscientious objectors."

28. "Number One Zionist"—Officially

The end of the war in November, 1918, meant no reduction in Julian's extra-judicial activities. Rather, it brought him increased involvement in Zionist and other Jewish affairs.

In December of that year, the American Jewish Congress was held in Philadelphia in accord with the arrangement agreed upon at the time of Brandeis' confirmation as a member of the Supreme Court.

For Zionism, this event was a major triumph. The Congress, acknowledged by all except the most pronounced anti-Zionist die-hards as the representative voice of American Jewry, substantially approved the Zionist program. It specifically endorsed, among other "peace aims," the establishment of a "Jewish commonwealth" in Palestine.

"It was nothing but a Zionist convention," one die-hard, Dr. Cyrus Adler, complained.

The real meaning of the Congress was this: In America, as elsewhere, the era of exclusive leadership in Jewish affairs by the "Big Names" had passed. Julian had been one of the "Big Names." Now, by collaborating with Brandeis in both Zionism and the Congress movement, he became a major bridge in a significant transition from well-intentioned dominance in Jewish affairs by "the Old Crowd" to a system in which the "little people" had a voice. Implicit in the changeover was the fact that East European Jews, the immigrants whose problems had occupied so much of Julian's career from the 1890's on, were then coming into their own as effective factors in American Jewish life. They had become, in truth, the backbone of the Zionist movement and of the American Jewish Congress.

Julian stressed the choice he had made in this respect by accepting election as president of the American Jewish Congress of 1918—the first American Jewish Congress, it should be noted, to distinguish it from its permanent successor organization by the same name, founded in 1922.

Moreover, prior to the convening of the *ad hoc* American Jewish Congress of December, 1918, he accepted still another major Jewish office—that of president of the Zionist Organization of America. Thus, in June, 1918, at the convention in Pittsburgh that created the Z.O.A., his identification with Zionism became complete, for all the world to see. Julian Mack had become, officially, America's "Number One Zionist."

There were those, then and later, who said that, for all his own prestige, "Judge Mack was merely a stand-in for Brandeis as head of the Z.O.A." Julian did not object to that view. If being Brandeis' "stand-in" meant representing Brandeis' views, then this statement —leaving off "merely"—was largely correct. This was, moreover, exactly the way he saw his role, and with gratification. Stephen S. Wise (then elected a vice-president of the Z.O.A.), Frankfurter, Benjamin V. Cohen, Jacob De Haas, Robert Szold, Eugene Meyer and Horace Kallen, among others in the leadership, all agreed that the leader, indubitably, was still Brandeis. Julian was, in effect, his "prime minister."

Why did Julian, rather than Brandeis, become president of the Z.O.A.?

Of course, the most logical choice for the presidency when the Z.O.A. was formed at the Pittsburgh convention would have been Brandeis. But shortly after Brandeis had gone on the Supreme Court, two years before, there had occurred an incident that brought him great embarrassment and annoyance. At a meeting to discuss the Congress idea, the handsome, mercurial Judah L. Magnes had incredibly questioned the "propriety" of Brandeis' presence there. It was not proper, he suggested, in view of his position as a Justice of the U.S. Supreme Court. Magnes' quibbling remarks got into the press, particularly *The New York Times.* As Julian later told Magnes—rebuking him as Julian seldom did anyone—Brandeis was "outraged."

Not long thereafter, various anti-Semitic publications, such as Henry Ford's *Dearborn Independent,* carried articles insinuating that Brandeis meant to use his position on the Supreme Court to become "King of the Jews." Brandeis' reaction was a determination to forestall repetitions of Magnes' blooper by refraining from public

participation in Zionist affairs. Accordingly, Brandeis' election as
president of the Z.O.A. was out of the question; he did, however,
accept the office of honorary president. He also remained as active
as before, though now on a private level, in Zionist affairs. But from
then on, it was generally assumed that when Julian spoke, or acted,
as president of the Z.O.A. it was Brandeis, too, speaking or acting.
So Julian became the voice as well as the collaborator of Brandeis.

Julian had not sought the honor of becoming the first president of
the Z.O.A. "I reluctantly accepted yesterday the Presidency of the
unified Zionist Organization of America," he wrote, on June 28,
1918, to a young friend, Henry Hurwitz, editor of the *Menorah
Journal*.

This was not false modesty. He genuinely felt that men who had
been active in Zionism much longer—specifically, Stephen S. Wise
and Jacob De Haas—were more entitled to the office if Brandeis was
not available. "There is not the slightest degree of undue humility in
my placing myself below you three," he told Wise.

But both Wise and De Haas had too many critics within the
Zionist movement to be considered seriously for the presidency in
1918, though Wise attained the office in 1936. Besides, neither of the
two men—not even Wise—had the kind of public image then
considered not only desirable but vital for the cause—the image of a
personage highly regarded by non-Jews as well as Jews, including
the leaders of the American Jewish Committee and even more
pronounced non-Zionists. No one filled that order better than
Julian Mack.

By then, all of his earlier ambivalence toward Zionism was gone.
"The problem that interests me most in Jewish affairs today is that of
Zionism," he told Henry Hurwitz. So when the Z.O.A. leadership
made its selection, Mack had no choice but to accept. His election
was nearly unanimous.

The presidency of the Z.O.A. was not an entirely happy period
for Julian. On the surface, his election indicated a harmonious
Zionist organization. But to sophisticated Zionists this was an
over-optimistic view. For, even as far back as the days of Theodor
Herzl, internal harmony had never been a sure aspect of Zionism.

Indeed, many Zionist leaders viewed division and controversy as a healthy climate that served to strengthen Zionism. If so, the Z.O.A., from Pittsburgh on, was destined to be a very strong organization indeed, for simultaneously with Julian's election there were planted seeds of inner conflict. One such seed was the decision that the Z.O.A. should have two administrative secretaries—Jacob De Haas as "general secretary" and Louis Lipsky as "secretary for organization affairs." Both brilliant, both wholly devoted to Zionism, these two men were not destined to work in tandem, personally or ideologically. It took no great gift of prophecy to foresee trouble in the De Haas-Lipsky arrangement.

Moreover, the basic virtue of Julian's election, representing the ascendency of "assimilated" Jews in Zionist leadership, was in reality a fundamental defect. Because of the old mutual distrust that existed between "Eastern" and "Western" Jews, the less "assimilated" Zionist leaders, as typified by Lipsky, later found it easier than might otherwise have been the case to join forces in a revolt against "the Brandeis-Mack group." When the rebellion came, it rocked the Zionist world, leaving lasting scars on many Zionists, including Julian.

Julian was not unaware that unhappy experiences could be in store for him as president of the Z.O.A. He had long been familiar with the simple fact of Zionist life that there were bound to be conflicts over goals as well as means. He himself had been involved in an explosion of divergent views within Zionism as far back as the summer of 1915. While vacationing with Jessie and Ruth at Mackinac Island, he read, to his dismay, a newspaper account of a gathering of Chicago Zionists at which the main speaker had been Pinhas Rutenberg, who later was to create the Palestine Electric Corporation. The report quoted Rutenberg as saying that the proposed Jewish state in Palestine would mean "a nation of which *all* Jews would be citizens," a position not in accord with official Zionism, as Julian understood it.

This piece of news nearly ruined his vacation. For Rutenberg's supposed statement, of course, raised the old bugaboo of "dual allegiance." Making matters worse for Julian, the story erroneously stated that he, Julian, had presided at the Chicago meeting and apparently endorsed the supposed Rutenberg statement.

He sent off an indignant letter to Nathan D. Kaplan, leader of the Chicago Zionists along with Bernard Horwich and Max Shulman.

"That is not my conception of Zionism. So far as political allegiance is concerned, I am an American and my citizenship is single. If a Jewish state is ever established, any Jew in the world will be at liberty to go to Palestine and become a citizen of that state, but he will be at liberty also to retain citizenship in any other political state. . . . I am curious to know whether the Zionists of Chicago, those whom you know, believe that Jews all over the world will become citizens of the Zionist state when it is established and therefore foreigners in their own country."

As it happened, Rutenberg had been misquoted. However, the issue of "dual allegiance" kept recurring, especially outside Zionist ranks. It was raised particularly by Julian's fellow members of the American Jewish Committee. Indeed, Brandeis, to whose attention Julian had called the alleged Rutenberg statement, took the opportunity to urge that Julian give his colleagues on the Committee some special "educating" on the subject. The anti-Zionists on the Committee, Brandeis observed, were harming Jewry by articulating the "dual allegiance" theme against Zionism.

"If there is any way," Brandeis wrote, "in which you can make clear to your friends on the American Jewish Committee, who have been so hostile to Zionism and Zionists, the dangers to which they are thus subjecting our people, you will be performing a very great service."

Julian, in fact, spent much time and energy trying to "make clear" to the Committee members the true Zionist concept of national citizenship. He had some success, but nevertheless, storms were continually aroused on that issue.

Julian himself, as president of the Z.O.A., stirred a squall that continued over a long period, though on an issue other than "dual allegiance." The cause was a well-publicized observation he had made in his presidential address at the 1919 convention of the Z.O.A. in Chicago: "Ninety per cent of all American Jews support the idea of the Jewish homeland in Palestine."

At a later time, such a comment would have been quite innocuous—and quite accurate. But in that day, it sent prominent anti-Zionists into frenzied outbursts, with shouts of "Not true! Not true!"

That such a mild statement could have stirred a violent controversy, and a bitter battle of press releases, was an indication of the shallowness of much of the debate in that era over the hope for a Jewish Palestine. Yet, it was precisely the shallowness of much anti-Zionist thinking that made the most trouble for Julian. Reason, he knew, seldom makes a dent on unreason. It was so with regard to Zionism.

Mainly, however, he concentrated on countering more basic misrepresentations made by anti-Zionist Jews, in particular the allegation of "dual allegiance." But perhaps the best answer to this shallow argument was the fact that such unchallengeably authentic Americans as Brandeis, Wise, Frankfurter, Henrietta Szold, Nathan Straus, and, of course, Judge Julian Mack of the U.S. Circuit Court, were fully committed to Zionism.

29. The Balfour Declaration

To conclude that the presidency of the Z.O.A. was mainly a time of conflict and frustration for Julian—or for the Z.O.A.—would be an error. True, the bitterest conflict still lay ahead. Yet this period was a time also of elation for him, especially as the number of *shekel*-paying Zionists soared by the tens of thousands. Though many converts were later to leave the ranks, the Z.O.A. roster began to include so many "big name" Jews that the Zionist movement seemed synonymous with the American-Jewish Establishment. Even Bernard Baruch became, if not a member, a contributor, as did Adolph Lewisohn and some of the Guggenheims.

As an even greater cause for rejoicing at that time, there was the issuance of the Balfour Declaration, which transformed the whole nature of the Zionist movement, and in the development of which Julian had had a part. In the words of Abba Eban several decades later, it was "the decisive diplomatic victory of the Jewish people in modern history."

Written in the form of a letter from Britain's Foreign Secretary Arthur James Balfour to Lord Lionel Walter Rothschild, honorary president of the Zionist Federation of Great Britain and Ireland, the Balfour Declaration was remarkably brief:

Foreign Office,
November 2, 1917.

Dear Lord Rothschild:

I have much pleasure in conveying to you, on behalf of His Majesty's Government, the following declaration of sympathy with Jewish Zionist aspirations which has been submitted to, and approved by, the Cabinet.

His Majesty's Government view with favour the establishment in Palestine of a national home for the Jewish people, and will use their best endeavours to facilitate the achievement of this object, it being clearly understood that nothing shall be done which may prejudice the civil and religious rights of existing non-Jewish communities in Palestine, or the rights and political status enjoyed by Jews in any other country.

I should be grateful if you would bring this declaration to the knowledge of the Zionist Federation.

Yours,
ARTHUR JAMES BALFOUR

Thus, at last, in the thirteenth year after his death, the hope of Theodor Herzl had been fulfilled: one of the Great Powers had given its support to his Zionist dream.

Contrary to the beliefs of some, that momentous declaration, celebrated by Jews from London to Pinsk, from Washington to Shanghai, did not come out of the blue. As already noted, it had its roots in a memorandum from Herbert Samuel; in the propaganda efforts of Aaron Aaronsohn and others; in semi-official discussions sparked by Sir Mark Sykes, the British Near East expert; and in Christian Biblical and Messianic stirrings along the lines of the Rev. Dr. Blackstone's memorial.

Behind the Declaration, too, were political factors—British war strategy and British aims for the Near East as a whole. Britain's hope was that an "Arab revolt" against Turkey, which Britain had encouraged and made possible, would leave Britain with a strategic foothold in the area—oil, sea lanes, and also Palestine. Another British aim was to increase Jewish support, especially in Russia and the United States, for the Allied cause.

All these motivations, and more, were in, and between, the lines of Lord Balfour's letter.

Obviously, the Balfour Declaration had not been tossed off lightly. Rather, it was the product of many minds, of much consultation, British and international, and of much debate in and out of the Cabinet. The final text was preceded by several drafts. Consideration was given to vigorous opposition from anti-Zionist British Jews. Also taken into account was an agreement—made in

1915, with Lawrence of Arabia in the picture—between Sir Henry McMahon, British High Commissioner to Egypt, and Hussein, Sherif of Mecca, later King of the Hejaz. Another factor was the Sykes-Picot agreement of 1916 between England and France, which provided for the division of certain areas of "influence" after the dismemberment of the Ottoman Empire.

When analyzed to see whether, and to what extent, it intended to be more than a mere endorsement of Zionism, the phraseology of the Balfour Declaration could have appeared unclear to those who wished to see it so. This "unclarity" was "studied," as Felix Frankfurter put it, and so, later on, allowed for divergent views as to its meaning. Yet at the time, the late fall of 1917, it was absolutely clear—and so proclaimed in contemporary official comments—that the intent of the Declaration was a Jewish homeland in Palestine which would eventually become a Jewish state.

Julian clearly understood the Declaration in those terms. For diplomatic reasons; i.e., in order not to agitate non-Zionists needlessly, he refrained from saying so at that moment, but later, defining the views of the Brandeis-Mack leadership, at the 1921 convention of the Z.O.A. in Cleveland, he was to declare openly:

> I have heard it said . . . that the majority in the Zionist Organization of America are not in favor of political Zionism, that they want a few colonies in Palestine, and nothing more. I cannot imagine from what speech, what writing, such misconceptions could have arisen. We believe in a Jewish nationality, and we believe that in the course of time, Palestine will be the Jewish National Homeland in every respect. . . . We want a living, breathing Jewish Nation in Palestine. . . .

For Julian, that affirmation was a momentous personal declaration. For he was well aware that in making it he went against the views of some important American Jews whose good will he valued—Louis Marshall, for example, who, though he helped implement the Balfour Declaration at the Paris Peace Conference, later said that all the Declaration had intended was the protection of Jewish settlements in Palestine and that the concept of a Jewish state was "dead." Julian was also aware of the differing view held by Chaim Weizmann, who, though destined to be Israel's first president, then, and for some time to come, held, at least publicly, to the concept of a Jewish "homeland" only.

Dr. Weizmann's stellar role in the origin and drafting of the Balfour Declaration is, of course, well known. Working with him were other European personages, such as Nahum Sokolow, Leopold J. Greenberg of the *London Jewish Chronicle,* Sir Mark Sykes, James A. Malcolm of the Armenian National Committee, and Rev. Moses H. Gaster, the *Haham* (Chief Rabbi) of the Sephardi community of London. Important roles were also played by members of the British cabinet, by Lord Alfred Milner, its colonial expert, as well as by Prime Minister Lloyd George and, of course, Lord Balfour himself. But among the figures greatly involved in the final draft of the Declaration were the American Zionists Brandeis, Wise, De Haas, Frankfurter—and Julian Mack. They constituted a kind of informal American committee on the Balfour Declaration who went over five basic drafts starting July 17, and ending October 31, 1917, when the British cabinet approved the final text.

How important was Julian's role here? Probably no more important than that of any of the four other American Zionists in the suggestions that were made and accepted, for there were no differences in approach among them. But his part was significant. In particular, he was notably vigilant in helping to change the words "Jewish race," in the draft submitted by Lord Milner on October 4, to "the Jewish *people.*"

Along with Brandeis, De Haas and Wise, Julian also strongly objected to phraseology in the same draft concerning the effect of the Jewish homeland on the status of Jews outside Palestine, on ". . . the rights and political status enjoyed in any other country by such Jews who are *fully contented* with their existing nationality (and citizenship)." When that text, cabled to America by Weizmann on October 10, was received in New York, the point was raised that the language, as Julian later explained, "places Zionism on a principle of discontent, which is most undesirable." So this passage, too, with Julian's help, was altered in the final version.

Another significant revision, also suggested by the Americans, was accepted for the final version. Stephen Wise, in his *Challenging Years,* recalled:

> Wilson sent the document to Justice Brandeis, and the latter forwarded it to me to be handed to Colonel House for transmission to the British Cabinet. De Haas and I were disturbed, as was Judge Julian W. Mack, upon whose wise and judicial counsel we often leaned, by the term in the document, "national home for Jews." De Haas and I bore the draft to Colonel House and suggested the change from "national home for *Jews"* to "national home for *the Jewish People."* House agreed at once to change the phrase and meaning, after discussing it once more with the President, which he did in our presence over a private wire to the White House.

Some of the foregoing, especially the references to Wilson and House, may be apocryphal, a consequence of confused or clouded memories after thirty years. But the textual change was made substantially as Wise related. It was a vital change, related to the concept of the Jewish state, and there is no doubt that Julian played a role in this phase of the transatlantic editing.

This belaboring of the historical record, all well documented, has been necessitated by the nature of much that has been written about the origins of the Balfour Declaration. For there developed a tendency to ignore, even to disavow, any American role in the text of the Declaration, let alone its implementation. Weizmann in particular once exhibited in public a curious aberration on this point. It occurred at the 1921 convention of the Z.O.A. in Cleveland after Stephen Wise, as a Brandeis-Mack partisan, had irritated Weizmann by declaring:

> I do not wish to detract from the honors that rightly sit upon the brow of Dr. Weizmann, and yet I must declare publicly, that it becomes a matter of public knowledge—Dr. Weizmann will be the first to admit it when he later speaks—the Balfour Declaration would never have been issued had it not been for

the moral prestige and loyal support of Justice Brandeis and his
associated American leaders.

Wise was then referring primarily to the *issuance* of the
Declaration. Weizmann's response, in a later speech, was:

> . . . Of course, they have rendered sterling serv-
> ice . . . [but] It is said, it is circulated, that the Balfour
> Declaration was framed here in America, was made here, that
> the text of this declaration was really framed here. There is not
> a vestige of truth in that statement. This is all I have to
> say. . . .

Obviously, Weizmann's memory, even so shortly after the event,
had become vague. However, he partially corrected himself after
Julian sent him a telegram reminding him of at least one revision "of
great importance" that had been suggested by the American
Zionists in October, 1917.

Weizmann had a great admiration for Julian. "Judge Mack," he
later told the 1921 convention, "is the one I am willing to go out of
my way for." Hence, on the next day, he gracefully admitted his
error in the matter of the Declaration.

> I am glad to take this opportunity [he told the convention] of
> making a correction in my speech of yesterday. I said that I
> heard here that the Balfour Declaration was framed here, was
> made here, and I said it is not true. In that form, it is not true.
> The Balfour Declaration was framed in London, as I said.
> [But] a change in the second part of the Balfour Declaration,
> as I find out now, was introduced here [in America] in the
> change in one phrase in the second part. It is considered an
> important change. . . .

"In the interest of truth, I will read a telegram from Judge Mack,"
he then added, thus setting the record straight.

But more important, to be sure, than to trace the evolution of the
text of the Balfour Declaration is to understand how it came to be

issued at all. Simply as a statement by the British Cabinet, the Declaration alone could not have led to the establishment of a Jewish homeland, for it had to be accepted by Britain's war allies, particularly the United States and France. In this area especially, certain facts about the origin of the Balfour Declaration still remain obscure half a century later. But two facts are evident. First, that the British mandate over Palestine, in accord with the Balfour Declaration, would never have been established by the League of Nations without the approval of the United States; and second, that the British Cabinet would never have issued the Declaration itself had it not been satisfied that President Wilson approved of it. All accounts agree that in this crucial aspect of the Declaration, the American Zionists, with Brandeis as the outstanding figure, were the vital factor.

Enter then here, in the scenario, President Wilson and his *alter ego* in foreign affairs, Colonel Edward M. House. Both men had high regard for Brandeis. If anyone could influence either of the two, it was Justice Brandeis.

As regards Wilson's attitude toward Zionism, the generally held view is reflected in Stephen Wise's *Challenging Years:*

> From the very beginning of his administration, Brandeis and I knew that in Wilson we had and would always have understanding sympathy with the Zionist program and purpose. . . . As I urged him one day to cooperate with the British government *re* the hope of the Balfour Declaration, he was touched, and soliloquized aloud, "To think that I, a son of the manse, should be able to help restore the Holy Land to its people!"

The conventional view was that Colonel House's position on Jewish Palestine corresponded to that of his chief.

Secretive and astute, House was a complicated personality, idealist and pragmatist at the same time. Since he greatly admired Brandeis for similar qualities, the general assumption was that he sympathized strongly with the Jews and Brandeis' Zionist program. In the end, so far as the available records show, he did help expedite the Declaration and its implementation. As De Haas notes in his masterly *History of Palestine,* all negotiations on the Declaration passed through House as well as Wilson.

Yet House was not, in fact, so dependable as was assumed. At times his conduct in regard to the Declaration was in direct contrast to what Wise had reported from London to De Haas on April 9, 1917:

> He is enlisted in our cause. There is no question about it whatever.

The truth is that there was some doubt about the attitude of Colonel House. As Balfour, for one, noted, House was sometimes guilty of anti-Semitism, and Leonard Stein, later political secretary of the World Zionist Organization and historian of the Declaration, was to state flatly that "House clearly disliked Jews and was irritated by the Zionists."

Had House had an independent personal choice, there probably would have been no American support for the Balfour Declaration.

The fact seems to have been that both Wilson and House—the two men were psychologically one, at the time—had to be kept in line. To do so was uniquely the task of Louis D. Brandeis; it was his vital and supreme contribution to the issuance of the Balfour Declaration.

Did the British Cabinet feel that it had Wilson's approval before Balfour handed his "Dear Lord Rothschild" letter to Chaim Weizmann? The answer, presumably, is yes.

Yet the way in which Wilson's approval was—or in fact was not—communicated presents a curious study in political and diplomatic obfuscation. The truth appears to be that Wilson behaved in a markedly ambivalent manner with respect to the issuance of the Declaration. This was so despite all his personal expressions to Stephen Wise and Brandeis and despite a favorable public statement made at the White House to a Jewish delegation, headed by Julian, *after* the Declaration had been issued. It may be that except for private, even secret, conversations with Brandeis, Balfour, and Sir William Wiseman, Wilson had gone no further officially than to hint to the British that he favored the Declaration, letting the Declaration be issued without any objection, while Brandeis served as conduit for Wilson's effective favorable hints at the critical point of the deliberations in London. The fact is that in October, 1917, when an official endorsement was requested by the British, and when it appeared that without his sanction the Declaration might never be issued at all, Wilson withheld direct official, or even "personal," communication on the matter.

What kind of charade was Wilson, champion of "open convenants, openly arrived at," conducting in the fall of 1917? Did he want to be in a position of saying that not he, but the British, were responsible for the disposition of Palestine?

The answer here might explain a riddle that meant considerable nervousness for Julian and his associates so long as Wilson was President. Julian, Brandeis, Wise, and their colleagues in America, as well as Weizmann and his associates in Europe, were all kept on tenterhooks by the "son of the manse" for months as to whether or not there would be a declaration at all. The pattern emerged notably in May, 1917, after the United States had become Britain's ally in the war and Lord Balfour had visited Washington. As Britain's foreign secretary, Balfour had come to the United States to cement the alliance. On his agenda, among other items, was Palestine.

It is now known that Balfour then informed Wilson of various secret agreements, no doubt including those made by British agents with France and Arab leaders concerning the Ottoman Empire, later called "the loot of the war." And Balfour not only talked with Wilson, but significantly also with Brandeis, who by then was functioning both as a Justice of the Supreme Court and as consultant to Wilson on problems related to the war.

As a consequence, Brandeis, on May 15, 1917, cabled to London, through State Department facilities, a message intended for Weizmann's information and to be passed on, to the effect that talks conducted by himself and Balfour with Wilson about Palestine had been "satisfactory."

This intelligence, however, was "not for publication," a specification which left the British Cabinet, as well as Weizmann, puzzled and unhappy, despite the accepted excuse for Wilson's reticence that the United States was not at war with Turkey and hence should not be involved—at least not publicly—in her dismemberment.

Meanwhile, the British Zionists were having trouble with British officials over the proposed declaration. As Weizmann suggests in his autobiography, the situation, in September, 1917, was apparently touch and go. French diplomats were balking. There had also mushroomed powerful opposition from anti-Zionist British Jews, voiced in particular by Herbert Samuel's cousin, Edwin Montagu, Secretary of State for India.

Behind Montagu was a group of Jews called the Conjoint Foreign Committee. Founded in 1878 jointly by the Board of Deputies of British Jews and the Anglo-Jewish Association—two British counterparts of the American Jewish Committee—this body acted as a "Foreign Office" for Jewish affairs. Its members raised the old bugaboos about "Jewish nationalism," which they abhorred, and about "dual allegiance," which they professed to fear, in order to jettison the proposed Balfour Declaration.

Montagu's statements suggested hysteria. Yet, he was influential enough to get the Declaration removed at one point from the agenda of the British Cabinet.

On September 4, 1917, Robert Cecil, Balfour's aide in the British Foreign Office, and, incidentally, a friend of Frankfurter and an admirer of Julian, sent a desperate cable to Colonel House:

> We are being pressed for a declaration of sympathy for the Zionist movement . . . [S]hould be very grateful if you felt able to ascertain unofficially if the President favours such a declaration.

House's response was to send Cecil's cable to Wilson, at the same time warning the President against expressing himself. In the Zionist movement "there are many dangers," he wrote to Wilson on September 7.

As a consequence, Cecil received no answer from Washington until September 11, when House finally cabled that Wilson felt "the time was not opportune for any definite statement, further, perhaps, than one of sympathy, provided it can be made without conveying any real commitment."

That dash of cold water was perhaps more House than Wilson. Undoubtedly, however, House administered it with Wilson's permission.

Weizmann then went into action with appeals to Brandeis. In one appeal, dated September 19, he included a proposed text for the Declaration, adding:

> May expect opposition from assimilationist quarters. Would greatly help if President Wilson and yourself would support text. Matter most urgent.

There were then two new main obstacles. First, there was the opposition from the Jewish Establishment in England, where a vociferously anti-Zionist "League of British Jews," similar to the later "American Council for Judaism," had been formed. Second, there was the reluctance of France to go along with the proposal.

Brandeis then understood that he would have to proceed with special caution. His first reaction was to suggest to Weizmann, presumably after talking with Colonel House, that Weizmann should get French and Italian diplomats to ask Wilson where he stood. The idea, apparently, was that, by this strategy, Wilson would be smoked out. After a second thought, however, Brandeis did a bold thing. On his own, he sent a cable—one backed up by his status as Supreme Court Justice and as a recognized close adviser to the President—stating flatly to Weizmann that "the President was in entire sympathy."

As a follow-up, Brandeis asked Colonel House to send Wilson a supporting memorandum. Colonel House acceded to Brandeis' request on October 7. The result, however, was more tension. For Wilson tucked House's memorandum away with a seeming casualness that doubtless would have appalled Brandeis, had he known.

In the end Wilson did respond. "I find in my pocket," Wilson wrote to House on October 13, 1917, "the memorandum you gave me about the Zionist movement. I am afraid I did not say to you that I concurred in the formula suggested from the other side. I do, and would be obliged if you would let them know it."

In the meantime, before Colonel House acted, and after a new and final draft of the Declaration had been prepared, London kept pressing for a more definite commitment from Wilson. Thus, on October 7, Weizmann cabled Brandeis:

> Most likely shall be asked to appear before the cabinet when final discussion takes place in about a week. It is essential to have not only President's approval of the text, but his recommendation to grant this declaration without delay. . . . Your support urgently needed.

Brandeis again got in touch with House. On October 16, House at last complied with Wilson's instruction to let the British Cabinet know where he stood. Thus satisfied by both Brandeis and House, the British Cabinet finally approved the Declaration for issuance.

Pertinent to the foregoing is the summation by R.H.S. Crossman, the British journalist-historian, from a perspective of 45 years, in the July, 1962 issue of *Commentary*:

"In 1917, the [U.S.] State Department was already resolutely anti-Zionist and it was only Brandeis' influence that saved the day."

The Secretary of State at the time was Robert E. Lansing. He did not approve of Zionist aims. This attitude was to pervade the State Department from then on; it was a stance with which more than one future President would have to contend. Lansing showed his colors clearly in a communication to Wilson on December 13, 1917. The communication, discovered in State Department files, called Wilson's attention to a number of requests that the United States make known publicly in a clear fashion its official position with respect to the Balfour Declaration, then some six weeks old.

"This emanates naturally from the Zionist element of the Jews," Lansing dourly advised the President. He went on to state that he was opposed to announcing any policy on "the final disposition of Palestine." Lansing then gave Wilson three reasons for this advice: first, that the United States had not declared war on Turkey; second, that "the Jews are by no means a unit in the desire to reestablish their race as an independent people"; and third, "that many Christian sects and individuals would undoubtedly resent turning the Holy Land over to the absolute control of the race credited with the death of Christ."

As might have been expected, Lansing's incredible third point produced an uproar when a somewhat garbled version of it became public. It was Julian who quieted down the unwanted ruckus with a public statement to the effect that Lansing had been misquoted and misinterpreted. Keeping in mind that Zionism had enemies in high places, Julian stated, with diplomatic equivocation, that Lansing was "really a friend of the Zionists"—though, in fact, the Secretary was not.

As for Wilson's reaction, Lansing noted at a cabinet meeting the next day that Wilson said that he was "forced to agree" with Lansing's letter, although "very unwillingly." According to Lansing, Wilson further observed that he "had an impression"—strange phrase—"that we had assented to the British declaration regarding returning Palestine to the Jews." But no statement on the Declaration, one way or another, was issued. Thus, Lansing had his way—temporarily.

To counter this stance, Stephen Wise, on August 27, 1918, went to see Wilson. A consummate persuader and a factor in Wilson's two elections, Rabbi Wise thereupon received a letter from Wilson, dated August 31, 1918, expressing the President's "satisfaction" over "the progress of the Zionist movement."

Later, Wilson made an even stronger pro-Zionist statement to a delegation from the newly-founded American Jewish Congress, headed by Julian, which called on the President at the White House on March 2, 1919. The meeting took place against the background of the Paris Peace Conference, from which Wilson had just returned for his celebrated "recess" and to which Julian's delegation was then preparing to go. A message to the President signed by 299 anti-Zionist Jews was then receiving wide circulation. Its burden was that the idea of a Jewish homeland should be scrapped altogether because of the alleged "danger" of "dual allegiance." This was a stab in the back, as Julian wryly noted, promoted largely by Julius Kahn, a Jewish congressman from California, and the

Cincinnati Reform rabbi, Dr. David Philipson, then president of the Central Conference of American Rabbis, who had officiated at Julian's wedding.

It was to counter this anti-Zionist attack that, together with Louis Marshall, Bernard G. Richards and Stephen Wise, Julian went to the White House that day in March, 1919. The delegation, after presenting Wilson with a "Memorial on Palestine" prepared by the American Jewish Congress, obtained the following statement from the President:

> I have before this expressed [to Rabbi Wise] my personal approval of the Declaration of the British Government regarding the aspirations and historic claims of the Jewish people in regard to Palestine. I am, moreover, persuaded that the Allied nations with the fullest concurrence of our Government and people are agreed that in Palestine there shall be laid the foundations of a Jewish Commonwealth.

By using the expression "Jewish Commonwealth," Wilson set off an uproar. The phrase, as related by Professor Frank E. Manuel in his study, *The Realities of American-Palestine Relations,* aroused dismay among certain Arabs in Cairo and also placed the American peace delegation "in a quandary." The U.S. adviser on "West Asia," William Linn Westermann, asked for an explanation from Wilson, who by then had returned to Paris. Westermann suggested that Wilson "either support his statement or outrightly deny the sponsorship of a Jewish Commonwealth."

"Wilson's reply was evasive," Manuel's account continues. His statement, the President said, had not been intended for quotation.

> All Wilson intended to do was to reiterate his support of the Balfour Declaration; he was specific in stating that the phrase "Jewish Commonwealth" went a "little further than" his intentions at that time. . . . The public use of the term "Jewish Commonwealth" by the President stood uncontradicted; Wilson then told the Commissioners in confidence that he had not meant anything more than the original Balfour Declaration.

Be that as it may, the fact that Wilson "meant" the Balfour Declaration seemed victory enough to the Zionists.

Wilson clearly understood that the British Cabinet, in issuing the Balfour Declaration, intended that a Jewish state should eventually be founded in Palestine. This had been made especially plain by David Lloyd George, the wartime Prime Minister, with whom Wilson had worked closely on the matter. "There could be no doubt as to what the Cabinet had in their minds," Lloyd George was to testify before the Palestine Royal Commission in 1937. "It was not their idea that a Jewish State should be set up immediately by the Peace Treaty. . . . On the other hand, it was contemplated that when the time arrived for according representative institutions to Palestine, if the Jews had meanwhile responded to the opportunity afforded them . . . and had become a definite majority of the inhabitants, then Palestine would thus become a Jewish Common- wealth."

Still later, in February, 1920, Wilson expressed to Secretary Lansing quite ardent support of the Declaration. At that time, the boundaries of Palestine were still under discussion by a conference of ambassadors in Paris. As president of the Z.O.A., Julian, together with others, had cabled a protest against the narrow boundaries that were being proposed, and Brandeis sent to Wilson a strongly worded letter on the matter. Narrow boundaries for the Jewish Homeland, he told Wilson, "would be a betrayal of the promises of Christendom." Wilson's response, though then unpublicized, once more put his support of Jewish Palestine on record in the State Department files. In forwarding Brandeis' "impressive" letter to Lansing, Wilson wrote:

> All the great powers are committed to the Balfour Declaration, and I agree with Mr. Justice Brandeis, regarding it as a solemn promise which we can in no circumstance afford to break or alter.

Such was one aspect of Wilson's record, but only one. As already noted, Wilson to the end had avoided making any direct communication to the British Cabinet on where he stood on

Palestine while the Cabinet was debating the issue. His record is further blurred by his refusal to send a greeting to the 1919 convention of the Z.O.A. in Chicago, where Julian was reelected president for a second term. His excuse was that the "delicate and dangerous" postwar world situation, including his ill-fated struggle for U.S. acceptance of the League of Nations, made such a greeting "imprudent."

Then, too, the memorandum which he wrote on the subject to his secretary, Joseph P. Tumulty, was hardly in accord with Stephen Wise's assessment of Wilson's attitude toward "the promoters of the Zionist movement."

"These gentlemen know the helpful position which the Government of the United States has assumed in this matter, and are a little too insistent upon a constant asseveration of our interest and sympathy," Wilson wrote.

A similar rebuff was tendered to Wise himself the following year when Wise, through Tumulty, asked to send a message to Wilson to the 1920 convention of the Z.O.A. in Buffalo that May, in celebration of the establishment of the British mandate over Palestine. Wilson made this penciled notation on Wise's request: "No. W.W."

How are we to explain Wilson's curious ambiguity, if indeed it was that? Was he shrewdly playing a double role to please Brandeis while seeking not to offend such Jewish anti-Zionists as Henry Morgenthau, Sr., who had been the finance chairman of his election campaign? Was he trying also to avoid offending another big campaign contributor, Charles R. Crane of the Chicago plumbing family? Crane was associated with both Julian and Brandeis in various social welfare causes, but he strongly opposed a Jewish Palestine. Was the President overly influenced by Crane's expressed admiration for "the Christian colleges in Beirut and Damascus," which then, as later, were powerhouses of pro-Arab agitation? Was he appeasing the State Department "crowd" that was traditionally opposed to any undertaking on behalf of Jews? Did he have qualms about supporting Britain's policy for the Middle East because he considered it not in accord with his proclaimed policy of the "self-determination of peoples"? Or was he wary of potential involvement in secret commitments and agreements among the British, the French, and assorted Arab sheiks, in view of the fact that he had proclaimed an end to "secret diplomacy"?

Perhaps the answers to these questions could be supplied only by the study made of Wilson, the idealist-politician, by Sigmund Freud in collaboration with William C. Bullitt. But the basic fact remains that Wilson did place, if at times indirectly, the sanction of the United States behind the Zionist dream, thanks in large part to Louis D. Brandeis, and also to Stephen Wise.

To be sure, the man who brilliantly masterminded the negotiations with the British Cabinet was Chaim Weizmann. Curiously in his memoirs, published over three decades later, Weizmann downgrades the role of Brandeis. But at the time the Declaration was issued, Weizmann was quite gracious in sharing credit with Brandeis.

"I need hardly say," he wrote to Brandeis on November 12, 1917, "how we all rejoice in this great event and how grateful we all feel to you for the valuable and efficient help which you have lent to the cause in this critical hour."

In his autobiography, Nahum Goldmann, for many years president of the World Zionist Organization, wrote of Brandeis:

> Brandeis occupies a major place in the Pantheon of Zionist leaders. If it had not been for his influence on Wilson, who in turn influenced the British government, the Balfour Declaration would probably never have been issued. And it is he who deserves the major credit for the essentially pro-Zionist policy of the American administrations of Roosevelt and Truman.

And Julian? More often than not his role would not even be mentioned in connection with the victory. Yet, as noted, his part had been considerable, in terms of specific details, and also because he was one of the inner circle, with all that this meant in terms of prestige and psychological support. As befitted his character, however, he was satisfied that chief credit should go to Brandeis; to Frankfurter for his important work for the cause, both in London and later in Paris; to Stephen Wise; to Jacob De Haas—and, of course, to Aaron Aaronsohn, who also had been effectively busy at the time in London and Paris. To be given "credit," however much deserved, was never important to Julian. One thing is certain: no one was more pleased than he that the Declaration had been issued. Aside from all else, it gave him, in his proselytizing for Zionism, a new argument with non-Zionist and even anti-Zionist friends. The idea of a Jewish homeland, he now argued, was "a war measure," and therefore to be supported if for no other reason but sheer patriotism. It was a powerful argument, to the discomfiture of the remaining die-hards.

He recognized, of course, that the Declaration by itself did not guarantee that the Homeland would indeed be established. Ben-Gurion put it correctly: the Balfour Declaration was "not self-enforcing." The Jews would have to fight for its implementation. Julian also recognized something else. Like most assimilated Jewish leaders, he had deplored the concept of "a Jewish vote," even though he had obtained his own judicial posts mainly due to the need of Mayor Harrison, and later President Taft, for the "Jewish vote." But the Balfour experience made plain to him one political fact of life: When the chips were down, politicians acted favorably on Jewish aims and needs because of practical pressures, including the votes and other political "clout" of Jews who spoke and voted as Jews. In all probability, he was forced to see that to a great extent even Woodrow Wilson was so motivated.

One other fact of life became clear to Julian, also in connection with Wilson. It was that even liberals, who were usually considered to bear good will toward Jews, could not always be counted upon to understand Jewish needs and aspirations; at times, like some elements in socialism, they would make common cause with the enemies of the Jews. To a Jew of Julian's background and outlook, the recognition that he could not trust all liberals on the Jewish "question," and specifically on Palestine, was a jolt. It did not shake him out of the liberal camp but it did cause him much perplexity and, at times, much pain.

30. War's End

Quite aside from the Balfour Declaration, the period of Julian's presidency of the Z.O.A.—from 1918 to 1921—was notably productive in other ways. For one thing, at the 1918 convention in Pittsburgh, the Z.O.A. adopted a set of principles that meant vital inspiration, albeit later some controversy, for the Jewish homeland in Palestine.

Highly Brandeisian in economic and social slant, these principles, known in Zionist literature as "The Pittsburgh Program," were intended as a code of social justice to guide the practical work of rebuilding Palestine:

> *First:* We declare for political and civil equality irrespective of race, sex, or faith of all the inhabitants of the land.
>
> *Second:* To insure in the Jewish National Home in Palestine equality of opportunity, we favor a policy which, with regard to existing rights, shall tend to establish the ownership and control by the whole people of the land, of all natural resources and of all public utilities.
>
> *Third:* All land, owned and controlled by the whole people, should be leased on such conditions as will insure the fullest opportunity for development and continuity of possession.
>
> *Fourth:* The cooperative principle should be applied so far as feasible in the organization of all agricultural, industrial, commercial and financial undertakings.
>
> *Fifth:* The system of free public instruction, which is to be established, should embrace all grades and departments of education.
>
> *Sixth:* Hebrew, the national language of the Jewish people, shall be the medium of public instruction.

The "Pittsburgh Program" was especially pleasing to liberal and labor Zionists even though the Po'ale Zion, the Labor Zionist party, remained outside the Z.O.A. The euphoric reaction of Henrietta Szold was typical. "I felt as though Isaiah and Amos were with us," she wrote to a friend about the Pittsburgh convention.

But there were hurdles ahead. One was the Peace Conference set to open in Paris six months later. To what extent would the leaders of the Great Powers act in Paris to ameliorate the plight of the Jews in Eastern Europe? How seriously would they consider the Balfour Declaration? These were crucially troubling questions. And by no means was there agreement on their solution among Jewish leaders in America, or abroad, let alone among the non-Jewish statesmen of the Powers.

On one postwar issue, however, there was unity among American Jewish leaders. They were determined that a massive effort of fund raising and fund distribution had to be mounted in behalf of all Jewish victims of the war, in Europe as well as in Palestine. Food, clothing, housing, medical care, transportation for homeless thousands, and commercial credit were required on an unprecedented scale for succoring the uprooted Jewish communities in Poland, Russia, Rumania, and Hungary.

The picture of the disaster suffered by European Jews, as portrayed by Horace Kallen, was labeled in some quarters as exaggerated. But Herbert Hoover, President Wilson's food administrator during the war, for one, shows in his book, *An American Epic,* that the extent of the tragedy was not overstated. Of Poland, where most of the stricken Jews were living, Hoover recalled:

> The homes of millions had been destroyed and many were living in hovels built of the rubble. . . . Industry was suspended . . . millions were destitute. . . . Typhus and other contagious diseases raged over whole provinces.

Hoover did not, however, mention an additional burden borne by the Jews: Anti-Semitism contrived to bar Jews from getting assistance through regular relief channels. Such help as they could expect had to come mainly from fellow Jews elsewhere. Over all, too, there was the specter of pogroms, some instigated because Jews were being succored by fellow Jews, others politically incited by Polish rightists on the allegation that "all the Jews sympathized with the Bolsheviks in Russia."

In all the various activities of Jewish organizations that went into action on behalf of European Jewry, Julian was deeply involved. Indeed, for some time he gave these concerns precedence even over Zionism. But the *Yishuv* was not overlooked. Fund raising for Palestine's Jewish community was stepped up to help it recover from the setbacks of the war and to enhance its ability to absorb new settlers. How active Julian was in all this was suggested by Stephen Wise's statement at the 1921 Cleveland convention:

> Mack, [Abba Hillel] Silver, and I together secured one-half to three-fourths of the money raised in America during the last five years for the Zionist cause.

All American Jews, Reform, Conservative, and Orthodox; Zionist, non-Zionist, and anti-Zionist; the irreligious and the mystically pious; the B'nai B'rith and other fraternal organizations; the women's organizations; labor and socialist Jews, along with "the rich"—all were enlisted in the appeal for funds for Palestine. Significantly, even Jewish elements still opposed to Zionism as such joined in that effort. Their rationale, one that Julian took great pains to encourage, was simple: Palestine was a haven for Jews in trouble, hence it was not to be boycotted, not by the most rigid anti-Zionists, not even by men such as Rabbi Hirsch, and certainly not by such outstanding "non-Zionists" as Louis Marshall, Felix Warburg, Herbert Lehman, and Julius Rosenwald, among others usually associated with the American Jewish Committee set. Their zeal in fund raising—and in making donations themselves—for fellow Jews, no matter where they might be—was sufficient to fulfill even the greatest expectations. Rosenwald alone, to Julian's particular satisfaction, gave what up to then had been the largest single charity contribution in either Jewish or American history for any one emergency cause—a check in the amount of one million dollars.

But it was not all rosy for Julian and his associates. Conflicts, some quite acrimonious, over budget allocations, were frequent. For example, though no one questioned the need to help Palestine, the extent to which relief funds should go there was often a matter of controversy. There was particular bitterness, especially among Zionists, when huge sums were raised to settle Jews in the Russian Crimea, a misbegotten project viewed by some as a substitute for rebuilding the Jewish homeland in Palestine.

In this dispute, Julian, despite his Zionism, characteristically took a middle ground. The Russian settlement should be helped *also*, he told Stephen Wise. He therefore declined to join in attacks on Julius Rosenwald and others who supported the Russian project. Again here and in other disputes, Julian's penchant for conciliation was at work, a major contribution to the general effort that saved the lives of hundreds of thousands of European Jews in a tragedy that was to be exceeded only by the Hitler holocaust.

Meanwhile, in December, 1918, there took place in Philadelphia the long anticipated meeting of the first American Jewish Congress, an epochal gathering. As Julian stated in his opening address as president of the Congress, it was the first time in American history "that Jews of all classes and factions have come together to deliberate for the welfare of the race."

His use of that once "horrid" word, "race," did not go unnoticed. Nor did the fact that he, the "Number One Zionist," had been chosen overwhelmingly as the leader of the Congress. This was a tribute to his personality and status, but, more important, it betokened recognition at last that the Zionists were an authentic element of the American Jewish community, a peer group along with the American Jewish Committee and the B'nai B'rith.

Most of them were there, the outstanding American Zionists, Louis Lipsky, Stephen Wise, Nachman Syrkin, Henrietta Szold, Horace Kallen, Felix Frankfurter, Robert Szold and Nathan Straus, Sr., among others. So, too, were some outstanding non-Zionists, such as Jacob Schiff, Louis Marshall, Henry Morgenthau, Sr., Adolph Kraus, and Cyrus Adler. There were socialists and financiers; lawyers, doctors, and merchants; trade unionists; representatives of Hadassah and the National Council of Jewish

Women; rabbis and other religious figures, notably faculty members of the Jewish Theological Seminary and of the Hebrew Union College; journalists; agnostics and believers; charity workers; intellectuals and the little-known "rank and file." Jews of the full spectrum of occupations and interests all joined, as Julian noted, for the common goal of helping other Jews regardless of nationality, denomination, or politics.

A dream of unity such as a Herzl might have envisioned had become reality.

Epochal, too, was the program adopted by the Congress. It included the basic decision that Jews should participate in the deliberations of the Paris Peace Conference and in the formulation of the peace treaties—as Jews. This was a major break with the previous tradition in America that Jews should not act as a separate group in general political affairs. In line with that decision Julian Mack, of the Zionist organization, and Louis Marshall, of the American Jewish Committee, were designated to lead a delegation to Paris—a clear signal that the Zionists and non-Zionists intended to cooperate. It was clear, too, that the Zionists were to be in the ascendancy. Julian was named chairman of the delegation, of which the majority was Zionist.

The delegation was given two main instructions. One was to work with other delegations to implement, at Paris, a Jewish "Bill of Rights" which had been adopted by the Congress, and which dealt with the rights of the millions of Jews in Eastern Europe who were to become citizens of the nations to be established, or enlarged, under the peace treaties—notably Poland, Rumania and Czecho-slovakia. The "Bill of Rights" called for the inclusion in those treaties of provisions guaranteeing "minority rights" for Jews along with other national minority groups. The agreements were to assure that all citizens "without distinction as to race, nationality, or creed" should "enjoy equal civil, political, and national rights"; that minority representation in legislatures and parliaments was to be provided for by law; that national as well as religious bodies were to be "accorded autonomous management of their own communal institutions," including schools; that no laws were to be enacted restricting the use of any language; and that the right of Jews to observe Saturday as their Sabbath would be protected.

In short, the American Jewish delegation was instructed to work in Paris to achieve a revolution in the historical situation of East European Jewry.

But more lastingly significant, in view of the eventual fate of European Jewry, was the other instruction given by the Congress to the delegation; namely, a specific directive with regard to Palestine. The delegation was

> to cooperate with the representatives of other Jewish organizations, and specifically with the World Zionist Organization, to the end that the Peace Conference may declare that, in accordance with the British Government's Declaration of November 2d, 1917 . . . there shall be established such political, administrative and economic conditions in Palestine as will assure, under the trusteeship of Great Britain, acting on behalf of such League of Nations as may be formed, the development of Palestine into a Jewish Commonwealth. . . .

Thus the 1918 Congress, going further than even Julian had thought prudent to urge, adopted, *in toto*, the Zionist dream. One young woman delegate, a member of Po'ale Zion, wrote of the proceedings to her husband in Milwaukee:

> . . . some moments reached such heights that, after them, one could have died happily. You should have been in the Hall when the resolution for Palestine was adopted. There were only two votes against it—German Jews. The Po'ale Zion played a tremendous part in the Congress. . . .

The delegate was Golda Meyerson, later known as Golda Meir.

Yet Julian, while also exultant, was not wholly euphoric as he adjourned the Philadelphia session. For the Allied peacemakers, including Wilson, Lloyd George, France's Clemenceau, and Italy's Orlando, with their entourages, were already meeting in Paris and reports of confusion were numerous. To begin with, the situation in Russia, where the Bolsheviks were gaining control, was disturbingly ambiguous.

Would Russia, under the Bolsheviks, directly or indirectly, help or hinder arrangements for a decent peace? Would Bolshevism become entrenched in Russia and, if so, how would the Jews be treated? Could the anti-Zionist Bolsheviks, among whom there were a number of Jews, be depended on to keep a pledge to outlaw anti-Semitism or would Jews in the "new" Russia still face discrimination and worse? At the time no one knew the answers to these questions, but the implications hung like a cloud over Paris and all the peace negotiations.

As for Poland, location of the main body of European Jewry, Julian, along with Louis Marshall, had had some equally disturbing conferences with Polish leaders, including the pianist-statesman Ignace Paderewski. These meetings left the distinct impression that the liberated "free Poland," which was expected to emerge from Paris, would be no land of freedom for the Polish Jews. Plainly, Paderewski, who was to become the first premier and foreign minister of Poland, was subservient to anti-Semitic demagogues, in particular one Roman Dmowski, leading agitator for a boycott of all Jewish businesses in Poland. Moreover, actual pogroms were being threatened or carried out, not only in the new Poland, but also in Galicia and in Rumania.

In November, 1918, Julian, as president of the Z.O.A., had received an alarming cable from London:

> . . . alarming news from absolutely reliable sources: Jews of all East European countries threatened by greatest danger. . . Wild agitation rousing basest instincts everywhere, especially Rumania-Poland. . . . Posters incite slaughter of Jews. . . . Black Hundred receiving arms from army, while Jewish self-defense impossible [due to] lack of arms. . . . At Warsaw Jews attacked in streets, and shops demolished, plundered. . . . Chief Commander Polish forces, General Vitold Orski, in proclamation dated October 8, denounces Jews as leaders [of] Bolshevism . . . all rabbis and directors [of]

schools, synagogues to be shot moment of beginning
Bolshevist activity. . . . Jewish population regards only hope
immediate effective international intervention. . . . In name
of these millions we urge help. Fulfill your duty, help save our
brethren.

Julian alerted not only the Z.O.A., but also other organizations,
such as the American Jewish Committee, the B'nai B'rith, to the
peril described in that cable. Mass meetings, as at the time of the
Kishinev pogroms, were held in New York, Chicago, and other
cities, all with the theme that the Peace Conference should *impose*
the "Jewish Bill of Rights" on the new nations—with the American
Jewish Committee, incidentally, more ardent in that regard than it
had been before Julian had presented them with the cable from
London. Louis Marshall in particular rejected outright the fears of
other non-Zionists that securing so-called "minority rights" for Jews
implied a "dangerous" recognition of Jewish "nationalism."

It was against this background that on March 6, 1919, four days
after the meeting with Wilson at the White House on the Balfour
Declaration, Julian sailed for Paris, to join other Jewish delegates
already there. He had an interesting Zionist companion on the S.S.
Aquitania on that voyage—Bernard G. Richards, the Boston
journalist who had so severely criticized Julian for his testimony
before the 1909 U.S. Immigration Commission on the question of
"What is a Jew?"

Julian, like most of his fellow Jews at the time, knew one
definition of "Jew" that hardly was challengeable: Jews were "people
in trouble." Although he had some confidence in the minority rights
treaty (a faith that future events did not justify) he was more certain
than ever of the promise held out by Zionism. What happened in
Paris would determine whether the Zionist dream could become a
reality.

31. Paris, 1919

In that first spring after the war, Paris was far from the carefree place Julian had enjoyed twenty years before, as a happy-go-lucky Harvard Law graduate on a Parker Fellowship. By all accounts, Paris in 1919 was confusion compounded. Diplomats, advisers, journalists, lobbyists, agents open and secret, and hangers-on by the hundreds had congregated there to make, or observe, the peace arrangements. The effect was a donnybrook into which Julian could not, and did not, avoid being drawn.

As soon as he had settled in his quarters at the Plaza on the Rue Montaigne, he found himself engulfed in the tension that pervaded the city. Nor was there much letup at any time during the weeks that he served as chairman of the American Jewish delegation, a post he later shared with Louis Marshall. Later, too, he became chairman of an international committee of various Jewish delegations, officially styled "Le Comité des Délégations Juives auprès de la Conférence de la Paix" (Committee of Jewish Delegations to the Peace Conference) out of which in the 1930's was to come the permanent World Jewish Congress.

There were times when he lost his usual aplomb. Thus, in a noteworthy diary of the conference kept by Lucien Wolf, the Anglo-Jewish spokesman and scholar, it is recorded in several entries that Julian had been testy and ill-tempered. Probably these surprising comments were prejudiced exaggeration, for Wolf did not agree with Julian on basic Jewish issues before the Conference. But the entries in Wolf's diary do indicate the strain to which Julian was subjected. "The whole period," he said, "was a most trying and nervous one for all [of] us Zionists."

He had some relief, however. For one thing, Julian for the first time met Chaim Weizmann. He found him, as did most persons, "wholly charming." There was no suggestion then of the bitterness that was to develop between the two men in later years. Julian's association with Weizmann, who later gave him a Bible inscribed "to the wise, great, and just judge," was a pleasant one.

Better still, Julian had in Paris the comforting presence of three of his most cherished friends. Felix Frankfurter, the consummate negotiator who had personal contact with many key Conference figures, was there as the official head of the American Zionist delegation, in effect, along with De Haas, the *ex officio* personal representative of Brandeis. Also in Paris was Benjamin V. Cohen, one of Julian's favorite former law clerks, who was acting in Paris and London as the principal drafter of written proposals for the Zionists. Under President Franklin D. Roosevelt, Cohen was to hold various posts, including counselor to the State Department.

Best of all, Aaron Aaronsohn was also there, helping to guide negotiations with Arab, British, and French spokesmen on Palestine, particularly with reference to the boundaries of the proposed Jewish homeland, on which Aaron was the prime expert of the Zionists. Julian thus found himself part of a congenial foursome that played a key role in much of the behind-the-scenes maneuvering on Jewish problems, a facet of the Peace Conference of 1919 which for the most part has gone unrecorded.

He had expected that the main problem facing him in Paris would be Arab opposition to incorporating the Balfour Declaration in the final peace arrangements. To his elation, he learned on his arrival that Frankfurter and Weizmann, powerfully aided by Aaronsohn, had obtained from the leading Arab at the Peace Conference, Emir Feisal (later king of Iraq), an endorsement of the Balfour Declaration. Indeed, Feisal had gone beyond merely approving the aims of the Zionists. In a much-publicized letter to Frankfurter, dated Paris, March 31, 1919 and affirming an earlier formal agreement with Weizmann in January of that year, Feisal had written:

> We Arabs, especially the educated among us, look with the deepest sympathy on the Zionist movement. Our deputation here in Paris is fully acquainted with the proposals submitted by the Zionist Organization to the Peace Conference, and we regard them as moderate and proper. We will do our best, insofar as we are concerned, to help them through; we will wish the Jews a most hearty welcome home.

It was a document that Arabs of a later day might do well to remember. True, Feisal had added to the original agreement a condition to the effect that he would consider himself bound by the agreement only if his hopes for British concessions to his people were fulfilled. Other Arabs were to exploit this reservation in an effort to portray Feisal's gesture of friendship for the Jews as meaningless, but that was still in the future.

At the same time, Hussein, Arab ruler of the Hejaz, also had agreed that for the good of all those who lived in the Middle East, Palestine should be restored to the Jews. The statements by Feisal and Hussein, along with the highly skillful presentations of Weizmann, Sokolow, and Ussishkin, plus the effective lobbying of Frankfurter and Aaronsohn, aided by "Lawrence of Arabia," among others, were influential with the peacemakers. The tenor of all their arguments was that Jews and Arabs, both of Semitic origin, could live peacefully together, and that, given the industrial, scientific and agricultural skills of the Jews, the restoration of a Jewish homeland in Palestine side by side with the establishment of new Arab states in the region would bring great benefits for the Arab population of the Middle East. Indeed, that concept was an essential element of Zionism: not hostility, but cooperation with the Arabs. The later myth that the Zionists had "ignored the existence of the Arabs" was an untruth.

Julian in Paris not only paid a good deal of attention, as did his associates, to the problems of the Arabs but also felt confident that the Arab nationalism emerging in the Middle East could develop side by side with Zionist aims in Palestine. As he later reported to the Z.O.A., Feisal's letter alone was "worth a great deal in making the Arab world realize that there is no antagonism between the Zionist aims and the best Arab interests."

True, some Arab elements in Egypt and Syria, hotly anti-Semitic and backed by foreign influences, had already begun to agitate against the proposal to allot part of tiny Palestine to the Jews. But at the time these elements seemed inconsequential. The friendly Arab attitude toward the idea of a Jewish homeland in Palestine appeared to be dominant, an ample justification for the optimism of Julian and other Zionists.

Even so, at Paris, Julian was greatly disturbed that some serious opposition to the Balfour Declaration did exist. His efforts to check this opposition took much of his time and energy. "I went to see Colonel House several times," he recalled. But the opposition that troubled Julian came not from Arabs, but from anti-Zionist Jews from England and France, and from certain non-Jewish Americans.

The distressing fact was that the official Jewish delegations from Britain and France were dominated by leaders who had little sympathy for the Balfour Declaration, or who were openly hostile. This in itself was serious enough, for it threatened to give the peacemakers an opportunity, if they chose to take it, of assuming that world Jewry was not committed to a Jewish homeland in Palestine. Even more serious was the opposition from two American non-Jews, Charles R. Crane, a wealthy midwestern manufacturer interested in the Christian missions in the Middle East, and Henry C. King, president of Oberlin College and prominent in the American Missionary Association. This busy pair commanded sufficient prestige to persuade President Wilson in Paris to send them to the Middle East to investigate the attitude of the local populations toward the projected Jewish National Home. Presumably, in the view of King and Crane, there would be no final decision about Palestine until they had made their findings. It was a quixotic situation since President Wilson and other heads of state had already indicated that the issue of Palestine was settled.

But quixotic or not, the King-Crane mission to the Middle East gave the Zionists in Paris some anxious days. Frank E. Manuel noted: "To the American (Protestant) missionaries in the Near East, the King-Crane expedition was a triumph which had vast horizons . . . a fresh reconsideration of the whole problem." Julian told in his report to the Z.O.A. how troublesome the matter was:

> There was continual danger, danger not yet past, of an harassing postponement. . . . The determination to appoint a commission to go to Syria for the avowed purpose of finding out what public opinion in Asia Minor wants, and the kaleidoscopic change of the commission and its departure, if,

when, and whether, engrossed our attention and really
distracted everybody. . . . And the serious thing about it was,
not that the commission was likely to change the situation, but
that it was throwing things into confusion, to increase the very
serious unrest that was prevailing in the entire Middle Eastern
region. . . .

King and Crane arrived in Palestine in June, 1919. On their
return that August, they submitted a report with such an
anti-Zionist, even anti-Semitic, bias that it was used long afterward
by anti-Israel propagandists, including especially the Number One
academic Arab apologist, George Antonius, author of *The Arab
Awakening*. But once again, Brandeis in Washington, alerted from
Paris, went into action with Wilson. In Paris, Julian, Frankfurter,
and Stephen Wise buttonholed Colonel House and other members
of the American delegation there. In the end, Wilson disowned the
King-Crane Commission and denied official status to its report.

And in addition, to Julian's intense relief, the U.S. delegation
in Paris stood by an earlier American official study on the "Palestine
Question," one that bore, among others, the signatures of Isaiah
Bowman of the Johns Hopkins University, James Shotwell of
Columbia University, and Sidney Mezes of the College of the City
of New York. It was a study that went further than even the Zionists
themselves had dared to go on Palestine, for it included the
following recommendations:

1. It is recommended that there be established a separate
State of Palestine.

2. It is recommended that this state be placed under Great
Britain as a mandatory of the League of Nations.

3. It is recommended that the Jews be invited to return to
Palestine . . . assured that it will be the policy of the League
of Nations to recognize Palestine as a Jewish state as soon as it
is a Jewish state in fact. It is right that Palestine should become
a Jewish state, if the Jews, being given the full opportunity,
make it such.

In short, a clear Zionist victory had been scored.

But victory over King and Crane, along with assumed Arab assent to Zionist goals in Palestine, did not mean clear sailing from then on for Julian and his colleagues in Paris. There remained the *Jewish* opposition not only to Zionist aims in Palestine, but also to the so-called "minority rights" provisions proposed for the treaties that created independent Poland and other new nations in Eastern Europe. This opposition was led by Lucien Wolf of England. Expecting defeat in their anti-Zionist stand, Wolf and his group offered only a half-hearted presentation of their views on Palestine, but they vigorously campaigned against some of the basic elements in the program for "minority rights" for the Jews in the newly-established East European states. In particular, Jewish delegates from Britain and France hotly opposed any reference to "national" rights, the old bugaboo that recognition of Jews as a national entity would cast a shadow over their status as loyal citizens in the countries where they lived.

Julian understood the position of the recalcitrant British and French Jews. It was a position that he himself had once held, but he could not sympathize with their determination to fight openly at the Peace Conference against the majority of world Jewish leaders. The matter, he saw, was mainly theoretical for the British and French Jews, but potentially a question of survival for the Jews in Eastern Europe, especially in Poland. If the Jews of that region felt the need for such provisions, he felt they should not be opposed.

Moreover, to Julian's great dismay, the opposition of the British and French Jews to "national rights" for Jewish minorities supplied powerful support to anti-Semitic Poles who wanted no treaty protections at all for Jews. It also encouraged vacillation on the issue by the American delegation, particularly Colonel House.

As David Hunter Miller, counselor to the U.S. delegation, noted in his diary on May 2, 1919, "House thought more of the Poles than he did of the Jews," and consequently "did not want to offend the Poles."

In the end, as on the Palestine issue, House refrained from overt opposition to the American-Jewish views on minority group rights and, after various private conferences, assured Julian that he would continue officially to do so. But House's personal feelings still meant danger, unless Jewish opposition to the program could be reasonably contained. A crisis for the Jewish delegations was precipitated by Lucien Wolf when he presented to the Big Four an independent Jewish program calling for *"some"* minority rights for the Jews in the new nations.

Aside from the fact that Wolf's presentation made no mention of "national" rights for Jews, the Jewish delegations from the United States and other countries were deeply offended by the "separatist" nature of Wolf's move. It was of a piece, they felt, with earlier action, denounced by Weizmann as "betrayal," on the part of Sylvain Lévi, of the Alliance Israélite Universelle, who had appeared before the Allied Supreme Council to oppose the Balfour Declaration. Intense bitterness flared. Prestigious mediators, particularly Americans, were badly needed. Julian was soon engaged in that role. Heartbreaking sessions marked these efforts, "a well-nigh hopeless task," as Julian phrased it.

"We had continued at it for about a week," he recalled, "and had given up." Then Louis Marshall arrived in Paris. He felt it his duty to try again, "and," Julian continued, "he went at it with very much hopefulness because, for many years, as head of the American Jewish Committee, he had been in constant contact with the representatives of the English organizations and of the Alliance Israélite of France. He worked unceasingly . . . did little or nothing for weeks except to attempt to bring about unity of action among all sections of Jewry. . . ."

But Marshall's efforts were not much more successful. They did, however, help achieve an agreement that all the Jewish delegations, representing some dozen countries, would at least meet together. Lengthy and at times stormy sessions, presided over by Julian, were held in the Consistoire Central at the Great Synagogue in Paris. Passionate speeches, Julian recalled, were made "in French, English, Hebrew, and also a camouflaged Yiddish." Menahem Ussishkin, the Russian Zionist leader, for one, blasted the non-Zionists mercilessly as "traitors." Sokolow of Poland threatened them with "ostracization from Jewry." As Lucien Wolf noted in his diary, Nachman Syrkin of the American delegation "twitted the Western Jews for being afraid [for] their own skins."

Julian stressed a basic point with the British and French Jews. "Even if you cannot agree with East European Jews it is still your duty to leave them alone; even if you believe they are mad and headed for self-destruction. It is *their* fate." It was a reasonable argument, but the British and French non-Zionists never yielded in their opposition to "national" rights for Jews.

Nor did they take a positive stand at Paris for a Jewish homeland in Palestine. They even refused to be a part of the international committee of Jewish delegations, which was then conceived by the Americans and others to achieve at least the *appearance* to the outside world of a unified, authoritative voice for Jewry at the Paris Peace Conference.

At one strained point, Julian, ever the conciliator, lunched with Lucien Wolf to seek his support for the unified group. For his pains he was subjected to a tirade. He "had been completely, and, I am afraid I must say, maliciously misinformed as to our attitude," Wolf, in his diary, later said of Julian. But Julian had not been misinformed, as Wolf's own diary, among other documents, makes indisputably plain. Not even the terrible reports of new pogroms in Poland that April, as the peace conference was in progress, softened the opposition of the Jewish delegations from Britain and France to treaty provisions designed to protect Jews from such outrages.

The news of the massacres and other "excesses" against Jews, some of them perpetrated by Polish government troops, plunged Julian and other Jewish delegates in Paris into deep anguish. Were the reports true? Non-Jewish delegates at the conference, including Ignace Paderewski, scoffed. So also, to Julian's chagrin, did a Chicago "friend," Chauncey McCormick, who, as a member of Herbert Hoover's food administration staff, served as adviser on Polish affairs to the U.S. delegation. It was all vastly exaggerated, McCormick assured Lucien Wolf and others. A similar view was expressed by Hugh Gibson, later the highly respected American Ambassador to Poland. But an American commission that investigated the situation found that unfortunately most of the reports from Poland had been only too true.

The non-Zionists did make one important concession. Recognizing, finally, that a public show of disunity among the Jewish delegations at the peace conference would be "bad for Jewry as a whole," they agreed, in Julian's words, to "a peace pact . . . while they would go their own way, they would not do anything directly antagonistic to the proposals that we deemed best to submit."

It was on this basis—"there was considerable gain in that," Julian later observed—that he accepted the chairmanship of the Comité des Délégations Juives auprès de la Conférence de la Paix, which then presented to the Allied Supreme Council a formal memorandum dated May 10, 1919.

Addressed to "Their Excellencies, the President and Members of the Peace Conference," this document declared, in the name of the world Jewish community, the desire of the Jews that the treaties establishing the new nations in Eastern Europe should include provisions for the protection of minority groups. Its language was substantially identical with the resolutions adopted by the American Jewish Congress in December, 1918. Appended to it was an impressive list of Jewish groups constituting the Comité des Délégations Juives auprès de la Conférence de la Paix:

> *AMERIQUE, ETATS-UNIS: Congrès Juif D'Amerique*
> *AMERIQUE CANADA:. Congrès Juif du Canada*
> *GALICIE ORIENTALE: Conseil National Juif*
> *ITALIE: Comité des Communautés, Fédération Sioniste, Fédération Rabbinique*
> *PALESTINE: Assemblée Constituante Juive*
> *POLOGNE: Conseil National Juif*
> *ROUMANIE: Publications officielles de la Fédération Sioniste, Union des Israélites indigènes et Union Po'ale-Sioniste*
> *RUSSIE: Conseil National Juif*
> *TCHECO-SLOVAQUIE: Conseil National Juif*
> *UKRAINE: Assemblée Nationale Juive*
> *ORGANISATIONS: American Jewish Committee; Bnai-Brith; Organisation Sioniste*
> *MANDATS PAR ECRIT: Grèce (Salonique), Translyvanie et Bukovine*

The signatures on the document were those of Louis Marshall, Leon Reich, Israel Rosoff, Nahum Sokolow, M.M. Ussishkin, Leo Motzkin—and "President: Julian W. Mack." Thus did Julian, once the personification of assimilationism, emerge officially on the world stage as the titular spokesman for the Jewish nationalists in world Jewry.

In years to come, there would be differences of opinion as to what, in fact, had been accomplished by the "Comité" which was headed first by Julian and later by Louis Marshall. But at the time of the Peace Conference, it was generally believed that the "Comité" had made crucial achievements for world Jewry. Despite the dismaying changes in years to come, this was largely true, for it was at Paris, 1919, that the legal foundation had been laid for the Jewish homeland in Palestine and, eventually, the State of Israel. It was out of the Paris Peace Conference that there came the League of Nations mandate over Palestine with its provisions for what Brandeis called a restored "Jewish Commonwealth."

The fate of the minority rights provisions was a different story. Though not exactly in the terms recommended by the international Jewish committee, provisions for Jewish minority rights were in fact inserted into the treaties that established the new states of Poland, Rumania, and Czechoslovakia. As David Hunter Miller, member of the U.S. treaty-drafting committee, noted in his diary, this was done "primarily" because of "American Jewish influence," and "largely" through "Marshall's and Mack's draftsmanship." In the end, these rights were eroded or simply ignored as Europe moved toward Hitlerism. As Horace Kallen, for one, pointed out, this was due largely to the failure of the League of Nations to make provisions for their enforcement. But the fact remained that, for the first time, such rights had been set forth in official, international treaties.

And finally, for the first time, there had come into being an officially recognized authoritative body to act as the voice of the Jewish community in international affairs. Julian, incidentally, always insisted that the main credit for the achievements in Paris was due not to him, but notably to Frankfurter and Marshall.

He and the other Zionists especially hailed Louis Marshall in this regard. Indeed, in his service in Paris Marshall had largely subordinated his personal views, even the policies of the American Jewish Committee, which he headed, to give loyal support to the majority Jewish view. As Horace Kallen once commented, Marshall, like Julian, had come "to regard public opposition to Zionism as an act of treachery to the welfare of Judaism."

Julian's generosity in distributing laurels came as no surprise to his close friends. "He always sought to calm the ruffled feelings of egotists and prima donnas with whom he worked and thus gave them credit not only for their own work, but [also] for his," Benjamin V. Cohen noted. "Even saints [whom] history remembers had much more of an ego than he had." Perhaps this explains why in the usual accounts of the Paris Peace Conference Julian's role, in a way the high point of his career in the service of American Jewry, is only mentioned in passing, or not at all.

32. Success and Tragedy

He had counted on taking off no more than four weeks from his judicial work for attending the Peace Conference. But to his dismay, the four weeks in Paris stretched to almost eleven, "working night and day," as he wrote to Schiff on March 24, 1919.

Even so, he left Europe before knowing the fate of the Zionist hopes for Palestine. On his return to the United States he was still "nervous" about the outcome, because certain Arabs and anti-Zionist Jews from England and the United States were stepping up their efforts to prevent the implementation of the Balfour Declaration. "The Arab situation is serious; how serious, no one can tell," he told Wise.

Julian's comments to Wise mainly concerned reports of outbreaks of anti-Jewish violence in Egypt and of certain Arab chieftains forming an organization which later was to become known as the Arab League. The allegation of these Arabs, who cited an obscure "Declaration to the Seven," dated June 16, 1918, was that British agents had promised them that the disposition of Palestine would depend on "the principle of the consent of the governed," and they argued, not without basis, that there had been some double-dealing by the British with respect to the Balfour Declaration.

But, as Julian reported to the National Executive Committee of the Z.O.A. on June 1, 1919, soon after his return to New York, he was confident that "in the end everything would come out right, come out as we expected." He even dropped on that occasion the caution with which he usually referred to the possibility of Palestine becoming a Jewish state. Hailing the certainty that Great Britain would be given a League of Nations mandate to govern Palestine, he optimistically added:

"I think, without going out and crying it from the housetops, we can go forward in our work with a feeling of full confidence that the foundations will be laid in Palestine for the development of an autonomous commonwealth."

There were, to be sure, other Zionists who even in that euphoric period did not trust British intentions in Palestine. They pointed out that the British military command in Palestine had forbidden the publication of the Balfour Declaration there, and that, as early as 1919, British soldiers had shown a strong disinclination to curb Arab terrorists in Haifa and Jerusalem.

One prescient Zionist who definitely mistrusted the British was Vladimir Jabotinsky. When Brandeis visited Palestine in July, 1919, Jabotinsky told him that he detected under the British mandate administration an atmosphere of pogroms, as in Russia. But, according to Jabotinsky, Brandeis replied: "This is not Czarist Russia. This is territory occupied by an Anglo-Saxon power . . . I believe in British justice." That was also Julian's over-optimistic faith.

He was too optimistic also at that Z.O.A. meeting in June, 1919 in giving his report on the minority rights clauses in the peace treaties. There had been serious compromises—"disastrous ones," De Haas had cabled to Brandeis at the time—on that issue. For, in order to appease anti-Semitic Polish nationalists, the phrase "national rights," with reference to the Jewish minority, had been omitted. Also dropped was a provision, drafted by Ben Cohen and Bernard Flexner, under which individuals, and not just nations, would have had the right to appeal to the League of Nations for the enforcement of measures protecting the minorities. But Julian was satisfied nevertheless, inasmuch as member nations at least were permitted to make such appeals. At the time, he assumed, again optimistically, that the United States would join the League.

Hence, he said:

> We can also look forward with confidence, in respect to national rights, though not under that name, [to] the substance of the things we asked for in the resolution of the American Jewish Congress; indeed, more than we asked for.

In this, he was to be proven wrong. The "Bill of Rights" was disdainfully ignored by the new Polish and Rumanian regimes. The League of Nations did nothing. Nor did Julian anticipate Woodrow Wilson's failure to bring the United States into the League, or the sad change in Wilson, following his stroke in Pueblo, Colorado, that caused Brandeis to remark to Stephen Wise in March, 1920, "I do not hold Wilson responsible, for he is no longer mentally or morally himself." But when Julian returned to New York from Paris that summer of 1919, these developments, like Britain's policies in Palestine, were still in the hidden future.

Buoyant as Julian was over the outcome of the Paris Peace Conference, his heart was heavy nonetheless over a great personal sorrow which the Peace Conference was to symbolize for him ever after: the mysterious death of Aaron Aaronsohn.

About May 10, 1919, the week before Julian was to leave Paris for New York, Aaron went over from Paris to London to get some maps and other materials for himself and Frankfurter for a visit to Palestine as members of the Zionist Commission. The Zionist Commission had been set up in 1918 by warrant from the British Foreign Office for the purpose of acting as a liaison between the British authorities and Palestine's Jewish community, coordinating postwar relief and reconstruction work in Palestine, helping establish friendly relations with Arabs and other non-Jewish communities and reporting on possibilities of further development of Jewish settlements and the country as a whole.

"[Aaronson] was to bring back an outfit for himself and Professor Frankfurter to wear in Palestine," Julian later reported to the executive committee of the Z.O.A., adding that Aaron, who "knew more about the land in Palestine than anyone," was to be "the head of a commission of experts who were to round up the entire work—all the engineering, agricultural and other work to be done."

He might have added that Brandeis at the time had been toying with the idea that Aaron might be the head of an eventual Jewish Agency for Palestine. A "Jewish Agency for Palestine" was, in fact, founded in the 1920's pursuant to a provision in the Mandate for Palestine, calling for the establishment of such a body for advising, and cooperating with, the Palestine administration in economic, social and other matters "affecting the establishment of the Jewish Homeland." In the beginning the functions of the Agency were carried out by the World Zionist Organization, of which Chaim Weizmann was then president.

Julian might have added, as Leonard Stein was to write some four decades later in his book *The Balfour Declaration*, that—as with

Julian himself—"descriptions of the events connected with the Balfour Declaration . . . usually [give] Aaronsohn less than his due, and underrate . . . his services to the Zionist cause"; likewise, that it was Aaronsohn who, more than any other individual, influenced Emir Feisal to write his letter to Frankfurter about the Arab endorsement of Zionist aspirations in Palestine.

When he left Paris for the Channel crossing to England, Aaron was in his usual sparkling mood. William C. Bullitt, then Wilson's confidant, and later Franklin D. Roosevelt's ambassador to Moscow and Paris, was to describe "how diplomats [in Washington] sat open-mouthed, astonished" by Aaron's insights and how they were "warmed by his picture of Zion." Bullitt also recalled chatting with Aaron at the Hotel Crillon in Paris shortly before his departure. Aaron then had enthusiastically told Bullitt that he expected "to appear before the Council of Four to plead for Zion," and amusedly asked Bullitt whether he thought that "Clemenceau, Orlando, Lloyd George and Wilson would understand if he [were to] ask that a particular five-acre field should be included in the Zionist State." Why? "Because," Bullitt wrote, "it contained a unique specimen of a wild plant, which should be preserved for the service of science and would be tended by the Jews, but might be neglected by the Arabs!"

Such was Aaron Aaronsohn, Julian's most delightful friend, whom Julian was not to see again. For Aaron Aaronsohn never returned from England. The last person of Julian's circle to see him alive was Benjamin V. Cohen, who was then in London on Zionist business. "I had lunch with him in London on the day he disappeared," Cohen recalled years later. "He was in good spirits, as usual, and when we parted, he said he intended to fly back to Paris. His disappearance was a great loss to Zionism."

The final assumption, as reported in the press, was that Aaron had drowned when a London-to-Paris mail plane, on which he presumably had obtained a seat for his return trip, had fallen into the English Channel. Rumor had it that the mishap had been no accident, but an act contrived by firebrand Arab nationalists who feared Aaron's influence. But these speculations were never verified.

Julian had expected Aaron to be back in Paris on May 15, 1919. When he did not show up, Julian concluded that he had decided to return by boat rather than by plane. As he wrote to Aaron's sister Rifka, Julian later learned from Bernard Flexner, who was in London with Ben Cohen at the time, that Aaronsohn had "telephoned from the field that the weather reports were such that he probably wouldn't fly." Apparently he had chosen to fly, after all. "At midnight when I came [to the hotel] from a meeting," Julian continued in his report to Rifka Aaronsohn, "I asked again; the next morning the concierge told me about a postal aeroplane accident & we knew the truth," or what he assumed to be the truth. Aaron's body was never found.

The most definite "official" report on Aaron's fate was a statement that Julian and Frankfurter sent to an insurance company in Switzerland more than two years later in connection with a policy on Aaron's life:

August 31, 1921

Gentlemen:

We do hereby certify that Aaron Aaronsohn, of Palestine, insured in your Company, proceeding from London to Paris by aeroplane, met with a wreck in the British Channel on May 15th, 1919. He was to have met us in Paris that night. He has never been heard from since. The wreckage was found the next morning, but no trace of him or of the pilot was ever discovered, and neither of them has ever been heard of since.

We are firmly convinced that he died in the wreck, and we do hereby jointly and severally guarantee unto you full and complete reimbursement of any and all sums that you may pay out on account of the insurance on his life, in case it should at any time be found that he is still alive.

Very truly yours,
(Sgd.) Julian W. Mack
(Sgd.) Felix Frankfurter
(Harvard Law School, Cambridge, Mass.)

La Bâloise Insurance Company,
Bâle, Switzerland

Probably it should be accepted as certain that Aaronsohn, who was so greatly responsible for Julian's conversion to Zionism, did in fact die in the English Channel, just as the Zionist dream was coming true. A symbolic suggestion of trouble ahead? Perhaps.

"I know Aaron would have wanted to end in some such way," Julian wrote to Aaron's sister, Rifka, "but it ought to have been in 25 or 30 years, not now."

33. *The Split*

More sorrow was directly ahead for Julian, an episode so wretchedly vexing for him that his unhappiness with the Commerce Court several years before seemed contentment by comparison: the split in the Zionist Organization of America, which came to a head at a special Z.O.A. convention in Cleveland in June, 1921, when the Brandeis-Mack leadership received a vote of "no confidence" and Julian resigned as president of the Z.O.A. "One must pay dearly for being a Zionist," he later remarked to Felix Frankfurter.

It was a time, incidentally, when the Zionist movement all over the world was riven by dissension that pitted friend against friend. In America, this turmoil emerged primarily as a confrontation, involving both principles and personalities, between the then two top leaders in world Zionism, Brandeis and Weizmann. Julian still sided loyally with Brandeis, but even so, he was caught in the middle. For, being much less rigid than Brandeis, and not having a need to be right on every issue, Julian characteristically tried to avoid a no-holds-barred clash. In that effort, he failed.

If not for Brandeis' unbending insistence on his convictions—perhaps his one great defect amidst his great virtues—could Julian have prevented the split? Benjamin V. Cohen, who was close to all the major participants on both sides and also was deeply involved in the episode as confidant to both Weizmann and Julian, has provided important insights on that question. In Paris, Julian and Weizmann stayed at the same hotel. They developed "warm personal relations . . . enjoyed each other's company regardless of agreement or disagreement on Zionist policy," Cohen recalled. But Weizmann, Cohen observed, was under pressure from East European Zionists to break with Brandeis.

A contributing factor here—which seemed a small matter on the surface—was Brandeis' habit of equating the resettlement of Palestine by Jews with the early settlement of America by the English Puritans, who, like the Palestine pioneers, had to meet and overcome all manner of hardships. Brandeis reiterated that point at

261

the Zionist Conference in London in July, 1920, the first
international gathering of the World Zionist movement following
World War I. Cohen, who was there, saw that when Brandeis
praised "Anglo-Saxon manhood in the early American colonial
period," this did not sit well with the Zionists from Russia and
Poland.

"The Europeans never forgot it," Cohen went on. "Brandeis was
in a sense, to them, an Anglo-Saxon *friend,* not a warm and
committed Jew. That does not mean Brandeis was not warm and
committed within himself. But the Europeans could never reach
that inner Brandeis."

At that conference Brandeis also practically called for an end of
the Zionist movement as it had been before the Balfour
Declaration. The building of the Jewish commonwealth, he
declared, now required not so much propaganda and "political
work" as "practical work," and this new approach in turn required
leadership, not by orators and the like, but by practical men of
affairs. Otherwise, he said, the needed funds from Americans would
not be forthcoming.

> It will be of little value to us to keep things as they are
> [Brandeis observed]. . . . We have reached a new era. . . .
> There has been a tremendous amount of talk in the past, and
> properly, of the political question, of political Zionism. The
> political question is important hereafter, but to my mind
> practically the whole of politics is: proceed efficiently in the
> building up of Palestine.

To the Europeans, Brandeis' reference to funds sounded like a
threat. Yet, contrary to later heated comments of his adversaries,
there could never be any doubt about Brandeis' commitment to the
upbuilding of the Jewish Homeland, for he gave a glowing report on
his visit to Palestine in 1919. What he saw had greatly moved him.
This was clear not only from his own report but also from a
comment by Lincoln Steffens, who happened to see Brandeis in
Paris just after his return from Palestine. On August 2, 1919 the
famous "muckraker" wrote from Paris to a friend:

[Brandeis] is a changed man. His trip to Palestine has affected him so that he even looks different. It's as if he had seen a vision. . . . He understands now, he said, why his people want that old country of theirs. It is very beautiful. "Like California," he said. And what it is proposed to do there, as for the Jews, will be for the Christians also. That's what he said, and somehow he made me feel that it was going to be done.

But Brandeis had seen in Palestine some things that had shocked him. There was, for instance, the high incidence of malaria, which was killing many pioneers and depleting the strength and energy of many more. There also was inefficiency, or what he considered inefficiency, in the disbursement of Zionist funds. His critics would insist that he was "obsessed" with the need for businesslike methods, that he placed "good bookkeeping ahead of good works in Palestine." But Brandeis did see waste, which he feared would frighten off prospective investors. He believed, moreover, that too much money was being spent on salaries for men who were not builders but "politicians."

Henrietta Szold, a peacemaker in the situation, who was then laying the groundwork for the great Hadassah medical organization in Palestine, unwittingly increased Brandeis' apprehensions about the waste of funds by telling him of Zionist publicists and others who were using office postage and telephones for personal business—a small thing, but one which Brandeis feared was typical of how Zionist funds were being squandered.

A report from Robert Szold on conditions in Palestine confirmed Brandeis in his own impressions of the need for new and more businesslike methods in Zionist work. Szold, then a young lawyer as practical and as socially conscious as Brandeis, was a "Brandeis-Mack man" whom Brandeis had picked as his representative on the Zionist Commission in 1919. Szold had hesitated about going to Palestine with the Commission because his wife, Zip Falk Szold, who later succeeded Henrietta Szold as president of Hadassah, was then expecting their first child. But Julian had gone to see the couple. "He was most persuasive that it was my husband's duty to accept the assignment," Mrs. Szold recalled. Weizmann, too, had specifically endorsed the choice of Szold as a member of the Commission, but perhaps he had come to regret it, for Szold was wholly a "Brandeisist" and had Brandeis' full confidence.

The report that Szold brought back from Palestine was detailed and carefully documented, but not a happy one. At a meeting at which Julian was present, Szold reported on the state of agriculture, education, industry and settlements in Palestine:

> The immigrants [he observed] have been coming at the rate of a thousand a month. It is really the outstanding feature of the present situation. They come in boat loads—and there is a panic every time a boat comes in. Nobody knows about it until it arrives.

No wonder Brandeis, always disciplined in managing his own affairs, remained staunch in his demand for a complete reorganization of Zionist activity.

At any event, Brandeis, at the London Conference in the summer of 1920, called for careful accounting procedures. Instead of an enlarged Zionist Executive, he urged a smaller one, to consist of no more than seven individuals, citing Bernard Flexner, the Chicago lawyer, as an example of the kind of individual he had in mind. As for fund raising he spoke out strongly against the "commingling" of "donation" and "investment" funds. They should be kept separate, he firmly argued. Moreover, he declared, "[Some] of the things we are doing now I think ought to end—that is, the political work in Palestine."

The proper medium for future political work, he added, was the British mandate machinery under Sir Herbert Samuel, who had been named High Commissioner for Palestine and in whom Brandeis had full confidence. "Samuel," he said, "was a man of eminent fairness and soundness, true to the Jewish cause as well as to the British cause and to the justice for which Great Britain stands." This statement was made before Samuel's attempts to appease the rioting Arabs made him *persona non grata* to many Zionists, including, to a large extent, even Brandeis.

The European Zionists, including some whose positions in Palestine would be abolished under Brandeis' program, were understandably shocked. Shmarya Levin, for one, gave witty but cutting vent to their indignation. Referring to Brandeis' concern for giving priority to the elimination of malaria in Palestine, he remarked: "He would hold up settling Jews there until the last mosquito is wiped out!"

Then, too, as Louis Lipsky was to emphasize following the split, the Europeans, and important American Zionists along with them, were upset by Brandeis' refusal to join a triumvirate which had been proposed to direct a restructured World Zionist Organization. It had been taken for granted that Brandeis would be the head of this triumvirate. This probably would have meant that Brandeis, and not Chaim Weizmann, would have been president of the World Zionist Executive and of the Jewish Agency. It was a dazzling prospect for Brandeis, not only from the Zionist point of view, but also in the eyes of the larger world. When various reports of what had been planned (some of them distorted, of course) were published in the press, the reaction of William Jennings Bryan, for one, was perhaps typical. "Glad to see," he wrote to Brandeis, "your name is mentioned in connection with the Presidency of the Jewish state. A great honor. I would be pleased to vote for you as President of the U.S."

But Brandeis accepted no more than the honorary presidency of the World Zionist Organization. To assume an active role in the triumvirate, he felt, would have necessitated his resignation from the Supreme Court, and he told Julian he believed he could serve Jewry, including Zionism, and even America, better by remaining on the Court. Julian, among others, agreed; it was a judgment that few persons, including Zionists, ever disputed. But from then on, most of the Europeans, as well as many of the American Zionists present in London, began to turn against Brandeis. So at least Louis Lipsky, writing in his *Thirty Years of American Zionism*, would maintain:

That was a decisive incident—the meeting of the Americans in the Council Chamber [of Zionist headquarters] at 77 Great

Russell Street. It was an intense moment . . . Mr. Brandeis
was invited to visit us. A number of addresses were delivered at
him—by me, as chairman, by Morris Rothenberg, by Israel
Brodie, by Abraham Tulin. We appealed to Mr. Brandeis to
assume membership in the Triumvirate, which meant, we had
no doubt, his personal leadership. Voices were filled with
emotion. We had been laboring in America for six years to
prepare Mr. Brandeis for the leadership. His name had been
repeatedly acclaimed. We had given unqualified support to his
policies. He had our admiration, respect and love. The time
had come for him to abandon the seclusion in which he had
enveloped himself, and to step into the open as the actual
leader in the making of the Jewish National Home.

This he declined to do. He had a number of reasons. They
seemed to satisfy at the time. . . . The reasons did not
matter. He could not accept, and did not accept. The
consequences were inevitable.

And Weizmann? He had wanted to maintain good relations with
Brandeis. At the outset, the two men had liked each other.
Moreover, Brandeis had gone to London prepared to follow the
advice given him by Frankfurter, who had long sensed a conflict
coming, particularly because of disparaging remarks De Haas had
been making to Brandeis about Weizmann. "I think it is only fair to
say," Frankfurter wrote to Brandeis from Paris, on March 3, 1919,
"that collaborative effort, even docility, could be imposed upon
Weizmann without difficulty. The closest and most cordial relations
between you and him are absolutely indispensable and I have not
the faintest shadow of a doubt that you will work together with the
happiest accord."
    Weizmann once actually kissed Brandeis' hand in gratitude for his
role in the cause they had in common. So Frankfurter was right.
    Benjamin V. Cohen's observations give an indication of Julian's
position with respect to Weizmann, and how this position differed
from that of Brandeis:

Dr. Weizmann [later] supported his European friends with whom Brandeis disagreed. Judge Mack liked and felt at home with Weizmann. Dr. W. and other European leaders did not feel at home with Brandeis, and Brandeis did not go out of his way to gain their personal confidence. Brandeis' temperament was in a sense alien to the temperaments of the European leaders. . . . They thought his feeling about Palestine was that of a stranger, not of a Zionist, although Brandeis was a good Zionist. With Mack, and also Frankfurter, they felt more at home.

While intellectually, Mack went along with Brandeis, his emotional reactions were quite different; *and from that you can draw your own conclusions what Mack might have done if L[ouis] D. B[randeis] was not in the picture. The breach would not have arisen in the form it did.* [Author's emphasis]

"Mack was not wishy-washy, as some said," Cohen further noted. "But he liked give-and-take in discussions and he could get along with those with whom he disagreed. He was much closer to Weizmann than the records probably show. If not for his loyalty to Brandeis, he might not have split with Weizmann at all, for he understood Weizmann's position."

But Iago-like figures were operating on both sides, some innocently, others perhaps less so. One of these was Jacob De Haas, Brandeis' "mentor in Zionism." Viewing himself as Herzl's spiritual spokesman and often recalling that Weizmann, by his own admission, had been a sharp critic of Herzl in the split in the Zionist movement in 1903 over the Uganda Scheme, De Haas clearly fed Brandeis' hostility toward Weizmann.

How strongly Brandeis was influenced in the crisis by De Haas is suggested by the result of one effort on the part of Julian to persuade Brandeis to hold De Haas in check. Brandeis' response as related by his biographer, Alpheus T. Mason, was a letter so "extravagant" in praise of De Haas that Mrs. Brandeis objected to its being sent. But Brandeis did tell Julian, "You, of course, do not expect me to change my view as to De Haas or to his usefulness to the cause."

Then there was the role of Shmarya Levin. It particularly pained and surprised Julian that Levin, his own mentor in Zionism, should be among those who egged on Weizmann in the feud with Brandeis. In a letter to Judah L. Magnes, in April, 1936, after Levin's death, commenting on Magnes' memorial tribute to Levin, Julian was to write:

> It is touchingly beautiful and it naturally deeply impressed me who had known him so well. . . . It always has been a deep regret of my Zionist life that he, more than anyone else, I fear, was responsible for the proceedings in 1921, due largely to that deep devotion and high opinion of Weizmann to which you, too, allude. He carried it, in my judgment, unfortunately too far at that time. It changed the face of Zionism in America, but my personal affection for him as a man never changed.

At one point, in April, 1921, Julian felt that he had worked out a compromise with Dr. Weizmann. Indeed, he believed that Weizmann had agreed to a joint statement that would have meant at least a truce. But such a statement was never issued. Julian felt that Weizmann had reneged on the urging of others, notably Louis Lipsky, who by then had resigned as secretary of the Z.O.A. to lead the rebellion of American Zionists against the Brandeis-Mack leadership.

There is, in fact, reason to believe that Weizmann decided that, regardless of his own preferences, he should go along with the Lipsky group of American Zionists. In this connection, Abraham Tulin, the father-in-law of Stephen Wise's daughter Justine, and a Brandeis-Mack negotiator, recalled:

> Judge Mack's role was to try to bring the two sides together in peace and harmony. That was my role too. We finally succeeded in coming to an agreement on all outstanding differences which satisfied both Justice Brandeis and Judge Mack, on the one side, and Dr. Weizmann on the other side; but this agreement was prevented from being implemented and put into effect by an aspiring younger group in the Z.O.A. who thought they saw an opportunity of taking the leadership

of the Z.O.A. away from the older and more famous men, such as Brandeis, Mack, and Wise.

There is yet another striking version of the story: an item in a New York Yiddish newspaper, the *Yidisher Tageblatt,* for April 19, 1921, the English translation of which has been preserved in the Mack and Brandeis papers:

WHY DID WEIZMANN BREAK WITH THE ZIONIST ORGANIZATION OF AMERICA?

On Saturday evening the officers of the Zionist Organization of America jubilantly told the editor of the *Jewish Daily News* that they expected there would be peace and that the negotiations would come to a satisfactory end Sunday morning. Asked on Sunday evening why there had been a break they answered that they did not know.

What happened? According to the entourage in the Hotel Commodore, this is what took place. Three men representing Dr. Weizmann, Mr. [Leonard] Stein, his secretary, Captain Abraham Tulin, and Judge Bernard A. Rosenblatt, met Mr. Samuel Rosensohn, representing Judge Mack, in the Yale Club Saturday evening and sat through the whole night drafting the document which has been published. They sent a copy to Judge Mack Sunday morning. The other copy was taken to Dr. Weizmann's rooms. Dr. Weizmann was willing to sign it but his friends were not. Dr. Levin threatened to return on the next boat to Europe and break Weizmann politically in Europe. Ussishkin and Rosensohn threatened to return on the next boat to Palestine and arouse all the Palestinians against Weizmann. Neumann and Lipsky and some others of the bitter-enders of the American minority threatened to go on the stump and break Weizmann politically in America. All of these three forces threatened and threatened and threatened, not against this agreement only but against all agreements. And having threatened Weizmann that his career as a Zionist leader would be at an end if he signed any agreement, and having subdued him to their wish, one of the group took from his pocket the manifesto and told Dr. Weizmann to sign now. Dr. Weizmann said he had not seen the Manifesto. They answered, "But we have seen it and we are satisfied. Sign here or we will fight you." He went into the next room, read the Manifesto and he signed it.

This story, which is accredited and was told with some glee at the Commodore, clearly explains that the fight is not a fight between Judge Mack and Dr. Weizmann. It is very evidently a fight between Dr. Weizmann and his own friends.

How much truth, how much speculation, how much rumor, did that article convey? A full answer has probably never been given. Several of the men named in it subsequently made flat denials. Most of them, incidentally, later patched up their differences with Julian and Brandeis, so that recriminations were blotted out, and all, or nearly all, was forgiven.

However, there apparently was enough substance in the article about the roles attributed in it to various leaders for Julian to have given it considerable credence at the time.

For Weizmann did renege, as Julian saw it, on the agreement that Julian believed had been reached.

Dr. Weizmann publicly denied this. Julian, however, published in *The New Palestine*, then the official organ of the Z.O.A., for April 22, 1921, a statement "To the Members of the Zionist Organization of America," that included the following unchallengeable assertions:

I regret deeply to be compelled to make the following statement: Sunday Dr. Weizmann abruptly terminated the negotiations which I have had with him and his associates for the past two weeks, in the hope of reaching common ground. . . .

When, on Saturday night, Dr. Weizmann finally and expressly assented that the Keren Hayesod should in the United States be exclusively a Donation Fund, I felt assured that the efforts for peace and united action had been successful.

The suggestions theretofore made in the course of our conferences were drafted during Saturday night by representatives appointed by Dr. Weizmann and myself. The draft was submitted to each of us Sunday morning. . . .

While the draft was under consideration, Dr. Weizmann advised me that he absolutely rejected it and without further statement or conference issued a proclamation, establishing —independent of the Zionist Organization of America—the Keren Hayesod Bureau in the United States. . . .

JULIAN W. MACK
President, Zionist Organization of America.

It was then that the issue was joined, making inevitable the split which, as Julian later told Magnes, "changed the face of Zionism in America," and also, as he might have added, on the international scene.

How had it happened that Julian Mack, usually so successful as a mediator, had failed so completely in this vital controversy?

Aside from his personal loyalty to Brandeis, and his belief in Brandeis' cause, which as he once observed to Wise was more important than loyalty to any one person, one explanation is that in the bitterness that raged, he was personally subjected to a good deal of abuse. As one example, Lipsky, in the heat of the feuding, leveled at Julian a charge which Julian took as a shocking reflection on his integrity. The accusation was that following Lipsky's resignation as secretary of the Z.O.A. Julian, as president of the organization, had ordered that all of Lipsky's mail—not only official Zionist communications but also personal letters addressed to him—should be intercepted. Later, Lipsky was to apologize and admit that his charges had been unfounded.

There was Iago-like activity around Julian also. Revealing in this regard is a note that Frankfurter sent to Brandeis on March 7, 1921, commenting on Julian's frame of mind. Apparently, Julian previously had not been as belligerent as Brandeis had wished.

However, after working with Julian on a summary statement related to the controversy, which was handed to Dr. Weizmann on his arrival in the United States, Frankfurter told Brandeis:

> I think you will agree that the summary is a good document. It shows what Mack can do. I feel as though his self-respect has been at last thoroughly aroused. Both his will and his brain are at last on the job.

At that point, Frankfurter, obviously, was not urging collaboration with Weizmann.

In short, Julian had been goaded into anger by Frankfurter, who a little later would telegraph Brandeis from Harvard: "Hope you will impress Mack necessity of dropping his concessions. . . ." Brandeis, incidentally, was adamant all along. Even Walter Lippmann, then editor of the *New York Evening World,* in what was perhaps his one definite venture in Zionism, tried his hand at peacemaking. In that connection, Frankfurter, on April 25, telegraphed to Brandeis at "Stoneleigh Court, Washington":

> ONLY FOR YOU. WALTER LIPPMANN WRITES HAS HAD TWO VERY LONG TALKS WITH W[EIZMANN] AND AT THE END HE ASKED ME TO ARRANGE AN OPPORTUNITY FOR MEETING WITH W. AND YOU, WALTER TO BE PRESENT TO TELL HIS POINT OF VIEW, WANTS TO REACH AN AGREEMENT IF HUMANLY POSSIBLE.

But Brandeis' answer was: "No. . . . No one should work with him."

Brandeis' response was predictable. Even his admirers, let alone his critics, found him "guilty" of "extreme rigidity." Harold Laski had a high regard for Brandeis. Yet, he once wrote to Justice Holmes that Brandeis "treats Zionists who do not agree with him like criminals . . . gives orders like an omnipotent sultan." There were some who believed this judgment to be true, though others saw Brandeis' rigidity as staunch dedication to correct principle—

the kind of dedication that caused him to send Julian a handwritten note on April 8, 1921, during Julian's negotiations with Weizmann:

> JWM. These have been trying days for all of us. Upon you the burden has been extra heavy. Throughout the negotiations you have done all that was possible to make our position understood. To hold firm to that position—whatever the issue—is demanded by the high ideals of the cause we have tried to serve and by our duty to those who had reposed confidence in our judgment and leadership.
>
> LDB

"There is no bridge between Washington and Pinsk," Weizmann later said of Brandeis' stance.

By then, indeed, there was no bridge any more. There might have been one, appropriately, in London, before attitudes hardened, as Ben Cohen suggests; namely, through action by Julian. He, rather than Lipsky, was supposed to have been there as the head of the American Zionist group, for he was still president of the Z.O.A. But Julian had been incapacitated by an attack of phlebitis, symptoms of which had begun to trouble him while he was still in Paris. So his doctors, as well as Jessie, insisted that instead of going to London he should "take the cure" at Hot Springs, Arkansas. Thus the one man who might have restrained Brandeis in London was not there.

At the 1919 convention of the Z.O.A. in Chicago, Julian again had been elected by an overwhelming majority to the presidency of the Z.O.A. In 1920, at Buffalo, he was reelected once more, along with the full Brandeis-Mack slate, although Julian had made it plain that there were differences between the American Zionists and the Zionists in Europe.

So, on the face of it, all had seemed serene in American Zionist circles. But under the surface, rebellion had been brewing. Nor could it be quelled; emotions were too strong for that, though afterwards students, as well as leading participants, would have difficulty in pinpointing what the monumental quarrel really had been all about.

In *Fifty Years of Zionism*, a brilliant analysis of Weizmann's autobiography *Trial and Error,* the historian Oskar K. Rabinowicz, after recalling the split that had occurred many years before between Weizmann and Theodor Herzl, reached an interesting conclusion:

> While the cleavage between Herzl and Dr. Weizmann was deep, no difference of any basic importance is traceable between him and Brandeis, so that the historian [Boehm] could rightly say that "on the whole it is to be stated that most things demanded by Brandeis . . . gradually have been executed."

To a large degree, this conclusion was borne out by events, including the establishment of the official Jewish Agency for Palestine and such private agencies as the Palestine Economic Corporation, in which non-Zionists such as Felix Warburg of Kuhn, Loeb & Co. were major figures. For those agencies, formed for the direction and financing of the upbuilding of Palestine, operated substantially along the lines that Brandeis had urged—and did so with the approval of Chaim Weizmann.

Pertinent, too, is a portrayal of Weizmann by his admiring friend, Sir Isaiah Berlin, of Oxford University. In a 1957 lecture on Weizmann, Sir Isaiah observed:

> When biographers came to consider his disagreements with the founder of the movement, Theodor Herzl, his duels with Justice Louis Brandeis, and with the leader of the extreme right wing Zionists, Vladimir Jabotinsky; or, for that matter, his differences with such genuine supporters of his own moderate policies as Sokolow, or Ben-Gurion, and many a lesser figure, they will—they inevitably must—ask how much of this was due to personal ambition, love of power, underestimation of opponents, impatient autocracy of temper; and how much was principle, devotion to ideas, rational conviction of what was right or expedient. When this question is posed, I do not believe it will find any very clear answer: perhaps no answer at all.

In other words, Weizmann was another Brandeis.

Thus a collision between Weizmann and Brandeis seems to have been inevitable, with Julian Mack, much to his distress, deeply involved because he was Brandeis' "Number One Knight." The collision occurred when Weizmann paid his first visit to the United States.

It was the division over Keren Hayesod, or the Palestine Foundation Fund, as it is known in English, that brought matters to a head. In setting up Keren Hayesod, the World Zionist Organization had acted counter to Brandeis' suggestions in various particulars. For one thing, Keren Hayesod was established as an international fund. Brandeis, however, had argued for the "federation" principle; i.e., that the Zionist organization in each country should have its own separate fund. Brandeis' suggestion was denounced as "separatism," or, worse, as "Diaspora nationalism"; as a "treasonable" negation of the Zionist principle that the Jews the world over formed one "nation." For another thing, the establishment of Keren Hayesod spelled rejection of Brandeis' injunction against the "commingling" of donation money and investment funds in one portfolio.

In the acrimonious dispute, it was alleged that the Mack-Brandeis Zionists objected to the Keren Hayesod setup because they intended to "drag their feet" in their effort to raise funds for Palestine in America, the main source of Zionist funds. This charge was not true. Julian had already announced that though the Z.O.A. intended to stay out of Keren Hayesod, it would establish a "Palestine Donation Fund" for the rebuilding of Palestine. But the insistence of the W.Z.O., under Weizmann, on going ahead with its program, in America as well as elsewhere, was the last straw so far as chances for a truce between the "Weizmannists" and the "Brandeisists" were concerned. That meant, as Weizmann admitted, that the W.Z.O. was going over the heads of the Brandeis-Mack Zionists in their own bailiwick, the United States; it was the clearest kind of challenge.

There were other "last straws," too, as far as Brandeis was concerned. One was a petty action attributed to Weizmann. While he was in England, Brandeis, because of his great prestige, had succeeded in getting two leading British Jews, Rufus Isaacs (later Lord Reading) and multimillionaire Alfred Mond (later Lord Melchett), both then non-Zionists, interested in giving financial assistance to the Jewish Homeland in Palestine.

"Brandeis wanted to go forward to build a Jewish state at once, practically, ideally," Robert Szold, who was also in London at the time, recalled. "He insisted that the best Jews, the Jews most capable for the purpose, be enlisted. He repeated and reiterated that the day of the Zionist speakers and propagandists was over. He had spoken to Lord Reading and Lord Mond to come in. The powers in the Zionist organization at the time were the old-time orators. They were not going to give up their power. Weizmann, behind Brandeis' back, went to Reading and Mond, to persuade them not to come in. Brandeis then said . . . 'We must therefore act, and act quickly.'"

Brandeis' intense anger was to be expected, though later Mond did help Palestine generously. It was to be expected also that he would be more firmly convinced than ever that Zionist activities should be directed, not by orators like Weizmann or Levin, or writers like Lipsky, but by "practical men of affairs." In a memorandum he subsequently prepared, later known as "the Zeeland Memorandum," because he had composed it aboard the *S.S.Zeeland* on which he sailed back to the United States from England, Brandeis wrote:

> The only consideration which we are at liberty to regard is efficiency . . . not to pick men because of what they may have done in the past. The only proper test . . . is fitness and efficiency. The man who is best fitted to perform a particular task must be selected. To my mind, it is an insult to a devoted Zionist to appoint him to office only because of services which he has performed in the past . . . the men who are to serve the cause of the Jewish homeland must have other qualities besides an understanding of the Jewish situation, of the Zionist situation in all the countries, an understanding of the Zionist past. . . .

In the conclusion of his "Zeeland Memorandum," Brandeis said:

> Furthermore, we must never lose sight of the fact that our plans should be such as to elicit the full cooperation of all Jews, those who do not want to build up the Zionist Organization, but who do want to share with the Zionist Organization in the upbuilding of Palestine.

In short, with Mack in agreement, Brandeis wanted to broaden, not to narrow, support for the Jewish Homeland, but understandably he offended some "old" Zionists. Among the "old" Zionists who were outraged was Menahem Ussishkin of Russia, who had been appointed by the W.Z.O. as head of Keren Hayesod. In this position he was the official who directed land purchases in Palestine. Brandeis considered Ussishkin too "undiplomatic" and also too prone to act on his own; these impressions were amply based on fact. Brandeis was shocked, too, that Ussishkin, without proper budgetary authority, should have purchased in the name of Keren Hayesod several thousand acres of land in the Emek region simply "because they were available." Later, Ussishkin was to be proven right in his judgment, and in time, Brandeis was to associate himself with Ussishkin on overall Zionist policy, notably in opposition to British schemes for "partition." He learned to appreciate Ussishkin's sterling, if bulldog, qualities. But in 1921 Brandeis could not stomach Ussishkin.

There was also Vladimir Jabotinsky. To Brandeis, who had met with him in London and in Palestine, Jabotinsky was an irresponsible, wild man. Many other Zionists for many years probably agreed with Brandeis' estimate of Jabotinsky. As in the case of Ussishkin, Brandeis probably was wrong, at least in part, in his evaluation of Jabotinsky, who consistently mistrusted the British mandatory authority. Jabotinsky's Jewish patriotism was beyond question. At London, in 1920, however, Brandeis insisted that Jabotinsky not be given any prominent role in Zionist affairs in Palestine and believed that Weizmann had promised to abide by his wishes. Yet, for Zionist political reasons, and because Jabotinsky then was a hero figure to many Palestinian Jews as a founder of the Jewish Legion, Jabotinsky was named to the Zionist Executive. To Brandeis this action was an unforgivable breach of faith. From then on, he became convinced that Weizmann was "untrustworthy." He never changed his mind; nor did Weizmann, as shown by snide remarks about Brandeis in his autobiography, ever "forgive" Brandeis for his attitude. So, as Robert Szold recalled, "It was in London, in July, 1920, that the break occurred."

Judge Bernard A. Rosenblatt, an American partisan of Weizmann, agreed:

> . . . at the London Zionist Conference of 1920 . . . the differences came to a head, largely, it seemed to me at the time, because Brandeis wanted to broaden the movement so as to include important [non-Zionist] figures of British Jewry, while Weizmann, understandably, may have feared that this might interfere with his acknowledged leadership. . . . Weizmann convinced me that the real issue was the integrity of Zionism as a world movement, which would be endangered by separatist and individual action on the part of American Zionists. . . . I was so convinced that unity was essential that I overlooked, as I later thought, the supreme importance of the economic program which Brandeis and Mack had formulated. . . . Be that as it may, Weizmann drew up a masterly document which I was to bring to the attention of the American Zionists.

Weizmann's "masterly document" was a declaration of war against the Brandeis-Mack Zionists. It was a war in which the majority of American Zionist leaders, in the various local Zionist organizations around the country, joined with Weizmann and his "knights," particularly Shmarya Levin, Ussishkin, Judge Rosenblatt, and, above all, Louis Lipsky. As a practical matter, of course, it was this defection of fellow Americans that produced the defeat of the Brandeis-Mack leadership.

Inasmuch as Julian, as the record shows, was able to work out a compromise, sincerely assuring Weizmann on April 25 that "no one wishes to impair the integrity of the World Zionist Organization," the question arises why the majority of American Zionists repudiated the Brandeis-Mack leadership. The answer seems to require psychological and sociological insights. It may well be that without fully realizing it themselves, most American Zionists, then mainly of Eastern European immigrant stock, had reacted adversely to the Brandeis-Mack leadership for some time. Theirs may have been an attitude common to old-time members of institutions when "converts" emerge as leaders; that is, they were emotionally susceptible to any issue which would bring out subconscious hostility toward "newcomers." Though this may not have been the whole story, it was probably a fundamental element in their opposition. Their attitude, if it existed, no doubt was hardened by the fact that the Brandeis-Mack leadership mainly represented "German" or "German-type" Jews, or so it seemed.

Were Jews who had gone to Harvard, who lived on Fifth Avenue, who bore names such as Meyer, Flexner, Szold, Frankfurter and Straus, as well as Mack and Brandeis, to be fully trusted with the fate of Zionism? It would not have been surprising if a majority of Zionists had instinctively tended to answer that question in the negative. For, in the 1920's, the old division, one that Julian had so long deplored, still existed between the "German" and the "Russian" Jews. In all likelihood it was this division that underlay the whole controversy which had erupted in American Zionism.

The controversy heated to a boil when Weizmann came to America in April, 1921. Julian had asked him not to come. It would be "unseemly," Weizmann was told, for a British Zionist to appear to be directing the Zionist movement in the United States. But Weizmann decided to make the journey nevertheless; his sole purpose, he said, was to achieve a compromise with the American Zionists. But to Brandeis, seconded by Julian, Weizmann's visit was a challenge to the Brandeis leadership, instigated by American Zionists who opposed him.

Weizmann then did a shrewd thing. Through Kurt Blumenfeld, a Zionist leader in Germany, he persuaded Albert Einstein to accompany him on his visit to the United States. Ostensibly, Einstein, already an ardent supporter of Zionism, made the journey to help raise funds for the Hebrew University in Jerusalem. But Weizmann's main motive in taking Einstein with him was to have Einstein's status as a world-renowned figure offset the prestige of

Justice Brandeis. The strategy was highly successful. As more than one observer noted, Einstein, who, like Weizmann, had never been to America before, was idolized "like a movie star." The commotion caused by his visit inevitably added much to the force of Weizmann's challenge to Brandeis. Moreover, Einstein entered directly into the fray. Thus, at one New York meeting, he dramatically said to fellow Zionists concerning Chaim Weizmann: "He is your leader—follow no other." His words rang out like those of an Old Testament prophet and influenced many against Brandeis.

To be sure, Einstein was then unsophisticated about politics in general and he had "bought" a prejudiced view about both Brandeis and Julian. Later, he became quite friendly with Julian and, after a visit with Brandeis soon after his arrival in America, he changed his mind about Brandeis, too. The visit to Brandeis was arranged by Jacques Loeb, the American Jewish scientist, at the suggestion of Bernard Flexner.

"When Einstein came back from the meeting with L.D.B., amazed and delighted, he said unequivocally to Loeb that he would stand to the utmost with L.D.B. and the Americans . . . that he was utterly sick of what Weizmann had done and was trying to do." So Flexner, who was later to help establish Einstein at Princeton, informed Frankfurter, who passed the word to Julian. But by that time, the damage had already been done. The controversy boiled down to the question of whether or not the Mack-Brandeis leadership was to receive the support of American Zionism. It was to settle the issue in a definitive and democratic way that the special convention at Cleveland was called for June, 1921. As president of the Z.O.A., Julian issued the convention call:

> Zionism in this country is menaced by forces of disruption. The Zionists of America are now called upon to express their opinion, to say the final word. . . . This convention will decide whether the forces in this country will remain unimpaired.

This was clearly a fighting statement, forecasting the mood of the convention that followed.

The Cleveland sessions began with apparent harmony. Both Mack, as chairman, and Weizmann, as a "distinguished visitor" (who was greeted with tremendous applause and the singing of *Hatikvah*, the Zionist anthem), addressed the convention. Both men called for "peace" within the organization.

Weizmann said: "I have no feeling against Judge Mack. He is the one I am willing to go out of my way for. . . ." Julian, in turn, expressed his admiration for Weizmann both as a man and as a Zionist. He then delivered a strong defense of his administration, one which prompted Brandeis, who was kept in close contact with the convention, to telegraph to Julian from Washington: "Your opening address was fine." Earlier, Brandeis had also told Julian, "Your statement is in very good form. The way is now clear and straight."

But it was obvious from the start that the vote would go against the Brandeis-Mack leadership, and that the majority of the delegates would stand behind Weizmann. They would regard the position of Brandeis as "technical," whereas Weizmann—and Lipsky—stood for "true Zionism." As Horace Kallen was to recall, the cries from the audience: "Our Weizmann!" and "Our Ussishkin!"—reflecting the identification of most of the delegates with "Pinsk" rather than with "Washington"—showed how the convention would go.

In vain did Frankfurter, Stephen S. Wise and Abba Hillel Silver, among others, seek to refute the allegations that Julian and Brandeis were "not Jewish Jews . . . good men, but lacking in Jewish hearts, without understanding of the Jewish people."

On oratorical complaints that Brandeis "laid down impossible rules," Frankfurter scored a point: "Moses also laid down rules; I suppose Moses did not 'understand the Jewish people.'"

But, as Julian had already observed before calling the convention to order, the followers of Weizmann and Lipsky had the votes. Robert Szold recalled:

> It was the old antagonism, which Judge Mack had always deplored, between Americanized Jews and the newcomers, with their allies from Europe. The Europeans, representing the "masses," were not going to give up their power. Let Mack

and Brandeis get out. Mack and Brandeis may have contributed mightily through the Balfour Declaration, but they were "strangers". . . . So the Europeans and their counterparts in America took control of the American Zionist organization from then until 1930.

A no-confidence resolution containing a harsh indictment was introduced by the opposition. It was adopted, 153 votes for, 71 against—a smashing rejection of Brandeis, and of Julian.

Julian took the repudiation with characteristic dignity. Despite his painful shock over what he considered to be deception by Weizmann, over attacks on Frankfurter, Ben Cohen and Robert Szold, and over the "turnabout" represented by Shmarya Levin's attacks on him, he appeared calm when he went to the rostrum after the vote.

"I accept, of course, what I foresaw long ago," he told the gathering. He then expressed thanks to the organization for "the opportunity to have [had] some share in the working out of the great problems which have confronted and, for years to come, will confront, Jewry."

Even under normal circumstances, his term of office would have ended with that convention. Accordingly, it would not have been necessary for Mack to yield his presidency formally to a new regime. But, as he had determined beforehand, "self-respect" required that in case he would be repudiated he should not hold the office of president "a single moment after the vote has been cast." So he submitted his resignation from the speaker's rostrum before the entire assembly of more than 200 delegates. Then he read to the convention a letter that Brandeis had written to him three days before. As was to be expected, this letter revealed Brandeis as uncompromising in adherence to his principles.

"Strict adherence to these principles is demanded by the high Zionist ideals," Brandeis wrote, adding: "We who believe in those principles . . . cannot properly take part in any administration of Zionist affairs which repudiates them. . . . [I present] my resignation as Honorary President. Our place will then be as humble soldiers in the ranks to hasten by our struggle the coming of the day when the policies in which we believe will be recognized as the only ones through which our great ends may be achieved."

Julian then announced that "by direction," name by name, almost the full membership of the National Executive Committee was also resigning—more than 30 in all. The list included some who recalled the earliest history of Zionism in America: Stephen Wise, who had been the first secretary of the Federation of American Zionists; Nathan Straus, an early convert from the ranks of the "German" Jews of wealth and status; Jacob De Haas, who had been an associate of Herzl himself; and Nathan D. Kaplan, of the old "Knights of Zion" in Chicago, the first group of organized Zionists in America. Also on the list were Horace M. Kallen, Dr. Harry Friedenwald, and a special group of men who, because of their ability and their personal attachment to either Brandeis or Mack, had been assigned to sensitive projects: Felix Frankfurter, Robert Szold, Bernard Flexner, and Benjamin V. Cohen.

The wholesale resignations marked the end of an era for the American Zionist movement, the era in which the influence and personality of Brandeis, with Julian his "Number One Knight" to the end, had been in the forefront of Zionist affairs.

34. A Zionist Still

There remained one satisfaction for Julian and his group. They had succeeded in keeping Hadassah, the tremendously vital American women's Zionist organization, out of the fracas. Especially Julian had felt that Hadassah's work in maintaining medical and other health functions in Palestine was too important for it to be caught up in Zionist "politics." So Henrietta Szold, the president of Hadassah, was told that she could be "neutral," a stance for which she and the pioneers in Palestine were always to be grateful. From then on, incidentally, Julian became a kind of honorary member of Hadassah, a symbolic father-figure upon whom its leaders were to lean for guidance during later troubled times.

Would the history of Jewish Palestine have been different if the split in American Zionism had not occurred, if Brandeis and Mack, Stephen Wise, Felix Frankfurter, Eugene Meyer, Bernard Flexner, Robert Szold, Nathan Straus, Horace Kallen and Benjamin V. Cohen had remained in Zionist leadership without an interregnum? These are fair, albeit "iffy," questions.

The answer could be in the affirmative; had that group remained as leaders of American Zionism, there might have been a stronger Jewish Palestine, and hence a stronger State of Israel, earlier than was the case. For it seems clear that if Brandeis, Julian and their associates had remained as the leaders, broader financial support might have come to Jewish Palestine in the 1920's, since these men probably would have been more successful in appeals to wealthy non-Zionist Jews than those who followed them.

True, nearly all of them, including Julian, eventually returned to the Z.O.A.; even Brandeis did so, though he became more secluded from public view with respect to Zionism than before. But before they did return, after 1928—at the earnest appeal of the leaders of the very elements who had forced their resignations at Cleveland— the Z.O.A. suffered a severe slump, both in membership and in fund raising. Weizmann, for one, pointed this out and perhaps regretted, from that viewpoint, that Julian's proposed compromise had not been worked out in 1921.

Perhaps that slump of the 1920's, which was not really checked until the effects of Hitlerism had begun to make themselves felt, would not have been so sharp if the Brandeis-Mack leadership had not been forced out. Then, too, because of Brandeis' departure, the Zionist movement suffered the loss of several particularly effective young men who had been drawn to Zionism by Brandeis, such as Eugene Meyer, the banker-economist, Dr. Alexander Sachs, and Lewis L. Strauss, who was to become chairman of the Atomic Energy Commission during the Eisenhower years. It may be conjectured, too, that if Brandeis had remained the acknowledged leader of American Zionism, the Zionist cause might have obtained a more effective hearing in Washington, especially with President Franklin D. Roosevelt, and that at least some of the sad history of American aloofness toward the idea of a Jewish homeland in Palestine, as well as indifference to the fate of European Jewry in the 1930's, might not have taken place.

Yet Julian and his associates, including Brandeis, felt no elation over the adverse developments that were to result from their ouster in Cleveland. There was no spirit of "I told you so." On the contrary, both Mack and Brandeis were greatly troubled. Julian, for one, made plain, in his valedictory following his repudiation at Cleveland, that he would remain loyal to the Zionist ideal: the upbuilding of the Jewish Homeland in Palestine. After announcing his resignation, he said:

> I further desire to state, not so much to you as to general Jewry, that no action which you have taken, no action which you will take, no action that you can take, will ever drive me, or any of the gentlemen whose names I have mentioned, from the ranks of membership in the Zionist Organization of America . . . and will never lessen by the slightest degree the intensity of our Zionism, our devotion to Palestine.

There were tears in the eyes of many of the delegates as he spoke. Many who had voted against him and Brandeis were among those who wept. But there also was no elation among the victors at Cleveland. It was probably symbolic that Emanuel Neumann, later head of the Z.O.A. and of the American Section of the World Zionist Organization, the delegate who had introduced the no-confidence resolution against the Mack-Brandeis group, was also the one to introduce a resolution thanking them "for inestimable services rendered by them to the cause of Zionism in a critical moment of its history." That signified an effort to heal the breach—a Mackian stance of conciliation that Julian, even while still smarting from bitter words at Cleveland, earnestly welcomed.

Although he was "out" of any official leadership role in the Z.O.A. for the seven or eight years that followed the vote in Cleveland, Julian nonetheless remained quite active in Zionist affairs. Shortly after the Cleveland convention, his group met at Pittsburgh, where, at a gathering over which he presided, the Palestine Development Council, Inc. was formed. This was a non-profit membership corporation, which supporters of Jewish Palestine, non-Zionist as well as Zionist, were invited to join. Its purpose, in line with the memorandum Brandeis had drawn up aboard the *S.S. Zeeland,* was to sponsor enterprises that would provide investment capital for Palestine. The object was to help immigrants to Palestine build homes, obtain equipment and enable them to be self-reliant.

Mack devoted much attention to the project. "Terribly busy, both in Court, and in Palestine matters, trying to get something going in the Palestine Development Council movement," he wrote to his brother William in December, 1921. Indeed, he who had so little personal interest in money now found himself almost obsessed with money questions—for Palestine. That did not mean, as critics of the Brandeis-Mack leadership charged at times, that he felt that American funds for the settlements were all-important. "Nothing can be more absurd," Julian once commented. "The people who are making the real contribution to Palestine are the *halutzim* tramping from Europe to get to Palestine, university men *and* women suffering hardships to build the roads and do the real work. All that we do in the way of giving money is insignificant compared to what *they* are doing." But he was aware that without funds from

American Jews the dream of Palestine restored could not be turned into reality.

Nor, as head of the Palestine Development Council and its parent, the Palestine Development League, did he confine his appeals to Zionists. "I am not now endeavoring to make converts to Zionism," he said in 1923. "I used to do that, up to 1919, the end of the war. I have ceased doing that because, if I can make converts to an interest in Palestine, the rest is apt to come. . . ."

He was also aware that financial support on a much larger scale—in hundreds of millions rather than in hundreds of thousands of dollars—would be needed, and that a great deal of capital and other resources would have to be arranged for, or created by, the *halutzim*—the Palestine pioneers—themselves, by their ingenuity and labor. Large-scale trade on world markets; scientific agriculture, with modern fertilizers and irrigation; massive economic planning—cooperative, partly socialist, partly capitalist, to promote initiative and enterprise; these objectives, Julian recognized, would all have to be pursued to build up a strong Jewish homeland, in large part by the kibbutzim and the Histadrut, the General Federation of Labor formed by the Jewish workers in Palestine in 1920. So the activity that greatly absorbed Julian in the early 1920's was, in fact, only on the order of a pilot model. But that was a time when both models and pilots, however small or uncertain, were needed to support future achievements.

Under the sponsorship of the Palestine Development Council there was formed in 1922 the Palestine Cooperative Company, Inc. with Julian as an active director. One of its major interests was to help organize and provide a portion of the funds for cooperative-type financial agencies in the Palestine communities, including credit unions. It also organized the Palestine Building Loan and Saving Association, Ltd., the first in the country, which as early as 1923 arranged funds for the construction of some 200 new houses, and went on over the years to play a role in assuring that streets and other improvements would be well planned. One early home loan was made to the Po'ale Zion leader David Ben-Gurion.

To help individual farmers, and operators of businesses which of necessity were on a modest scale then and for some time to come, was a major interest of the Cooperative Company. In addition, the company participated in the initial financing of two of the largest and most important enterprises of the new Palestine and later of the State of Israel. One was the hydroelectric power project on the Jordan River initiated by Pinhas Rutenberg. Another was the world-famous Dead Sea potash enterprise.

In 1926, there came into being the Palestine Economic Corporation for channeling investment funds into the Jewish Homeland. In effect, this corporation was a successor to the Palestine Cooperative Company, but with the added participation of such prominent non-Zionist Jews as Felix M. Warburg, Louis Marshall, and Herbert Lehman. In substance, the Palestine Economic Corporation was the outcome of a merger of the bulk of the assets held in Palestine by the Reconstruction Committee of the Joint Distribution Committee and by the Palestine Cooperative Company, together with subscriptions from non-Zionists who by then were prominent in non-political efforts to build the Jewish Homeland in Palestine. This, it should be noted, was in fact a fusion of the Brandeis *and* Weizmann concepts of aid to the Jewish Homeland.

The Brandeis-Mack leadership was represented in the Palestine Economic Corporation notably through Robert Szold, who from 1926 on was variously its vice-president, vice-chairman of the board, president, and chairman of the board. The corporation was non-political, but it worked closely with the official world Zionist movement, the Zionists in Palestine, and the Brandeis-Mack group. In essence, it represented the implementation of the basic concepts of the Brandeis-Mack leadership as to how American Jewry could be expected to help in the development of Jewish Palestine. After the State of Israel was created, the Palestine Economic Corporation continued as the PEC Israel Economic Corporation, with Brandeis-Mack figures still in top roles.

In addition, charitable activity, begun immediately after the Cleveland episode, with Julian participating along with Brandeis and others of their group, was conducted by Palestine Endowment Funds, Inc. This agency was set up to receive and administer donations for charitable, scientific, religious and educational objectives, including the Hebrew University in Jerusalem. Julian served as president from its founding until he was succeeded by Robert Szold 20 years later. Associated with him were Brandeis, Benjamin V. Cohen, Mary Fels, Dr. Harry Friedenwald, Louis S. Posner, Sol Rosenbloom, Samuel J. Rosensohn, Nathan Straus, Jr., Julius Weiss and Stephen S. Wise.

A number of the major American gifts for housing, health, research, scholarships, and educational activities that were to continue in the State of Israel were made through Palestine Endowment Funds, Inc. Gifts from Brandeis himself, including funds from his estate after his death, totalled more than $600,000 and were used for such purposes as settlement aid, housing, youth work, the education and training of mechanics and craftsmen, chemical research, water exploration, and the extermination of malaria. The Funds gave voluntary legal and financial advice—with Julian serving among the volunteers—to prospective donors.

Thus, weaving in and out of the story of the development of the Jewish Homeland into what became the State of Israel, the names of Brandeis and Mack continued to appear at every level: ideological, educational, economic and charitable. Almost every major suggestion they made over the years had its impact on what finally was done. In 1972, the Fund observed its fiftieth anniversary, with Robert Szold still as chairman.

By the 1970's, in addition to gifts from Brandeis and other early donors, the Palestine Endowment Funds—its name changed to PEF Israel Endowment Funds, Inc.—included the following endowments: the Felix Warburg family gift of $500,000; the Max and Jessie Cohen Estate of $300,000 for immigrant housing developments; the Julius and Marie Scheider Foundation Fund for the Neuropsychiatric Department at the Hebrew University; the Boris Margolin Institute for Technical Education at Beersheba; the Drs. Rosa and Dora Einhorn Dental Clinic at Tel Aviv University; the Bertha V. Guggenheimer Fund for playgrounds supervised by Hadassah; and the Sol Schwartz and Rachel Etting Cohen Funds for music scholarships at the Music Teachers' Training College of Tel Aviv. The PEF also supervised the Sol Rosenbloom Fund for Jewish Studies at the Hebrew University; the Max Schloessinger scholarship for Islamic studies at the Hebrew University; the Friedenwald funds for ophthalmology and medicine, the Israel B. Brodie Memorial Fund for scientific research (named after the Zionist who for many years was the fund's representative in Palestine) and the high school at Kiryat Shmoneh established by the Danciger Estate.

In 1966, there was established, in association with the PEF, a Center of Applied Science at the Hebrew University which has played a key role in the industrial development of the State of Israel. This center, which led to the establishment of the Graduate School of Applied Science and Technology, bears the name of Robert Szold. But in a large sense, because Brandeis and Julian Mack were Szold's mentors in Zionism, it is also a memorial to the zeal of Mack and Brandeis for the development of the Jewish State.

Nor did the Brandeis-Mack group confine its pro-Zionist activity to the work of the PEF and other special organizations. In 1930, when the Z.O.A. came upon "hard times," including a great decline in its membership, the Brandeis-Mack group, in effect, was summoned from its "exile" to restore strength to the American Zionist organization. Representing Brandeis and Julian, Robert Szold then became official leader. Julian, after turning down pleas that he return as president, accepted the title of "honorary president." Thus, the split was mended at last.

35. Harvard Again

In 1922, the year after the split in the Z.O.A., Julian went through yet another harrowing conflict over a Jewish "question," this time at his own beloved Harvard University. Back in 1919, Julian had been elected to Harvard's Board of Overseers, the first Jew to hold that position. He was reelected for a second six-year term in 1927, and yet again in 1937, thus becoming directly involved in the shaping of Harvard's policies.

To be an Overseer at Harvard was a distinction that he especially appreciated, for no one took the concept of "alma mater" more seriously than he. He "paid his way," too, as Overseers were tacitly supposed to do, by helping get gifts of money for Harvard. As might have been expected, the prospective donors he sought out were mainly Jewish.

Indeed, he made a special point of encouraging Jewish contributions to the university, on the theory that a monetary kind of "assimilation" between the American Jewish community and the New England aristocracy, represented by Harvard, would be good for both. He himself, with Jessie, established a scholarship fund at Harvard with a gift of $3,000—"seed money," he said, to attract other contributions to the fund. It was his second fund, following the one he had set up in honor of Ames.

He had "hardly" expected to be elected as an Overseer that first time in 1919, he confided to Horace Kallen. "Boston decides," he said, meaning the "proper" Bostonians who usually made up the majority of alumni casting ballots at Cambridge on Commencement Day, "and they don't want a Jew, I imagine." But he had been elected, probably in large part because of a situation that was then building up toward an explosive episode.

By the 1920's, the number of Jewish students at Harvard College, including many described as being of "immigrant" stock—meaning East Europeans who had not yet attained affluence—was about 20 per cent of the total student body. In the schools of law and medicine, the number of Jews was even larger. All this seemed to

291

trouble a number of Harvard people, and not only "proper" Bostonians such as Harvard's president, A. Lawrence Lowell. Some Jews also were concerned. These included "Jewish snobs," as Louis Marshall once called them, who, Marshall felt, sent their sons to Harvard "to be away from other Jews."

This situation, exceedingly painful to Julian, came to a head during his first term as an Overseer. It was a predicament that he could have side-stepped—as other Jews had in the past—and would in the future. But he characteristically responded; a kind of "Joseph," it might be said—the successful brother unable to desert his father's "other sons."

Because of his strong sentimental attachment to Harvard, he had let himself believe that Harvard, of all institutions, would never be involved in anti-Jewish discrimination. He seemed not to have taken into account the fact that the Harvard of the 1920's, in certain superficial but nevertheless important aspects, was as different from his own Harvard of the 1880's as narrow, ancestor-worshipping A. Lawrence Lowell, its president in the 1920's, was different from the tolerant, cosmopolitan Charles W. Eliot, whom Lowell had succeeded in 1909. At any rate, in the spring of 1922 Julian was shocked when President Lowell asked him, as an Overseer, to approve a proposal that would limit the number of Jewish students admitted to Harvard College. In short, he was asked to endorse a form of *numerus clausus*, a "Jewish quota" such as was often used in anti-Semitic European states.

It has been said that A. Lawrence Lowell—who may or may not have been consciously anti-Semitic—looked upon Julian not as just another Overseer, but as a kind of "Jewish ambassador" on the Board of Overseers, one with a dual capacity: representing the Jewish world to Harvard, on the one hand, and the Harvard community to the Jewish world, on the other. If this was so, it would explain why he put his proposal to Julian before presenting it to the full board. It was also said that Lowell, noting Julian's loyalty to Harvard, and noting also his benign style, never "pushy"—a word that seemed to come easily to Lowell when he sized up "acceptable" Jews—felt that Julian was "somebody with whom he could do business."

Be that as it may, just as in 1909 Julian had engaged in a verbal encounter with a Cabot Lodge over the "Jewish problem," he now exchanged even more serious ripostes with a Lowell over the same problem. This, incidentally, made a point which a social historian might view as ironic confirmation of the progress achieved by some sons of immigrants in America. For in this confrontation A. Lawrence Lowell and Julian William Mack functioned as equals —both officers of Harvard University.

For Harvard to adopt a "Jewish quota" struck Julian as perhaps potentially more dangerous to the status of the Jews in America than even the attacks upon Jews then current in Henry Ford's publication, the *Dearborn Independent.* Ford's attacks on Jews were disturbing enough, but they came from an individual. On the other hand, for an American institution as prestigious as Harvard to adopt a policy which seemed to imply that Jews as a class were "undesirable" could have been interpreted as an authoritative sanction of anti-Semitism in the United States. Such was Julian's reaction. It was also the reaction of other Jewish leaders when Lowell's scheme became generally known.

Julian had tried to persuade Lowell to drop the "quota" idea before the matter became public. But he did not succeed. Clearly Lowell had raised the issue with him, not in order to explain it to him or to get his reaction, but to persuade him to be an advocate of the proposal both to the Jewish community and to his fellow Overseers.

In fairness to Lowell, it should be recorded that he sincerely viewed his proposal as less brutal than was generally understood. For example, he felt it was generous that no Jewish applicant for admission to the freshman class would be rejected if he passed the examinations given for academic ability. The "quota" procedure was to be applied "only" to Jews who wished to transfer to Harvard from other colleges, and "only" to those who had not fully passed the examinations but normally would have been admitted nevertheless as a matter of traditional Harvard practice. Lowell had expected Julian to concur when he wrote to him:

I think you understand very clearly the object as we see it. It is the duty of Harvard to receive just as many boys who have come, or whose parents have come, to this country without our background as it can effectively educate; including in education the imparting, not only of book knowledge, but of the ideas and traditions of our people. Experience seems to place that proportion at about 15%. That number we ought to take; but if we take more than we can bring into contact with our student body, we shall do those we do receive far less good, and to the detriment of the institution. We are trying in this to pursue the policy which, if pursued by all colleges, would be for the greatest interest of everyone concerned. What do you think of the method of accomplishing the result that we have suggested?

The key to Lowell's thinking, of course, was his emphasis upon the "traditions of our people," by which he meant the Anglo-Saxon New England culture. He felt, he would say, that the presence of too many students of non-Anglo-Saxon background would so change the "cultural atmosphere" at Harvard that all students would be deprived of much that the university had to offer. In fact, he argued that if his proposal were carried, Jewish students who were admitted to Harvard would themselves benefit from the resultant decrease in anti-Semitic feeling. Thus he expected the Jews themselves to support the "quota" idea.

Julian refrained from giving Lowell "a definite opinion" about the plan immediately. "My impressions, however, are entirely against it because of my belief that if anything of this kind is to be done, it should be done in the frankest possible way," he wrote to Lowell. At one time Lowell had told Julian of reports that Jewish students accounted for a large proportion of the cases of dishonesty on the campus, including the theft of library books. Julian asked for the facts, saying that he wanted such data before expressing his opinion on Lowell's plan. That is, he adopted the stance of judge, with the hope of getting Lowell to admit that his "quota" plan was based upon incorrect assumptions—or upon prejudice.

An apocryphal, but nonetheless pertinent, story about the alleged library book thefts at Harvard was later to be told by Frankfurter to

Prof. A.M. Bickel of Yale. In this version, Julian had come to Frankfurter crestfallen because Lowell had claimed that 50 per cent of the book thefts from the main Harvard library during a certain period had been committed by Jewish students.

> Frankfurter, who knew his Lowell, said, "Why don't you go back and ask President Lowell what the statistical basis of his statement is? What was the total number of thefts of which 50 per cent were committed by Jewish students?"

> Judge Mack went back and asked that question, to which President Lowell sheepishly replied: "Two." In short, a total of two thefts had been discovered, one of which had been committed by a Jewish student.

Apocryphal or not, Frankfurter's story was indicative of some of the arguments advanced in support of a "Jewish quota" as the issue was debated on and off the Harvard campus.

At one point Julian asked Lowell to explain how it would be determined which Jews were "desirable" and which were not. Obviously, he suspected that Lowell considered the East European Jews—the later "immigrants"—as the "undesirables." But Lowell responded evasively. Soon he even stopped further efforts to bring Julian around. In May, 1922, he simply advised Julian in a coldly formal letter that "the Faculty" had voted to implement his plan. The "vote" stated that transfer students, and those who up to then would have been considered for admission even if they had not completely passed their examinations, would not be admitted, unless the Admission Committee, even if it was satisfied "as to their mental attainments and moral character is convinced that their presence as members of the College will positively contribute to the general advantage of the College." Also, that "pending further action by the Faculty, in making its decisions in these cases, the Committee be instructed to take into account the resulting proportionate size of racial and national groups, in the membership of Harvard College."

If the issue had rested there, European-style discrimination in education would have been introduced at Harvard. The frank mention of "racial and national groups" made this apparent.

But the matter did not rest there. "I am calling a meeting of the Overseers for June 5th, at which I shall submit these votes, with other matters," Lowell wrote. Then the issue, for the first time, became a matter for the Board of Overseers.

Lowell at the same time presented to the Board a "vote" by "the Faculty" authorizing him to appoint a special committee "to consider principles and methods for more effectively sifting candidates for admission."

The Board approved the establishment of such a "sifting" committee, although it was to be one representing the University as a whole, not just the College. The deliberations of the Board were not made public, but its authorization of the "sifting" committee had the effect of postponing a decision one way or another until that committee would have submitted its report. Lowell apparently believed that his proposal would be accepted by the Overseers if the committee approved. Julian, on the other hand, hoped that the committee would understand that any system of admission adopted at Harvard should be in accord with American democratic principles, which meant that the principle of admitting students on the basis of race and national origin should be rejected.

In writing to Lowell about the composition of the "sifting" committee Julian said:

> One thing is clear to me. This committee must have men on it who thoroughly appreciate the point of view that Jerome Greene and I emphasized and that the Overseers adopted, namely, that while the question of the larger number of Jews now going to the College has provoked this inquiry, the problem to be considered by the Committee is a very much broader one, namely, [what is] the duty of Harvard University and all of its Departments, in view of its history, its traditions and its place in the life of the American people, [with] reference to the admission of students to any Department in the University, the nature and character of the tests, and the limitations, if any, to be placed upon any one or more groups,

however differentiated from other groups in American life? This involves fundamentally a consideration of the place and the obligations of Harvard College and Harvard University in the life of the American people and in the future.

I trust that this broadening of, or rather change in, the nature of the inquiry originally proposed by the Faculty of Arts and Sciences has been made clear to that body and will be made clear to the Committee.

Lowell did not concede to Julian that the nature of the inquiry should be changed. Nor would he accede to Julian's request that Frankfurter be named as one of the "sifting" committee of 13 faculty members. Lowell frankly admitted that Frankfurter was unacceptable "because undoubtedly he holds your views." Lowell did appoint to the committee three Jews, Paul J. Sachs of the Fine Arts Department, Dr. Milton J. Rosenau of the Medical School, along with Harry A. Wolfson—but not Felix Frankfurter.

Though greatly attached to Wolfson, Julian felt that he was "too philosophical" to put up the kind of fight that would be needed. He went far in his efforts to urge Frankfurter upon Lowell. "I am firmly convinced," he wrote to Lowell, "that to leave off the Committee the one Jew on the Faculties who is uniquely fitted for this work would carry an obvious significance. Primarily in the interest of Harvard—and, frankly, [I] say that in this problem I am always thinking primarily of Harvard's interest—I want to avert any such danger."

But Lowell was adamant against Frankfurter.

The committee submitted its report to the Overseers in April, 1923. It rejected the proposed "Jewish quota" but it did recommend some revisions in the system of admitting students to Harvard College that indirectly affected Jews. These changes included reducing the proportion of students admitted from large cities in the East and North, and increasing the proportion to be admitted from small cities and from rural areas in the West and South—the objective being that Harvard College should become more definitely a "national" institution. The practical effect, it was presumed, would be that the character of the college student body would more nearly reflect the character of the nation as a whole, certainly with respect to the proportion of Jews and other groups. Thus, in effect, it could be expected that Lowell's objective of holding down the proportion of Jews in the college would be achieved, but without overt racial or religious tests. On this point, the committee specifically declared:

> Concerning proportional representation, your committee is unanimous in recommending that no departure be made from the policy of equal opportunity for all, regardless of race and religion. Any action liable to interpretation as an acceptance of racial discrimination would to many seem like a dangerous surrender of traditional ideals.

The report went further, stating:

> Under the circumstances, the introduction of any novel process of scrutiny appears inexpedient. Even so rational a method as a personal conference or an intelligence test, if now adopted here as a means of selection, would inevitably be regarded as a covert device to eliminate those deemed racially or socially undesirable, and, however fairly conceived and conducted, could not fail to arouse damaging suspicion.

The Board of Overseers adopted the report, and resolved that:

> . . . in the administration of rules for admission Harvard College will maintain its traditional policy of freedom from discrimination on grounds of race or religion.

Despite the assumed practical effects of the committee's decision, the result was viewed as a disavowal of prejudice against Jews, a victory, if not a complete one, for Julian and other Jewish leaders, as well as for the liberal press, notably *The New Republic* and *The Nation*, which had exposed and denounced Lowell's scheme.

Lowell himself felt that he had suffered a rebuff. "Since his return from England Mr. Lowell has felt so much concerned about the Report of his committee of inquiry that he has been silent on the subject, and has become so nervous and agitated that he has been compelled to leave his work and go away for rest and quiet," ex-president Eliot reported to Julian. Still alert at the age of 89, Eliot had cooperated with Julian in efforts to have Lowell's proposal defeated, cooperation which, Julian felt, had played an important role in the resolution of the matter.

Of Julian's role, Horace Kallen wrote that "without his sharp intervention" the Lowell proposal "might have won out by default." Brandeis, among others, agreed. He had been watching the situation carefully and had discussed it privately with Julian and with Felix Frankfurter. "You and Felix have done a fine job at Harvard," he wrote to Julian after the Overseers' action. "But of course," he added, "you've scotched the snake, not killed it. There is larger work that remains to be done." This was true not only for Harvard, of course, but for a number of other "top" colleges in years to come.

There was a sequel. For later, Lowell provoked a situation with regard to black students similar to the Jewish quota issue. Earlier, he required all freshmen students to live in the then new dormitories that formed Harvard Yard, his special pride. But when a black student, Roscoe Conkling Bruce, Jr., son of a Harvard graduate, applied for a room in these dormitories, he was told that he could not live there. In Lowell's curious view, the presence of the young black student would "impinge upon a right of the white students"; namely, not to have to live with a Negro. Again there was a fight. Here, too, Julian took a leading role and, assisted by a number of students, including Corliss Lamont, son of the partner of the House of Morgan, won a victory.

"He does not like to fight," Stephen Wise said of him, with the Harvard incidents in mind, "but he can battle like a lion for a man or for a cause."

Also, he could still go out of his way to further the careers of young people. In June, 1922, he was impressed by the commencement address given at Harvard by a bachelor degree candidate on "The Present Condition of the Negroes in the United States." He spoke to Julius Rosenwald about the young orator. Rosenwald made it possible for the black student to continue his studies for a doctorate. The young man was Dr. Mordecai W. Johnson, who became a noted educator and was for many years president of Howard University. "It was Julian Mack," he later said, "who opened my way."

36. "No Jew Can Touch That Ground. . . ."

After the Harvard episode, Julian entered upon a bittersweet time, especially in the year 1923. He was turning 57 and had begun to show signs of aging. His diabetes became more pronounced, with symptoms of heightened fatigue, and eye trouble that especially disturbed him in view of his increasing workload at court. He was distressed also by the deterioration in Jessie's health, with indications of nervousness that later developed into a breakdown.

Then, too, in 1923, for the first time, his daughter Ruth, the "apple of his eye," brought him heartache. For Ruth, who in 1917 had married a bright young physician, Dr. Hermann Blumgart, a Harvard graduate of whom Julian was very fond, announced that she was getting a divorce and going off to Vienna to study and undergo psychoanalysis with Dr. Sigmund Freud. "Julian was broken up when Ruth told him that," a relative recalled.

The outside world, too, dealt Julian some harsh blows. From Munich, in 1923, came news of the "beer hall putsch" of Adolf Hitler. The "putsch" failed, but Julian's sensitivity to any threat to his fellow Jews alerted him to a new ordeal for European Jewry ahead.

Moreover, from Dearborn, Michigan, there came rumblings of new anti-Semitism in America that seemed more serious than any such outbreak since the Leo Frank case in 1914: Henry Ford's venture into Jew-hatred through his newspaper, the *Dearborn Independent*. Week after week, in the tone of the "Protocols of the Elders of Zion," which it incredibly endorsed, Ford's paper attacked American Jews as despoilers of American virtues and slipped in clever insinuations against prominent Jews such as Brandeis, Schiff, Bernard Baruch—and Julian Mack.

Leading Christian personages, such as Chief Justice William Howard Taft and his eventual successor, Charles Evans Hughes, joined leading Jews, including Julian, in upbraiding Ford. Yet Ford was to continue his childish but vile anti-Semitic propaganda for several years. It was in 1923 also that the Teapot Dome scandal

301

exploded after the death of President Harding. The scandal caused
Julian much pain. As a U.S. judge, he was, after all, a member of
the government which, as he viewed it, had been sullied by the
affair. It was not a happy time for an American idealist.

One experience, however, in that otherwise gloomy year brought
Julian much pleasure. For that summer, accompanied by Jessie, he
visited Palestine.

This, the first of Julian's three visits there, strengthened his
conviction that the Jewish people would be able to establish a
successful homeland in Palestine. Some prominent Jews still did not
believe so, still argued that the land could not support a sizable
Jewish population, or that Arab opposition would prevent the
creation of a Jewish homeland there. Julian used his on-the-spot
observations to refute such pessimism.

His speech at a gathering in New York in October, 1923, reflected
the impressions he had gained on his visit. He combined sentiment
with practicality. "Go out and see the land of our forefathers for
yourselves," he urged.

> You will be touched, you will be cheered, you will be inspired.
> No Jew can touch that ground without thinking of the glories
> of his people in the past, without wondering about the work of
> his people in the present, without praying and hoping that the
> dreams of our ancestors may become true in the future, for
> the benefit of the Jewish people that will be in Pales-
> tine . . . and to the infinite benefit, we hope and believe, of
> all mankind.

But, he added, it must not be imagined that Palestine would
become "a Jewish land, a predominantly Jewish land, overnight. It
is going to take years and years."

He recalled a bloody Arab attack on Jews at Petach Tikvah in
1921, but held out hope that Jews and Arabs nevertheless would be
able to get along with one another:

> In Petach Tikvah, the Arabs in large numbers came and
> attacked the Jewish settlements. You see the men, young and

old, who defended the colony. You listen, as a Jew, with deep interest and high excitement, to the story of that conflict. You rejoice that a handful of Jews not only were able to withstand several thousand Arabs, but came off highly successful in the whole conflict. . . . A mere handful of Jews, who knew that if they must give their lives, it meant the salvation, not merely of that colony, but perhaps of all the colonies.

Perhaps more wonderful is the story of the peace that came this year. The Arabs came to seek re-establishment of peace, with their neighbors, and acknowledged they had been wrong, a tribute to the Jew. The Jew . . . re-established the peace that now reigns there. That is the spirit that can exist between the Arab of Palestine and the Jew of Palestine, if the Arab of Palestine will but be left alone by political leaders and jealous landlords.

He glowingly described the then new city of Tel Aviv, "formerly a suburb of Jaffa, now a completely Jewish city," and also Jerusalem, to which many Jews had returned, "to live, not just to die," as they had in former years. But to "get the real thrill of Palestine," he said,

you must go into the colonies. You must see and meet and speak to the men and women who came over 40 years ago. You must listen to the story of their struggle; you must see their oases in the desert, created by Jewish hands. You must compare these colonies with . . . Arab colonies. Then you begin to appreciate, not merely what the Jews can do, but what Palestine has inspired the Jew to do, and what Palestine means for the Jewish people, not only the old men and women, but their sons and daughters born in Palestine. . . .

He had in mind particularly Zikhron Ya'akov which, of course, he and Jessie visited in order to meet members of Aaron Aaronsohn's family, including Aaron's aged father and his sister, Rifka. They visited Athlit to see, as Julian wrote, "what was left of Aaron's Experimental Station. . . . The Turks did enormous damage to the place. It was a sad spectacle for me."

Bittersweet memories of his beloved friend, Aaron, flooded him, strengthening him in his determination to continue his efforts for Zionist aims, despite the unhappy split in the Z.O.A.

Thus, on his return from Palestine in 1923, although officially "out" of Zionist leadership, he came to be very much "in" the movement in a wider sense. He stepped up his own efforts on behalf of Palestine, and sought to build confidence in the larger Jewish world regarding the potential of the land. But his emphasis now was more on the Homeland than on Zionist ideology. Indeed, his attitude anticipated a comment which David Ben-Gurion was to make years later to the effect that when the Homeland would become reality, the "old" Zionism would no longer exist.

Julian, for one, recognized that changed circumstances made it desirable and necessary that divisions within the ranks of the Z.O.A. should be healed or soft-pedaled, for the sake of the Homeland. It was in this spirit that most of the Brandeis-Mack group, including Julian, began to return to posts of leadership in the "new Zionism."

37. Last Years

After the split, the Harvard episode, and the Palestine visit, Julian had twenty more years of what, except for his final period, could be called his usual full life. There was for him continued involvement in Jewish affairs and in general issues such as the Sacco-Vanzetti case; further activity as an Overseer at Harvard, and the interest he took in his many protegés, including, in the 1930's, refugees from Hitler's Germany. Too, in this period he assumed with added gusto the role of *paterfamilias* in the Mack family, not only to Ruth, who was by then a promising psychoanalyst first in Vienna and later in New York, but also to her husbands (she was married and divorced twice), his granddaughter Matilda, and to his brothers and sisters and *their* families.

But mainly now the emphasis of his activity was on his role as U.S. Circuit Judge. Suddenly, or so it seemed, by the 1920's his image was no longer that of a young judge from Chicago who had caught the imagination of the New York bar and the public with his innovative ways and with conduct that had given him the image of a kind of "character." He was by now seen as a pillar of the Federal bench, one to whom the appellation "distinguished jurist" deservedly applied.

As for Jewish affairs, including Zionism, he was consulted on almost every issue, and his name appeared on the letterheads of practically every Jewish organization of the time. Viewed now as an "elder statesman" in Jewry, he was often called in as a mediator when dissensions developed, as they often did among various organizations.

In particular, over more than a decade he spent much time in attempting to bridge the dissension that marked the founding of the Hebrew University in Jerusalem. Though questions of curriculum and administration were involved, much of the trouble had stemmed from the personality of Judah L. Magnes, the first president of the University. Much of the conflict also centered on Albert Einstein. Julian and many others had hoped that Einstein,

305

having turned his back on Nazi Germany, would join the faculty of the University. But although he was greatly interested in the University in Jerusalem, Einstein declined to associate himself actively with the University's scientific program because he had strong objections to some of the views held by Dr. Magnes. Einstein had been on the board of the University but by 1929 he felt bound to resign unless certain changes were adopted. Julian devoted much effort to avert Einstein's resignation, which would have been a hard blow to the institution. Thus he had much correspondence, and many personal conferences, with Einstein on the subject. In the summer of 1934 Einstein wrote to him (in German):

Watch Hill, June 9, 1934

Dear Judge Mack:

I thank you for the untiring patience which you have devoted to our long correspondence about the matter. I shall let it rest now but beg you at the Board meeting to urge that in the final text precaution is taken that Magnes is not in a position to sabotage the efficacy of the Academic Board through postponement of its meetings. After the experiences which I have had with him I do not doubt that he will try it. I will not occupy myself with the matter any more before I receive the report of the Board meeting to read.

Now I would further beg you urgently to prevent, as far as possible, that the matter be put up to the uninitiated in such a way as if I had already at this time obligated myself to join the Board. This depends naturally entirely upon the regulations, which the Board will decide upon. I hope very much that our efforts will lead toward removing the undignified conditions in the University which through the report were so clearly set forth in so thanksworthy a manner.

With cordial greetings to you and your wife,

Yours,
(signed) A. EINSTEIN

In the end—though it took years—a settlement was reached which substantially satisfied Einstein and the others, but not without much aggravation to Julian and other leaders, including Weizmann. The solution was to "promote" Dr. Magnes to the rank of chancellor, but with less authority than he had enjoyed as president of the University.

All along, too, Julian gave liberally of his time to the Palestine Economic Corporation and various other pro-Palestine activities, including the establishment of a proper memorial for Aaron Aaronsohn in the form of an agricultural project at the Hebrew University. He took an active interest also in a workshop school for children in Tel Aviv which had been sparked by Horace Kallen's sister, Deborah, and which was ultimately named for Julian. He was concerned, too, about the increasing hostility of Arab politicians toward the Jewish Homeland; all the while, he also maintained his interest in the American Jewish Committee and in the problems of the Jews of Eastern Europe who, more than a decade after the end of World War I, were still in serious economic straits.

Indeed, to his family, secretaries, friends, and colleagues on the bench, he seemed perpetually in a bewildering maelstrom of meetings, telephone calls, and correspondence quite apart from his judgeship. "He did not merely lend his name to movements," recalled Benjamin V. Cohen, who kept up an association with him long after he had gone on to a busy career of his own. "He was *active*, a doer. There was no limit to the projects he would take on, the people he would help, not half-heartedly, but wholeheartedly. As a consequence, he seemed always rushed—and always late in getting out his judicial opinions." His worry about those delays added to the "busy" image that he presented, a man constantly on the go, with coat-tails still flying as they had been in his younger days when Jacob Schiff had wondered whether he ever slept.

Nevertheless, despite the aura of perpetual motion that he exuded, he somehow also managed, more than ever, to project a primary image of himself as a sedate, dignified jurist. Esteem for him as a jurist was at its greatest and most universal. "He knew the common law like a modern Lord Coke," observed Murray Gurfein, one of his law secretaries who later himself became a Federal judge.

"Not even Brandeis or Frankfurter surpassed him in legal knowledge," Ben Cohen recalled—and his judgment was not merely based on affection. In short, more than ever, Julian Mack was the distinguished judge who happened also to be an esteemed, liberal American Jew.

In the late 1920's and well into the 1930's his services as a "relief" judge for district and appellate work were especially appreciated. This was so particularly in the Southern District of New York, which included New York City. There the amount of court business, especially after Prohibition went into effect, was usually beyond the capacity of the regular district judges to handle expeditiously; it was therefore necessary for Julian to deal with motions by which cases were expedited toward conclusion or appeal. Of his work in this "*nisi prius* field," Judge Augustus Hand, for one, hailed him. He had "long thought Julian Mack a judge with scarcely an equal," Hand was to say.

In addition to such service, and sitting *en banc* with other circuit judges in reviewing lower court decisions, he presided over trials and handled receiverships, the latter especially during the Great Depression. He was notably assigned cases involving complicated financial affairs, and also certain especially "delicate" cases with political or other implications that made his selection desirable because of his recognized impeccable standing.

In 1923, for example, he was designated to preside at the controversial trial of Marcus Garvey, the black leader who wished to take his people back to Africa and who had been charged with using the mails to defraud through the sale of shares in his Black Star shipping line. Julian showed a great deal of sympathy for Garvey and clearly tried to help him, though in the end the so-called "Black Moses" was convicted and given a prison sentence.

Julian also presided over the Prohibition-law perjury case against the theatrical producer, Earl Carroll—the celebrated "bathtub gin" matter which was played up by the press because of the allegation that Carroll had given a party at which girls had bathed in tubs of gin. He sat as judge also in a sensational breach of contract case involving Lillian Gish, the movie star, and the equally sensational prosecution of the editor of a blackmail sheet who had been accused of having extorted money from Peggy Hopkins Joyce, among other "celebrities."

He presided, too, in 1926, at the trials of Harry M. Daugherty, Attorney General of the United States under Harding, and of Colonel Thomas W. Miller, former Alien Property Custodian, who had been accused of wrongdoing in the administration of alien property seized during World War I. These were among the most publicized trials of the era. All along, too, cases involving bootleggers and other racketeers were assigned to him, including prosecution of "Big Bill" Dwyer, known in the New York area as "the king of the bootleggers."

If Julian, whose forte was civil law, felt sensitive about presiding over criminal cases, Brandeis assured him that he should not be troubled about them. The "crime wave," as the press referred to the increase in law violations that marked the 1920's, was really a "deluge," Brandeis wrote to Julian in 1924, adding that the problem called for "the best efforts" of the judiciary. "I'm glad you are having the Criminal session; you could not be better employed," Brandeis wrote to him in 1926.

That year he was involved in the censorship stir over H. L. Mencken's *American Mercury* for its publication of "Hatrack," the story of a prostitute in a small Missouri town. To challenge efforts to ban publication of such material in Boston, Mencken sold copies of his magazine in Boston himself in order to be arrested by Boston police. This aspect of the case got the publicity. But a potentially more serious action was a little-known effort to have the U.S. Post Office ban the magazine from the mails. Julian heard a petition for an injunction to restrain the Post Office from handling the magazine. He denied the petition, making it clear that he opposed unreasonable censorship. "I may be wrong," he commented, "but I have some pretty strong opinions regarding the right of freedom of the press and censorship of the average human being." Technically, his decision set no precedent, but it discouraged further harassment of the *Mercury*. "We rejoice that this act of stupidity or malice has been overruled by Judge Mack," said *The Nation*.

It was during this period, too, that Julian was much disturbed over the Sacco-Vanzetti case. Ordinarily, because of his position, he would have been only a spectator at that tragedy. But Felix Frankfurter was deeply involved in efforts to prevent the execution of the two radicals and Julian, out of loyalty and friendship for Frankfurter, found himself embroiled in the affair.

Judicial propriety kept him from joining in public statements on the Sacco-Vanzetti matter, but he helped raise funds for the defense committee in Boston, prevailing upon Julius Rosenwald, among others, to contribute. He also helped in trying to get persons who he thought would be influential with Governor Alvan T. Fuller of Massachusetts to urge the governor to prevent the execution of the prisoners. That effort, of course, failed.

Adding to Julian's distress over Sacco-Vanzetti was the role of Justice Brandeis. For, while he sided with Frankfurter in the case, Julian strongly defended Brandeis for declining, as had Justice Holmes, to hear a petition to have the U.S. Supreme Court review the case, a step that would have meant staying the executions.

Aside from legal aspects, Brandeis cited personal relationships as a reason for not acting. For both Mrs. Brandeis and Mrs. Glendower Evans, who was occupying the Brandeis residence in Dedham and was regarded as a member of the Brandeis family, had befriended Sacco's wife, allowing her to stay at the Brandeis home while her husband was in the Dedham jail. In addition, Mrs. Evans was a leader in the fight to save Sacco and Vanzetti. Hence, Brandeis felt he could not intervene without being open to the charge of bias.

The radical press heaped denunciations upon Brandeis. Even Horace Kallen criticized him. It was Julian who defended Brandeis. The "great legal wrong in this case was that a prejudiced man should have sat as a judge in the case," Julian wrote to Kallen. Under the circumstances, he said, Brandeis' becoming involved in the case would have permitted Judge Thayer's supporters to charge Brandeis, too, with being prejudiced. Besides, Julian continued, if Brandeis believed there was no legal justification for action, his taking jurisdiction would have meant exercising "czar-like powers" and "violating his oath of office."

"My own interest," Julian added, "was in the preservation of law and justice as the rule that should govern men. It was the violation, as I viewed it, of the rules that, under our jurisprudence, should prevail that excited my interest, and I may say my very deep interest and activity. But if LDB, to right a wrong, had himself done the utterly unjudicial thing that you seem to think he should have done, I should have been the first to denounce it and him. Such an act would have been a much greater danger to civilization than the actions of [Judge] Thayer and [Governor] Fuller combined."

The exchange that followed between him and Kallen was the most painful that Julian had ever engaged in, involving as it did two of his most beloved friends. Even worse for him was the action by a commission, dominated by President Lowell of Harvard (once again a "villain" in Julian's life), that Governor Fuller of Massachusetts had appointed to advise him on the Sacco and Vanzetti case. The Lowell commission recommended that Fuller should not prevent the executions. "It is terribly crushing," Julian wrote to Frankfurter on hearing the news from Boston. "It is too crushing to think about."

To a large degree, for Julian, as well as others, the Sacco and Vanzetti case suggested implications about America that went even beyond the issue of fair jurisprudence. For the passions that it provoked created uneasiness among perceptive observers about the social fabric of America as a whole. There seemed to be extraordinary prosperity. But labor was restless, and so was the farm population. Both the major political parties were clearly heading toward schisms in a deepening struggle between "conservatives" and "progressives" over issues old and new involving social and economic justice. Radicalism seemed rampant. Indeed, Julian's own court calendar reflected, as it later turned out, a gathering crisis—the Great Depression lay just ahead—through cases involving anti-trust actions, receiverships, bankruptcies, and the like, all indicating unhealthy fissures below the surface of the so-called "Coolidge-Mellon prosperity," cases that brought Julian some of the most arduous judicial work of his entire career.

The cases included an especially complicated anti-trust action brought by the government against the Sugar Institute, an association formed by leading sugar corporations, which the government alleged had been set up for fixing prices in violation of the law. The case involved literally millions of words in testimony, as well as documents and arguments so complicated that Julian found it difficult to reach a decision. "He was very troubled about the Sugar Institute case," his law clerk, Herbert S. Marks, recalled. Not until March, 1934, after more than three years, did he finally file an opinion enjoining some of the practices of the institute, but approving others, an opinion that was to be upheld by the Supreme Court. For years, it was a landmark decision in the anti-trust field.

While still working on the Sugar Institute matter, he was placed in charge of the receivership of the Interborough Rapid Transit lines of the City of New York. Originally this far-flung receivership had been in the hands of Judge Martin Manton, who was later impeached. Manton had assigned the case to himself while sitting in the District Court, a practice which was considered highly irregular.

In the fall of 1933, Chief Justice Charles Evans Hughes of the Supreme Court ordered the case transferred to Julian, "for the good of the service," as Brandeis wrote to him.

Taking on this receivership meant that Julian was deeply involved for several years in the operations of the New York subway system. He had to approve purchases of supplies, labor union arrangements, and similar matters which, in effect, made of him as much a businessman as a judge.

In the midst of the subways receivership, Julian was also assigned to hear a celebrated action against a mammoth utility enterprise, the Associated Gas and Electric Company, a holding company. This case, aside from its monumental legal aspects, involved Julian in a painful personal to-do. Attorneys for the corporation had asked for a change of venue, seizing upon the coincidence that the *Survey Magazine*—on whose board Julian still served—had carried an editorial attacking the formation of holding companies in general and the Associated Gas and Electric Company in particular. The editorial was cited by the attorneys for the company—an impressive array of legal minds from the largest law firms of the country—as grounds for disqualifying Julian from hearing the case, the first such challenge to him in his entire career.

It was clear that the company lawyers felt—not without basis—that Julian had held "New Deal" views on holding companies. Indeed, earlier, in a technical maneuver, they attempted to prevent his hearing the case altogether, on the grounds that he had been assigned to it by Judge Manton, whereas they maintained that only the Chief Justice could assign "this particular jurist." Chief Justice Hughes sent a telegram stating that Judge Mack had been designated to act in all courts of the Second District. It was then that the lawyers fell back on the *Survey* editorial.

Under Federal Court procedure, Julian could have ruled on the petition for change of venue himself. But, recalling a 50-year-old Federal statute permitting a second Federal judge to rule on such a petition, he asked Judge Robert P. Patterson—later Secretary of War under Harry S. Truman—to make the decision so as to eliminate any question of personal bias. According to Patterson's ruling, the charge that Julian might have been influenced by the *Survey* article—which, by the way, he had never even seen—was "ridiculous" and "frivolous." So Julian retained jurisdiction and, after some grueling sessions, ruled that the company had been mismanaged and had to be reorganized under the National Bankruptcy Act.

The incident was a depressing one for Julian. In 1937 a case of even more "New Dealish" character came to him when the Electric Bond and Share Company challenged the constitutionality of the Public Utilities Holding Company Act, a key measure of the early Franklin D. Roosevelt years. It was a case with historic repercussions, for Julian's decision, upheld by the Supreme Court, led to the enforced dissolution generally of large utility conglomerates and, as one side effect, to the later emergence of Wendell L. Willkie as a strong Republican candidate against Roosevelt in 1940. It was also the last major litigation that Julian was to hear. For that fall, when he was 71, he suffered a stroke. It was considered mild, but left him a partial invalid; the most pronounced symptom at first was a blurring of his vision.

"I thought you had changed the light bulbs," he said to Jessie one day. "I did," she answered. He realized then that his eyes had been affected. Obviously, that meant that his days as a judge were numbered. With the aid of magnifying lenses and the special assistance of secretaries, he carried on for some months. He reluctantly but bravely faced the fact that his active life was nearing its close. Friends and family urged him to resign from the bench and retire from all his outside activities. "Not yet," he said. There was still too much to do, especially in the outside activities, especially for fellow Jews.

As time went on, he began to notice lapses of memory; he would read something and not be able to retain what he had read. At times, these symptoms disappeared, but they recurred often enough to make him realize that he would definitely have to give up full-time work on the judicial bench. Always the optimist, he deprecated the seriousness of his condition; he remained on the bench and continued many of his activities, especially those on behalf of Palestine. But his condition was serious enough for his daughter, then married to the musicologist Mark Brunswick, to leave Vienna to be near him. She set up a home and office above her parents' apartment on Fifth Avenue.

Ruth's decision pleased Julian, not only for its own sake, but also because he was greatly worried about her remaining in Vienna after Hitler had annexed Austria in March, 1938. She and her husband were indeed in danger because they had run something of an underground movement in Vienna to save Jews marked for arrest by the Nazis.

As early as 1933, Julian had written to Horace Kallen: "Ruth writes that apparently things are quiet in Vienna, but I am sure they appreciate [that] they are on a volcano." In 1935, Ruth had forwarded to Julian a memorandum that forecast what lay ahead in Germany and Austria under Hitler, one so impressive and ominous that Julian sent it to Brandeis, who in turn forwarded it to the U.S. Department of State. Brandeis then made to Julian a prophetic observation: "All the German Jews should leave Germany. What happened to Spain should now happen to Germany." What the State Department did, if anything, about the letter, nobody ever found out.

On September 1, 1938, Julian wrote to Kallen:

> While my condition, except as to the eyes, is very satisfactory,
> I am nevertheless under orders to abstain from judicial and

other mental activities as well . . . I personally can do little reading, practically none except the headlines. . . . I try to keep in touch with Palestine affairs and with matters Jewish in this country and only wish I could be much more active.

He was, in fact, too active. That was true also before he had suffered his stroke and was probably a factor in his illness. For example, in the summer of 1936, he had presided over the World Jewish Congress in Geneva. Then, too, from the time Hitler came to power in Germany, he worked with various agencies to bring Jewish professors and their families out of Germany, to resettle them and to place them in universities in the United States, notably the New School. He also helped get positions for some of the refugees on the faculty of the Hebrew University in Jerusalem, an institution in which he continued to take a great interest. All this entailed many conferences, much correspondence, and considerable heartache.

He did not forget members of his parents' family in Germany. For this purpose he created the Mack Family Fund—part of the money for which came from beneficiaries of a trust fund that had been established by his Uncle Max many years before. He had announced his plan in a letter to all his relatives:

To the Children and Grandchildren of Wm. J. Mack:

As March 22, 1936, marks our father's (grandfather's) one hundredth anniversary, I purpose at that time starting a Mack Family Fund with an initial contribution from me of not less than $1,000. . . .

The conditions in Germany are such that, in my judgment, it is absolutely imperative for every young Jew to emigrate from there, and it is equally the duty of those of their blood who possibly can do so, to aid them financially and otherwise. . . .

In a manner reminiscent of his father's brother, good Uncle Max Mack, who had helped him go to Harvard, he signed the letter: "Uncle Julian."

With his help, one young cousin in Germany, Jacob Steinberger, went to Palestine, settling in Kibbutz Ein Gev. From there, some 25 years later, after a visit to Ein Gev by David Ben-Gurion, then Prime Minister of Israel, Steinberger recalled: "I had an opportunity to speak to Mr. Ben-Gurion about my cousin, Judge Mack, [and] he was pleased that one of Judge Mack's relatives was living in Israel. He said that the Judge had been a very good Zionist, probably in a more deep-felt way than even Judge Brandeis and other members of his group."

In February, 1962, on learning that Julian's biography was being planned, Ben-Gurion again had occasion to recall Julian with admiration, writing:

> I am very glad . . . that the biography of Judge Mack is being written at last . . . I met him when I visited the United States (several times) and was impressed by him as a devoted Jew, a good Zionist, a man of sound logic and a warm heart. . . . [T]his illustrious Jew is eminently worthy of a literary memorial that will preserve the character of a great American Jewish personality for the generations to come.

Among the things for which the future Prime Minister was grateful to Julian and to Brandeis was the special fund raising effort in which the two men engaged during the late 1930's. These funds were used for propaganda against the British opposition to Jewish immigration into Palestine, and for Haganah, the underground defense force of Palestine's Jewish community.

It was a period of shock after shock. It was as though the world, like Julian himself, had become stricken—and in the area in which Julian was most concerned. For Great Britain by then had begun its betrayal of the Balfour Declaration in order to appease Arab rioters and terrorists.

In September, 1939, Brandeis wrote to Julian concerning Palestine: "My confidence in our ultimate success remains intact." But by then even he, who in 1919 had so confidently upbraided Vladimir Jabotinsky for mistrusting "Anglo-Saxon justice," recognized that Great Britain was reneging on its promise to the Jews. He also realized that, just as Hitler had won over Arab nationalists bent on destroying the Jewish Homeland, British leaders, including even the previously self-proclaimed "Zionist" Winston Churchill and many of his Labor Party opponents, were for appeasing the Arab nationalists.

In October, 1937, Julian expressed to E. N. Mohl, executive of the Palestine Economic Corporation in Natanya, his views on a British proposal, submitted earlier that year, for a "partition" of Palestine into two sovereign states—one Arab, one Jewish—with part of the country (including Jerusalem, Bethlehem and Nazareth) remaining under British mandate:

> Our group under the leadership of the Justice (Brandeis) is unalterably opposed to partition, and we purpose in every way in our power to endeavor to educate both the Jews and the American public, and to the extent of our ability, the British, on what we conceive to be the utter worthlessness of partition.

> We are under all circumstances opposed to acceptance. If ultimately it should be imposed upon us, then, of course, we want to have the best and largest possible State, but so far as we are concerned, it will be an imposed and not an accepted State.

Julian, as well as Brandeis, then felt that establishment of a Jewish state at that point would mean a trap; that a weak, truncated Jewish state such as the one proposed by the British would eventually be destroyed by intransigent Arabs, with the British looking on and doing nothing. All the while, Hitler grew in power and in hostility toward the Jews.

After World War II, of course, the *Yishuv*, under Ben-Gurion's leadership, did accept the partition of Palestine, on the basis of which the State of Israel was proclaimed in 1948. Would Julian and Brandeis have approved? It may be set down as certain that they would have approved the decision. They did not, as some critics alleged, "ignore" the "Arab problem." They were quite aware of the risks inherent in the situation of a small Jewish state surrounded by Arab countries. Rather than "ignoring" that situation, or foolishly minimizing it, they were concerned about it, and they always firmly urged the fullest possible Zionist cooperation with the Arabs in and outside Jewish Palestine. It was a cardinal principle with them to extend the hand of friendship to the Arabs even after the Arab terrorists had perpetrated the most outrageous attacks upon the *Yishuv*. Certainly it was Julian's policy, though he was unwavering in his support of the idea of a Jewish state, to cooperate with the Arabs. Like Brandeis, he was always sure that in the end the Jewish settlers in Palestine would have the fortitude, the courage, and the intelligence to overcome all perils. But he was certain, too, that the path ahead would not be easy.

There were other shocks for Julian, too, including certain aspects of the policies of Franklin D. Roosevelt which he, a supporter of Roosevelt, did not like to concede existed. He approved most of Roosevelt's economic policies; if anything, he privately felt that the "radical" New Deal was not radical enough. He was delighted, too, that Benjamin V. Cohen had become one of Roosevelt's major advisors, along with Frankfurter. In June, 1935 Roosevelt paid Julian the compliment of inviting him to dinner at the White House to trade "wine-taster stories that I think will amuse you."

As a jurist, however, Julian was not at all pleased with Roosevelt's "court-packing" proposal, not even though Frankfurter ardently supported it. In his opposition, Julian shared Brandeis' view and found himself in the painful position of having to act as mediator between Frankfurter and Brandeis to keep them from parting as associates over the issue.

But there was another thing which Julian found even more distressing. This was what seemed to him the inexplicable and unconscionable attitude of the Roosevelt administration toward the matter of rescuing Jews in Germany and elsewhere from the Hitler peril. Later, it was to become clear that thousands, perhaps millions, of Jews in Europe might have been saved from the Hitler holocaust had Roosevelt, and Winston Churchill, made more of an effort to do so.

Fortunately, it may be said, Julian's illness spared him the greatest shock of all: the massacre of European Jewry. The beginnings of the slaughter that doomed six million Jews in Nazi-held Europe first became known in 1942, following the entry of the United States into the war. But by then, Julian's condition was such that he was really not aware of the tragedy that was unfolding. The sad reports were being kept from him. Even if they had reached him, it was doubtful that he would have really comprehended them. Outwardly, he did not seem mentally incapacitated. Indeed, he enjoyed company, liked to have people read to him, and in general was his usual cheerful self. Yet his mind had begun to slip markedly. He knew this—and accepted it. The prominent lawyer, C. C. Burlingham, after a visit in May, 1943, recalled: "How brave and cheerful he was."

"You know, I enjoy being read to, but afterward I can't tell what was read to me. But I have no pain, and, for that I am grateful," Julian told a friend.

He probably never knew that Brandeis had died in the fall of 1941.

Back in 1938 he had suffered a deep personal blow: the death of Jessie. True, some friends felt that Jessie had been a disappointment as a wife to Julian. For she shared few of his social interests. Indeed, she had remained a non-Zionist, true to her own "Cincinnati Reform" upbringing. Perhaps she was really anti-Zionist. Yet Julian was loyal to her. He cherished her even though, as when they first met, she needled him about his interests. With moving tenderness and concern he cared for her throughout her long illness, which began with a nervous breakdown and ended in her death from lung cancer on November 30, 1938. Both Julian and Ruth were with her at the end. A week later, from his wheelchair, Julian wrote to Dr. Weizmann in London:

> Thank you for your kind inquiries about our health. I am getting along, although still entirely out of commission and confined to the room. But last week Jessie passed away—fortunately without pain because of the use of opiates. . . .

They had been married forty-two years.

38. The Gentle End

Two quiet years passed. Then, on July 24, 1940, Julian had occasion to write another letter. Directed to members of his immediate family, and marked "Very Confidential," it read in part:

> Mark's mother, Ruth's mother-in-law whom we all call Cec, is coming here on or about August 31st to become my wife within, at most, a couple of weeks thereafter. She went back to California at the beginning of July on my insistence that, alone and not with me, she should think over the entire situation very carefully and only then reach a final decision. The result has been what I had hoped for; she is, therefore, winding up her household affairs out there quietly, comfortably, and without hurrying too much, and by returning at the very end of August instead of now she will escape most, if not all, of New York's probable hottest weather.

> I am, of course, very happy to add that Ruth approves this step and says that, if I had consulted her in advance, Cec is the only person that she would have selected for me. Mark, too, agrees with her, and Til [Matilda] is overjoyed at the prospect and particularly at having her only surviving maternal grandparent here.

> In the light of the continual improvement in my general condition, despite certain permanent encroachments of illness, my own physician, as well as a couple of intimate friends who are excellent physicians, also approve this step to my greater happiness, with the caution, of course, that we must not forget both my illness and my actual years, despite my general feeling that I am little more than middle-aged instead of 74. Naturally, knowing full well the need of keeping this advice ever in mind and always heeding it, we shall thoroughly follow it.

On October 8, 1940 he wrote to Chaim Weizmann:

> On September 4, I was married to my daughter Ruth's
> mother-in-law, Cecile Brunswick. . . . I am feeling quite
> well, though naturally, at all times terribly saddened by world
> events.

The ceremony was performed by Rabbi Stephen S. Wise. The
next day, all the members of the family who were in New York,
together with some 30 or 40 good friends, joined Julian and Cecile
for "tea, etc., from 4:30 to 7:00, naturally informal."

A week after Julian's remarriage, he received a cordial letter from
Franklin D. Roosevelt, to whom he had sent his resignation from
the bench:

> Dear Julian:
>
> Very mixed feelings—I just hate the thought of your leaving
> the Bench—and at the same time I am made very happy in
> your marriage and send all my blessings to both of you.
>
> F.D.R.

The years that followed were peaceful for him. "Cec" Mack, a
soft-spoken, gentle, and good-humored woman, "warm and
devoted," in the words of one of Julian's secretaries, was a good
companion to him in his last years.

He spent his days quietly, enjoying visits from old friends in his
home, writing occasional letters, enjoying the presence of his
daughter after so many years of separation while she had lived in
Vienna, and of the grandchild, Til, who later became a social
worker. His greatest pleasure was listening to Cec reading to
him—far into the afternoon. Once in a while they ventured on a
short vacation to a nearby resort, but for the most part Julian was
confined to his apartment on Fifth Avenue. Describing this period
in his life, a beloved niece, Eleanor Mack Lowenthal, said, "I visited
him once just after he had awakened from a nap. I told him how
well he looked after his nap. And he answered me, 'I enjoyed the

nap—preparing for the long sleep.'"

The "long sleep" began as he quietly slipped away while sitting in a chair on September 5, 1943, precisely as his Uncle Max had died in Cincinnati 36 years before.

The month before he died, there was held in New York an emergency American Jewish Conference, the equivalent of the 1918 American Jewish Congress. Representatives of practically every Jewish organization in America took part. And at that conference, American Jewry at last, in a united voice (save, ironically, for a small, inconsequential group headed by a son of Julius Rosenwald) called for the establishment in Palestine, not merely of a vague Jewish "homeland" or "commonwealth," but a sovereign Jewish State—the future State of Israel.

On the motion of Stephen Wise, who knew that Julian was dying, the Conference named him an honorary officer. By its very convocation at this point in Jewish history the Conference symbolically placed a seal of approval on the career that was about to come to an end. It was a seal of victory honoring Julian's long and ardent efforts to enlist the support of American Jewry for the Jewish State that was to be proclaimed five years later, not just as an answer to anti-Semitism but to the age-old desire of self-respecting Jews—"manly" Jews, to use one of Brandeis' favorite adjectives—to have a homeland for themselves and for all those who wished it because, as Julian would have said, "it was right."

There was no conventional funeral. With his friend and associate in Zionism, Stephen Wise, presiding, an informal memorial service was held at Rabbi Wise's Free Synagogue in New York City—informal because, Dr. Wise explained, "Julian Mack was not the kind of man who would want a funeral or formal eulogy." Then, as Julian had requested, his body was cremated.

The following November there was a moving ceremony at Ramat HaShofet, the flourishing kibbutz that had been named in his honor at the express direction of his one-time adversary, Menahem Ussishkin. Henrietta Szold, who owed so much to Julian—as he had to her in the understanding of the Jewish people—was present at the Ramat HaShofet ceremony. She spoke not only of Julian, "my warm and faithful friend," but also of Brandeis, of Aaron

Aaronsohn, of Shmarya Levin, and of many others whose lives had been so closely interwoven with that of Julian Mack.

Also present was Robert Szold, by then himself well known both in the law and in Zionism, one of those young men whom Julian had helped and who represented that Brandeis "Round Table," of which he, together with Julian, had been one of the "knights." His words, spoken as he stood with others on the soil of Palestine in tribute to Julian, formed a true estimate. Julian, said Robert Szold, "represented a perfect synthesis of Americanism and Zionism. . . . He was a great judge, a great American, a great humanitarian, a great Jew, and a great soul."

Another authentic estimate was the summary-conclusion of Julian's life in the biographical sketch written for the *American Jewish Year Book* by Horace M. Kallen:

> His life was, through its long last illness, right up to its contracted last moment, one brave, willing affirmation. He took what he had to take, and he stood up without flinching, saying *Yes* to life. Thinking of him, one thinks of the words of another great Jew, Baruch Spinoza: "A free man thinks of nothing less than death, and his wisdom is not a meditation upon death but upon life." Julian Mack was a free man.

BIBLIOGRAPHY

Aaronsohn, Aaron, *Diary*, ed. Rifka Aaronsohn, Israel.

Aaronsohn, Alexander, *With the Turks in Palestine*, Boston, 1916.

Abbott, Edith, "Grace Abbott: A Sister's Memories," *Social Service Review* (Vol. 13), Chicago, 1939.

Abbott, Grace, *The Immigrant and the Community*, New York, 1917.

Adams, Samuel Hopkins, *Incredible Era: The Life of Warren Gamaliel Harding*, Boston, 1939.

Addams, Jane, *My Friend Julia Lathrop*, New York, 1935.

——, *Peace and Bread in Time of War*, New York, 1922.

——, *The Spirit of Youth and the City Streets*, New York, 1909.

——, *Twenty Years at Hull House*, New York, 1924.

——, *Second Twenty Years at Hull House*, New York, 1935.

——, et al., *The Child, the Clinic and the Court*, New York, 1925.

Adler, Cyrus, *I Have Considered the Days*, Philadelphia, 1941.

——, *Jacob H. Schiff, His Life and Letters*, Garden City, 1928.

——, with Margalith, Aaron M., *With Firmness in the Right: American Diplomatic Action Affecting Jews, 1840–1945*, New York, 1946.

Agar, Herbert, *The Saving Remnant*, New York, 1960.

Aldington, Richard, *Lawrence of Arabia*, London, 1969.

Andrews, Wayne, *Battle for Chicago*, New York, 1946.

Asbury, Herbert, *Gem of the Prairie: An Informal History of the Chicago Underworld*, New York, 1940.

Baker, Liva, *Felix Frankfurter*, New York, 1969.

Baldwin, Roger N. and Flexner, Bernard, *Juvenile Courts and Probation*, New York, 1914.

Barnard, Harry, *The Standard Club of Chicago, 1869–1969*.

Baron, Salo W., *A Social and Religious History of the Jews* (2d ed.), New York, 1952.

Bentwich, Norman, *For Zion's Sake: A Biography of Judah L. Magnes*, Philadelphia, 1954.

——, and Helen, *Mandate Memories, 1918–1948*, New York, 1965.

Berlin, Isaiah, *Chaim Weizmann*, London, 1958.

Bernheimer, Charles S., *The Russian Jew in the United States*, Philadelphia, 1905.

Birmingham, Stephen, *Our Crowd: The Great Jewish Families of New York*, New York, 1967.

Blankfort, Michael, *Behold the Fire*, New York, 1965.

Bogen, Boris D., *Jewish Philanthropy*, New York, 1917.

Borchsenius, Paul, *The History of the Jews*, New York, 1965.

Bowen, Louise DeKoven, *Growing Up With a City*, New York, 1926.

———, *Open Windows*, Chicago, 1946.

Brandeis, Louis D., *Business: A Profession*, Boston, 1933.

———, *Other People's Money and How the Bankers Use It*, New York, 1932.

———, *Zionism and Patriotism*, New York, 1915.

Breckinridge, Sophonisba P., and Abbott, Edith, *The Delinquent Child and the Home*, New York, 1916.

Bregstone, Philip, *Chicago and Its Jews*, Chicago, 1933.

Brunswick, Ruth Mack, "Reminiscence of Sigmund Freud," *Psychoanalytic Quarterly*, 1940, ix

Burns, James McGregor, *Roosevelt: The Lion and the Fox*, New York, 1956.

Carsel, Wilfred, *A History of the Chicago Ladies' Garment Workers Union*, Chicago, 1940.

Chamberlain, John, *Farewell to Reform*, New York, 1933.

Chicago Civil Liberties Committee, *Pursuit of Freedom: A History of Civil Liberty in Illinois, 1787–1942*, Chicago, 1942.

Chyet, Stanley, "Ludwig Lewisohn," *American Jewish Archives*, November, 1959.

Clark, Ronald W., *Einstein: The Life and Times*, New York, 1971.

Cohen, Israel, *The Zionist Movement*, London, 1945.

Cohen, Morris R., *A Dreamer's Journey*, Boston, 1949.

Cohen, Naomi W., *Not Free to Desist*, Philadelphia, 1972.

Croly, Herbert, *The Promise of American Life*, New York, 1964.

Cronbach, Abraham, "Autobiography," *American Jewish Archives*, February, 1959.

Cronon, Edmund Davis, *Black Moses: The Story of Marcus Garvey and the Universal Negro Improvement Association*, Madison, 1955.

Dallek, Robert, *Democrat and Diplomat: The Life of William E. Dodd*, New York, 1968.

Darrow, Clarence, *The Story of My Life*, New York, 1932.

Daugherty, Harry M., *The Inside Story of the Harding Tragedy*, California, 1932.

Davis, Allen F., and McCree, Mary Lynn, eds., *Eighty Years at Hull House,* Chicago, 1969.

DeHaas, Jacob, *Louis D. Brandeis,* New York, 1929.

———, *History of Palestine,* New York, 1934.

Dilliard, Irving, ed., *Mr. Justice Brandeis, Great American, 1856–1941,* St. Louis, 1941.

Dillon, Emile Joseph, *The Inside Story of the Paris Peace Conference,* New York, 1920.

Dimont, Max I., *Jews, God and History,* New York, 1962.

Dodd, Martha, *Through Embassy Eyes,* New York, 1939.

Dodd, William E., Jr., and Dodd, Martha, eds., *Ambassador Dodd's Diary, 1933–1938,* New York, 1941.

Dreiser, Theodore, *A Book About Myself,* New York, 1922.

———, *The Financier,* New York, 1927.

Dubnow, S.M., *History of the Jews in Russia and Poland,* Philadelphia, 1916.

Dugdale, Blanche E.C., *Arthur James Balfour,* New York, 1937.

Eban, Abba S., *My Country,* New York, 1972.

———, *My People,* New York, 1969.

———, *Voice of Israel,* New York, 1969.

Einstein, Albert, *Ideas and Opinions,* New York, 1954.

Engle, Anita, *The Nili Spies,* London, 1959.

Epstein, Ralph C., *GATX: A History of the General American Transportation Corporation, 1898–1948,* New York, 1948.

Eytan, Walter, *The First Ten Years: A Diplomatic History of Israel,* New York, 1958.

Fairchild, David Grandison, *The World Was My Garden,* New York, 1941.

Farrell, John C., *Beloved Lady: A History of Jane Addams' Ideas on Reform,* Baltimore, 1967.

Felsenthal, Emma, *Bernhard Felsenthal, Teacher in Israel,* New York, 1924.

Filler, Louis, *Crusaders for American Liberalism,* New York, 1939.

Fineman, Irving, *Woman of Valor: The Life of Henrietta Szold,* New York, 1961.

Fink, Reuben, ed., *America and Palestine,* New York, 1945.

Flexner, Bernard, *Mr. Justice Brandeis and the University of Louisville,* Louisville, 1938.

Fraenkel, Osmond K., ed., *The Curse of Bigness,* New York, 1934.

Frank, Jerome N., *Courts on Trial,* Princeton, 1950.

———, *Law and the Modern Mind,* New York, 1930.

Frank, Philipp, *Einstein: His Life and Times,* New York, 1947.

Frankfurter, Felix, *The Case of Sacco and Vanzetti,* Boston, 1927.

———, ed., *Mr. Justice Brandeis*, New Haven, 1932.

———, *Of Law and Life and Other Things That Matter*, ed. Philip B. Kurland, Cambridge, Mass., 1965.

———, *Felix Frankfurter Reminisces*, with Harlan Phillips, New York, 1960.

Freedman, Max, ed., *Roosevelt and Frankfurter, Their Correspondence, 1928–1945*, Boston, 1968.

Funk & Wagnalls, *The Jewish Encyclopedia*, New York, 1903–04.

Glanz, Rudolf, *Studies in Judaica Americana*, New York, 1970.

Glazer, Nathan, *American Judaism*, Chicago, 1957.

———, and Moynihan, Daniel P., *Beyond the Melting Pot*, Cambridge, Mass., 1970.

Golden, Harry L., *A Little Girl Is Dead*, Cleveland, 1965.

———, *Only in America*, Cleveland, 1958.

Goldman, Eric F., *Rendezvous with Destiny*, New York, 1952.

Goldman, Solomon, ed., *The Words of Justice Brandeis*, New York, 1953.

Goldmann, Nahum, *The Autobiography of Nahum Goldmann*, New York, 1969.

Gottheil, Richard James Horatio, *Zionism*, Philadelphia, 1914.

Grusd, Edward E., *B'nai B'rith: The Story of a Covenant*, New York, 1966.

Gunther, John, *Taken at the Flood: The Story of Albert D. Lasker*, New York, 1960.

Haber, Julius, *The Odyssey of an American Zionist*, New York, 1956.

Hackett, Francis, *I Chose Denmark*, New York, 1940.

Halperin, Samuel, *The Political World of American Zionism*, Detroit, 1961.

Handlin, Oscar, *Adventure in Freedom: Three Hundred Years of Jewish Life in America*, New York, 1954.

———, *The Uprooted: The Epic Story of the Great Migrations That Made the American People*, Boston, 1951.

Harrison, Carter, *Stormy Years*, New York, 1935.

Hecht, Ben, *A Guide for the Bedevilled*, New York, 1944.

———, *Gaily, Gaily*, New York, 1964.

Heller, James G., *Isaac M. Wise, His Life, Work and Thought*, New York, 1965.

Hertzberg, Arthur, ed., *The Zionist Idea*, Garden City, 1959.

Herzl, Theodor, *The Complete Diaries of Theodor Herzl* (5 vols.), New York, 1960.

———, *The Jewish State*, new ed. New York, 1970.

Hess, Moses, *Rome and Jerusalem*, New York, 1943.

Hirsch, Emil G., *My Religion*, New York, 1925.
Hoffmann, Banesh, in collaboration with Dukas, Helen, *Albert Einstein, Creator and Rebel*, New York, 1972.
Holmes, John Haynes, *Palestine Today and Tomorrow*, New York, 1929.
Hoover, Herbert, *An American Epic* (3 vols.), 1959-61.
Horwich, Bernard, *My First Eighty Years*, Chicago, 1939.
Howe, Henry, *Historical Collections of Ohio*, Cincinnati, 1907.
Howe, Irving, and Gershman, Carl, eds., *Israel, the Arabs and the Middle East*, New York, 1972.
Howe, Mark DeWolfe, ed., *The Holmes-Laski Letters, 1916-1935*, New York, 1963.
Hull, Cordell, *Memoirs*, New York, 1948.
Ickes, Harold L., *Autobiography of a Curmudgeon*, New York, 1943.
———, *The Secret Diary of Harold L. Ickes*, New York, 1953.
Janowsky, Oscar I., ed., *The American Jew, A Composite Portrait*, New York, 1942.
———, *The Jews and Minority Rights, 1898-1919*, New York, 1933.
———, *Nationalities and National Minorities*, New York, 1945.
Jewish Frontier Anthology, New York, 1967.
Johnson, Gerald W., *An Honorable Titan: A Biographical Study of Adolph S. Ochs*, New York, 1946.
Jones, Ernest, *The Life and Work of Sigmund Freud*, New York, 1961.
Josephson, Matthew, *Sidney Hillman, Statesman of American Labor*, Garden City, 1952.
———, *Zola and His Times*, London, 1929.
Kahn, Roger, *The Passionate People*, New York, 1968.
Kallen, Horace M., *Of Them Which Say They Are Jews*, New York, 1954.
———, *Utopians at Bay*, New York, 1958.
———, *Zionism and World Politics*, Garden City, 1921.
Karp, Abraham J., ed., *The Jewish Experience in America*, New York, 1969.
King, Willard L., *Melville W. Fuller, Chief Justice of the United States*, New York, 1950.
Kinsley, Philip, *The Chicago Tribune: Its First Hundred Years*, Chicago, 1943-46.
Klausner, Joseph, *Menahem Ussishkin, His Life and Work*, New York, 1942.
Konvitz, Milton R., *Civil Rights in Immigration*, Ithaca, 1953.
Korn, Bertram W., *The American Reaction to the Mortara Case*, Cincinnati, 1957.
Laqueur, Walter Z., *A History of Zionism*, New York, 1972.

Laski, Harold J., *The American Democracy*, New York, 1948.

Learsi, Rufus, *Fulfillment: The Epic Story of Zionism*, Cleveland, 1951.

———, *The Jews in America*, Cleveland, 1954.

Lebeson, Anita Libman, *Pilgrim People*, New York, 1950.

Lerner, Max, *America As a Civilization*, New York, 1957.

Leslie, Shane, *Mark Sykes: His Life and Letters*, London, 1923.

Levin, Alexandra Lee, *The Szolds of Lombard Street*, Philadelphia, 1960.

———, *Vision: A Biography of Dr. Harry Friedenwald*, Philadelphia, 1964.

Levin, Meyer, *In Search*, New York, 1950.

———, *The Settlers*, New York, 1972.

Levin, Shmarya, *Forward From Exile*, Philadelphia, 1967.

Levinger, Lee J., *Anti-Semitism Yesterday and Tomorrow*, New York, 1936.

———, *A History of the Jews in the United States*, New York, 1961.

Lewisohn, Ludwig, *Israel*, New York, 1925.

———, *Upstream, an American Chronicle*, New York, 1922.

Lief, Alfred, *Brandeis: The Personal History of an American Ideal*, New York, 1936.

———, *Democracy's Norris*, Harrisburg, 1939.

Linn, James Weber, *Jane Addams*, New York, 1935.

Lipsky, Louis, *A Gallery of Zionist Profiles*, New York, 1956.

———, *Thirty Years of American Zionism*, New York, 1927.

Litvinoff, Barnet, *Road to Jerusalem*, London, 1965.

Livingston, Sigmund, *Must Men Hate?* Cleveland, 1944.

Lloyd George, David, *The Truth About the Peace Treaties*, London, 1938.

Lovett, Robert Morse, *All Our Years*, New York, 1948.

Lowdermilk, Walter C., *Palestine, Land of Promise*, New York, 1944.

Lowenthal, Marvin, *Henrietta Szold, Life and Letters*, New York, 1942.

———, *The Jews of Germany*, New York, 1936.

Mandelbaum, Bernard, ed., *Assignment in Israel*, New York, 1960.

Manuel, Frank E., *Realities of American-Palestine Relations*, Washington, 1949.

Marcus, Jacob R., *Essays in American Jewish History*, Cincinnati, 1958.

———, *Studies in American Jewish History*, Cincinnati, 1959.

———, *Memoirs of American Jews, 1775-1865*, Philadelphia, 1955.

———, *The Rise and Destiny of the German Jews*, Cincinnati, 1934.

Markmann, Charles Lam, *The Noblest Cry: A History of the American Civil Liberties Union*, New York, 1965.

Mason, Alpheus T., *Brandeis: A Free Man's Life*, New York, 1946.

———, *Harlan Fiske Stone*, New York, 1956.

Masters, Edgar Lee, *Across Spoon River*, New York, 1936.

———, *Tale of Chicago*, New York, 1933.

McWilliams, Carey, *Brothers Under the Skin*, Boston, 1943.

———, *A Mask for Privilege*, Boston, 1948.

Meinertzhagen, Richard, *Middle East Diary, 1917-56*, New York, 1960.

Meites, Hyman L., ed., *History of the Jews of Chicago*, Chicago,1924.

Miller, David Hunter, *My Diary at the Peace Conference*, 1919.

Monsky, Daisy, and Bisgyer, Maurice, *Henry Monsky*, Washington, D.C., 1947.

Morgenthau, Henry, Jr., *From the Morgenthau Diaries*, Boston, 1939-47.

Morgenthau, Henry, Sr., *All in a Lifetime*, Garden City, 1925.

Morse, Arthur D., *While Six Million Died*, New York, 1968.

Naiditch, Isaac, *Edmond de Rothschild*, Washington, 1945.

Nathan, Robert, et al., *Palestine: Problem and Promise*, Washington, 1946.

Nevins, Allan, *Ford: The Times, the Man and the Company*, New York, 1954.

———, *Herbert H. Lehman and His Era*, New York, 1963.

Nutting, Anthony, *Lawrence of Arabia*, New York, 1961.

The Occident, a daily, ed. by Isaac Leeser in Philadelphia, 1843-68.

Oppenheimer, Heinz R., "Florula transiordanica; révision critique des plantes recoltées et partiellement determinées par Aaron Aaronsohn au cours de ses expéditions (1904-1908) en Transjordanie et dans le Wadi-el-Araba . . . avec des journaux de voyages d'Aaron Aaronsohn . . . et une notice biographique d'Alex Aaronsohn." Originally published as an article in the Bulletin of the Botanical Society of Geneva, Vol. 22, 1930. Reprinted in 1931 in the form of a memorial booklet by the Aaronsohn family of Zikhron Yaakov, Israel.

Parkes, James W., *A History of the Jewish People*, Chicago, 1962.

———, *Whose Land? A History of the Peoples of Palestine*, Baltimore, 1949.

Philipson, David, *The Reform Movement in Judaism*, New York, 1967.

Pierce, Bessie L., *A History of Chicago*, New York, 1937.

Pinsker, Leo, *Road to Freedom*, New York, 1944.

Podhoretz, Norman, ed., *The Commentary Reader*, New York, 1966.

Polier, Justine Wise, and Wise, James W., eds., *The Personal Letters of Stephen S. Wise*, Boston, 1956.

Polk, William R., Stamler, David, and Asfour, Edmund, *Backdrop to Tragedy*, Boston, 1957.

Pringle, Henry F., *The Life and Times of William Howard Taft*, New York, 1939.

———, *Theodore Roosevelt: A Biography*, New York, 1956.

Proskauer, Joseph M., *A Segment of My Times*, New York, 1950.

Pusey, Merlo, *Charles Evans Hughes*, New York, 1951.

Rabinowicz, Oskar K., *Fifty Years of Zionism*, London, 1950.

Raisin, Max, *Great Jews I Have Known*, New York, 1952.

The Reform Advocate, ed. by Emil G. Hirsch from 1891 to 1923 in Chicago.

Reznikoff, Charles, ed., *Louis Marshall, Champion of Liberty* (2 vols.), Philadelphia, 1957.

Riis, Jacob A., *How the Other Half Lives: Studies Among the Tenements of New York*, New York, 1957.

Rischin, Moses, *The Promised City: New York's Jews, 1870-1914*, Cambridge, Mass., 1962

Robinson, Jacob, et al., *Were the Minorities Treaties a Failure?* New York, 1943.

Roche, John P., *The Quest for the Dream: The Development of Civil Rights and Human Relations in Modern America*, New York, 1963.

Rosenberg, James N., *Unfinished Business*, Scarsdale, 1967.

Rosenblatt, Bernard A., *Two Generations of Zionism: Historical Recollections of an American Zionist*, New York, 1967.

Rosenfield, Leonora D. (Cohen), *Portrait of a Philosopher: Morris Raphael Cohen in Life and Letters*, New York, 1962.

Roth, Cecil, *The Magnificent Rothschilds*, New York, 1962.

Ruppin, Arthur, *The Jews of To-Day*, New York, 1913.

Russell, Francis, *The Shadow of Blooming Grove: Warren G. Harding in His Times*, New York, 1968.

Sachar, Abram L., *A History of the Jews*, New York, 1965.

———, *Sufferance Is the Badge*, New York, 1939.

Sachar, Howard, *The Course of Modern Jewish History*, Cleveland, 1958.

Sacher, Harry, *Israel: The Establishment of a State*, New York, 1952.

St. John, Robert, *Ben-Gurion*, Doubleday, 1959.

Sampter, Jessie, ed., *Modern Palestine*, New York, 1933.

Samuel, Viscount Herbert, *Grooves of Change*, Indianapolis, 1946.

Samuel, Maurice, *Blood Accusation: The Strange History of the Beilis Case*, New York, 1966.

————, *Level Sunlight*, New York, 1953.

————, *Little Did I Know*, New York, 1963.

Schachner, Nathan, *The Price of Liberty: A History of the American Jewish Committee*, New York, 1948.

Schappes, Morris U., *A Documentary History of the Jews in the United States, 1654-1875*, New York, 1950.

Schechtman, Joseph B., *Rebel and Statesman: The Vladimir Jabotinsky Story*, New York, 1956.

Schwarz, Leo W., ed., *Great Ages and Ideas of the Jewish People*, New York, 1956.

————, ed., *The Menorah Treasury*, Philadelphia, 1964.

Shirer, William L., *Rise and Fall of the Third Reich: A History of Nazi Germany*, New York, 1960.

Shubow, Joseph S., ed., *The Brandeis Avukah Annual of 1936*, Boston, 1932.

Smith, Gene, *When the Cheering Stopped: The Last Years of Woodrow Wilson*, New York, 1964.

Smith, Howard K., *Last Train from Berlin*, New York, 1942.

Sokolow, Nahum, *History of Zionism, 1600-1918*, New York, 1969.

Steffens, Lincoln, *The Autobiography of Lincoln Steffens*, New York, 1931.

Stein, Leonard J., *The Balfour Declaration*, New York, 1961.

————, *Zionism*, New York, 1926.

Stone, Goldie, *My Caravan of Years*, New York, 1945.

Stone, Irving, *Clarence Darrow for the Defense*, Garden City, 1941.

Strauss, Lewis L., *Men and Decisions*, Garden City, 1962.

Sullivan, Mark, *Our Times: The United States, 1900-1925*, New York, 1932.

Survey, The (periodical)

Survey Graphic (periodical)

Sward, Keith, *The Legend of Henry Ford*, New York, 1948.

Sykes, Christopher, *Crossroads to Israel*, Cleveland, 1965.

Syrkin, Marie, ed., *A Land of Our Own: An Oral Autobiography of Golda Meir*, New York, 1973.

Szold, Robert, "Louis Dembitz Brandeis," *Hadassah Newsletter*, Dec. 1941-Jan. 1942.

Teller, Judd, *The Jews: Biography of a People*, New York, 1966.

Tharp, Louise Hall, *Mrs. Jack: A Biography of Isabelle Steward Gardner*, Boston, 1965.

Todd, Alden L., *Justice on Trial: The Case of Louis D. Brandeis*, New York, 1964.

Tuchman, Barbara, *The Guns of August,* New York, 1962.

Vallentin, Antonina, *The Drama of Albert Einstein,* New York, 1954.

Villard, Oswald Garrison, *Fighting Years,* New York, 1939.

Viteles, Rose R., *An American in Israel,* Jerusalem, 1960.

Voorsanger, Jacob, ed., *The Chronicles of Emanu-El of San Francisco,* San Francisco, 1900.

Vorspan, Albert, *Giants of Justice,* New York, 1960.

Voss, Carl Herman, *Rabbi and Minister: The Friendship of Stephen S. Wise and John Haynes Holmes,* Cleveland, 1964.

——, ed., *Stephen S. Wise, Servant of the People: Selected Letters,* Philadelphia, 1969.

Waldman, Morris D., *Nor By Power,* New York, 1953.

Weinberg, Arthur and Lila, eds., *The Muckrakers,* New York, 1961.

Weisgal, Meyer W., ed., *Theodor Herzl: A Memorial,* New York, 1929.

——, *Meyer Weisgal—So Far,* New York, 1972.

——, and Carmichael, Joel, eds., *Chaim Weizmann: A Biography by Several Hands,* New York, 1962.

Weizmann, Chaim, *Trial and Error,* New York, 1966.

Werner, Morris Robert, *Julius Rosenwald,* New York, 1939.

White, Andrew Dickson, *Autobiography of Andrew Dickson White,* New York, 1905.

Wiernik, Peter, *History of the Jews in America,* New York, 1931.

Willkie, Wendell L., *One World,* New York, 1943.

Wilson, Edmund, *The American Earthquake: A Documentary of the '20s and '30s,* Garden City, 1958.

Wirth, Louis, *The Ghetto,* Chicago, 1956.

Wise, Isaac Mayer, *Reminiscences,* ed. by David Philipson, New York, 1945.

Wise, Stephen S., *As I See It,* New York, 1944.

——, *Challenging Years: The Autobiography of Stephen S. Wise,* New York, 1949.

——, and DeHaas, Jacob, *The Great Betrayal,* New York, 1930.

Wolf, Edwin II, with Fleming, John F., *A.S.W. Rosenbach,* London, 1961.

Wolf, Simon, *The American Jew as Patriot, Soldier and Citizen,* Philadelphia, 1895.

Woodward, C. Vann, *Tom Watson,* New York, 1938.

Yaffe, James, *The American Jews,* New York, 1968.

Zborowski, Mark, and Herzog, Elizabeth, *Life Is With People,* New York, 1952.

Ziff, William B., *The Rape of Palestine,* New York, 1938.

334

Private Papers, Documents, and Correspondence

Aaron Aaronsohn papers (diary, correspondence, etc.); Rifka Aaronsohn Memorandum on Julian W. Mack; American Jewish Archives; American Jewish Committee Minutes, 1906–1943; Board of Inquiry on Conscientious Objectors, papers in National Archives; Louis D. Brandeis papers. Chicago Tribune Collection on Julian W. Mack; Cleveland Convention of the Zionist Organization of America Report (1921); Federal Court Reports; Federation of American Zionists Minutes, 1914–1918; Felix Frankfurter papers; Murray Gurfein Memorandum on Judge Mack; Harvard University Archives; Hughes High School (Cincinnati Archives); Illinois Appellate Court Reports; Illinois Supreme Court Reports; Horace M. Kallen papers; Frederick P. Keppel—Report to Secretary of War Newton D. Baker ("Statement Concerning Treatment of Conscientious Objectors in the Army"); Ira Aaron Kipnis, *American Conscientious Objectors During the First World War* —M.A. thesis, University of Chicago; Max Lowenthal Memorandum on Julian W. Mack; Mack Family papers from Max Lowenthal; Julian W. Mack papers; Julian W. Mack report on the Paris Peace Conference—1919; Julian W. Mack Student Assistance papers; Herbert Marks transcript of interview by Harlan Phillips concerning Judge Mack; New School for Social Research papers; New York Times collection on Julian W. Mack; Northwestern University Law School Archives; Oral History (Columbia University) tapes (Oral History Collection: Reminiscenses of Roger N. Baldwin, C. C. Burlingham, Homer Folks, and others); Palestine Development Council records; Palestine Economic Corporation correspondence; Bernard G. Richards Memorandum on Julian W. Mack; Julius Rosenwald papers at University of Chicago; Jacob Schiff papers; Robert Szold papers; William Howard Taft papers, Library of Congress Collection; U.S. Immigration Commission Report; Felix Warburg papers; John Wigmore papers, Northwestern University; Lucien Wolf diary; Zionist Archives in New York; Roger N. Baldwin, Memorandum on Julian W. Mack; Henry P. Chandler, Memorandum on JWM; Benjamin V. Cohen, Memorandum on Julian W. Mack; Felix Frankfurter, interview on Judge Mack by Harlan B. Phillips; Felix Frankfurter, miscellaneous letters; Mack and Tandler family letters; William J. Mack (brother), Memorandum on Julian W. Mack; Rosenthal law firm miscellaneous papers.

Individuals Consulted

James Abajian, Harry Alderman, Rose Alschuler, Roger N. Baldwin, Russell W. Ballard, David Barnard, Ruth E. Barnard, Samuel J. Baskin, Edward L. Bernays, Alexander M. Bickel, Jessie F. Binford, Dr. Hermann Blumgart, Samuel Brodsky, Edward Chayes, Iva Cohen, Robert Cromie, John P. Cullen, Stanley Chyet, Ruth Davenport, Richard Demuth, Irving Dilliard, Justice William O. Douglas, Helen Dukas, Marjorie V. Edwards, Joseph Eisenstat, Bennett Epstein, Morris L. Ernst, Irving Fineman, Mrs. Jerome Frank, John Hope Franklin, Dr. Anna Freud, Ernest Freund, Paul A. Freund, Herbert A. Friedlich, Susan Brandeis Gilbert, Beatrice Mack Goldberg, Eugene Goldman, Mrs. Alice Goldsmith, Erwin N. Griswold, Boris Guriel, David Ben-Gurion, Carl Haessler, Mrs. William S. Hanna, James G. Heller, Judith Bernays Heller, Harry B. Hershey, Ira Hirschmann, John Haynes Holmes, Matilda Juliana Brunswick Hosford, Israel Hosiosky, Clare and C. E. Israel, Philip Jaffe, Oscar I. Janowsky, Mrs. Irma Jacobs, David Karno, Judge Irving Kaufman, Freda Kirchwey, Sebastian Kletzky, Edith P. Kubly, Harold L. Kudan, Corliss Lamont, David Levinson, Arnold Levy, Charles F. Linnen, Harry L. Lodge, Eleanor Mack Lowenthal.

Louis L. Mann, Jacob R. Marcus, Herbert S. Marks, Alpheus T. Mason, Nicholas John Matsoukas, Irene Moran, Julian Morgenstern, Dr. Lillian G. Moulton, Philip C. Neal, Fred P. Nickless, Jr., Garrison Norton, R. H. Peck, Harlan B. Phillips, Jacob S. Potofsky, Roscoe Pound, Joseph M. Proskauer, James A. Rahl, William R. Roalfe, Robert Rosenthal, Bernard A. Rosenblatt, Howard Sachar, Joseph Schaffner, Judith A. Schiff, Helen Schwab, Gertrude Foreman Schwartz, Sidney Schwartz, Austin W. Scott, Murray Seasongood, Claire B. Shetter, Rabbi Joseph S. Shubow, Rabbi Edgar E. Siskin, Dr. Alfred P. Solomon, Leonard Stein, Hirsh Steinberg, Yaakov Steinberger, Leon Stolz, Roberta B. Sutton, Thomas W. Swan, Mrs. Robert Szold, Dr. Norman Treves, Signe Toksvig, William M. Trumbull, Abraham Tulin, Carl Herman Voss, David R. Watkins, Arthur Weinberg, Meyer W. Weisgal, Milton C. Weisman, Julius Weiss, C. W. Wickersham, Harry Austryn Wolfson, Wendell L. Wray, Dr. Ernest Zeisler, Paul B. Zeisler, Paul Zeisler, and many others.

INDEX